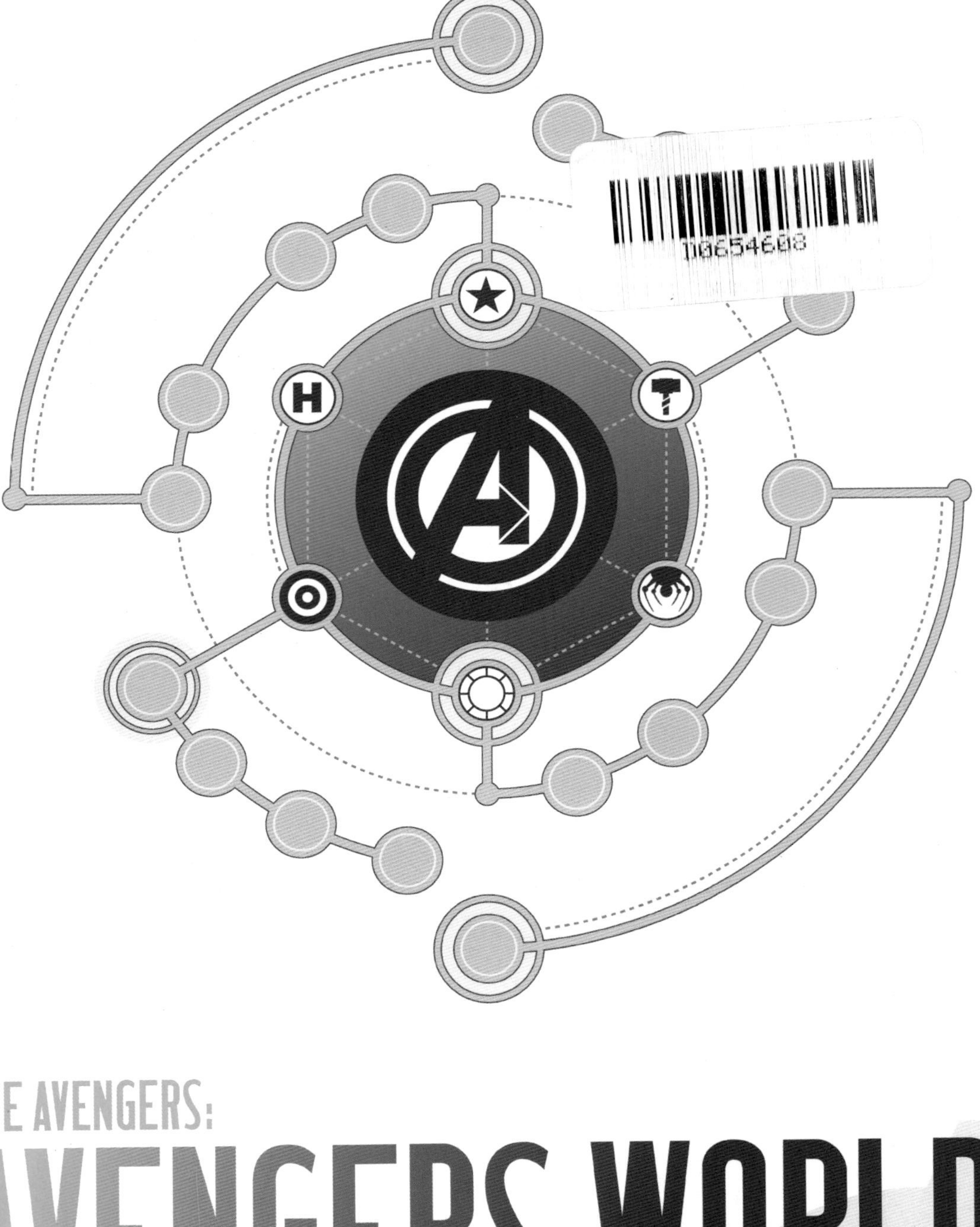

THE AVENGERS:
AVENGERS WORLD

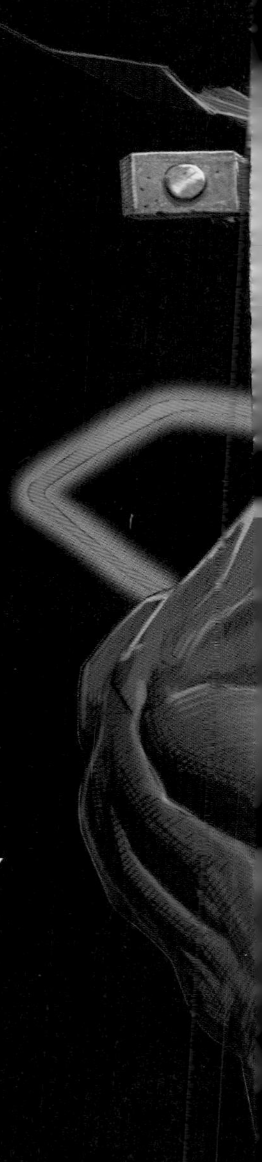

AVENGERS WORLD

WRITER: JONATHAN HICKMAN
ARTISTS: JEROME OPEÑA & ADAM KUBERT
COLOUR ARTISTS: DEAN WHITE, JUSTIN PONSON, MORRY HOLLOWELL, FRANK MARTIN, RICHARD ISANOVE & FRANK D'ARMATA
LETTERER: VC'S CORY PETIT

COVER ARTISTS: DUSTIN WEAVER & JUSTIN PONSOR

ASSISTANT EDITOR: JAKE THOMAS
EDITORS: TOM BREVOORT & LAUREN SANKOVITCH
EDITOR IN CHIEF: AXEL ALONSO
CHIEF CREATIVE OFFICER: JOE QUESADA

PUBLISHER: DAN BUCKLEY
EXECUTIVE PRODUCER: ALAN FINE

AVENGERS: AVENGERS WORLD contains material originally published in magazine form as AVENGERS Vol. 5 #1-6. First printing 2013. Published by Panini Publishing, a division of Panini UK Limited. Mike Riddell, Managing Director. Alan O'Keefe, Managing Editor. Mark Irvine, Production Manager. Marco M. Lupoi, Publishing Director Europe. Ed Hammond, Reprint Editor. Angela Hart, Designer. Office of publication: Brockbourne House, 77 Mount Ephraim, Tunbridge Wells, Kent TN4 8BS.
Printed in Italy. ISBN: 978-1-84653-536-9

Do you have any comments or queries about this graphic novel? Email us at graphicnovels@panini.co.uk

MARVEL
marvel.com
© 2013 MARVEL

FSC
www.fsc.org

MIX
Paper from responsible sources
FSC® C005613

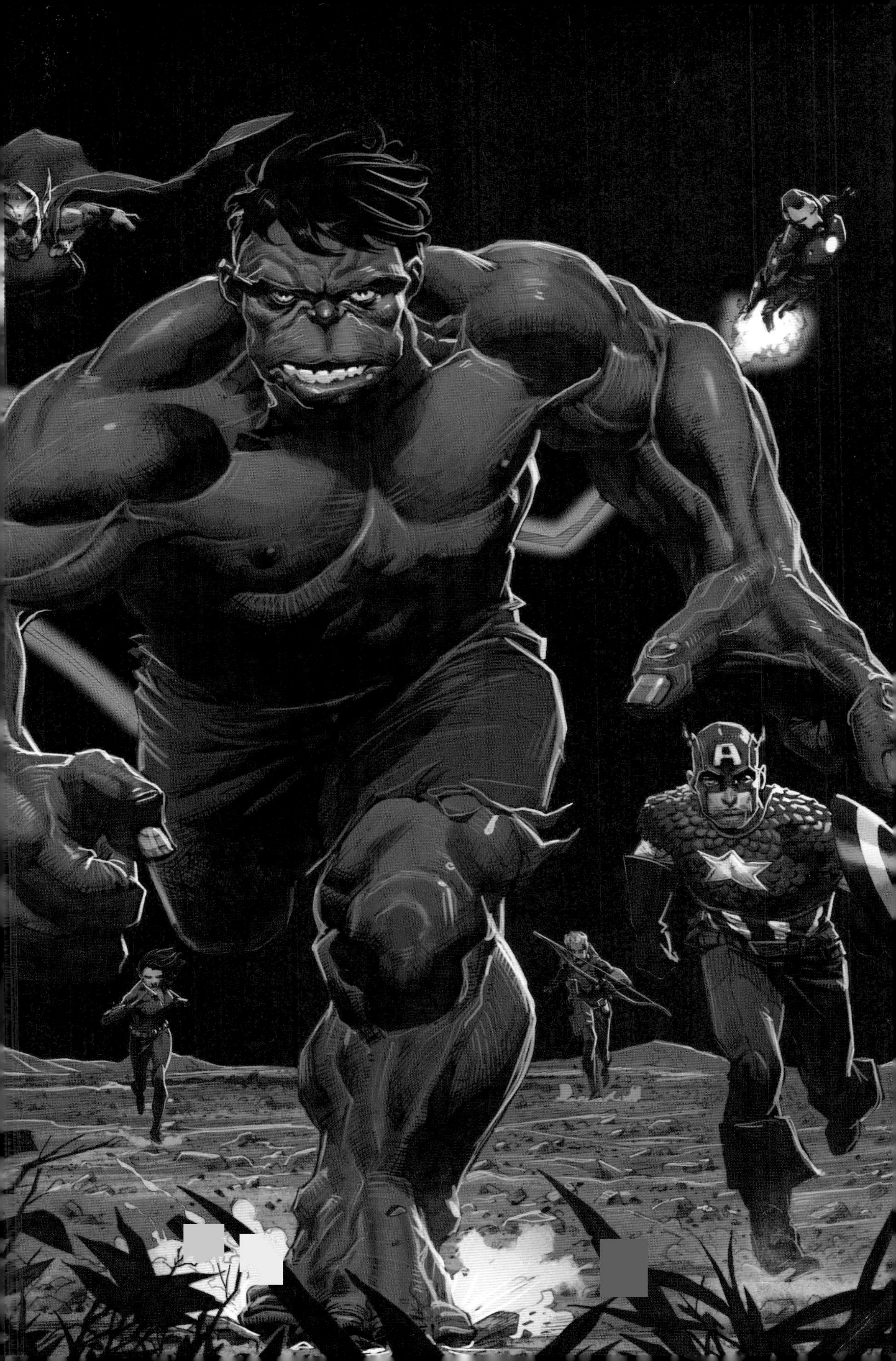

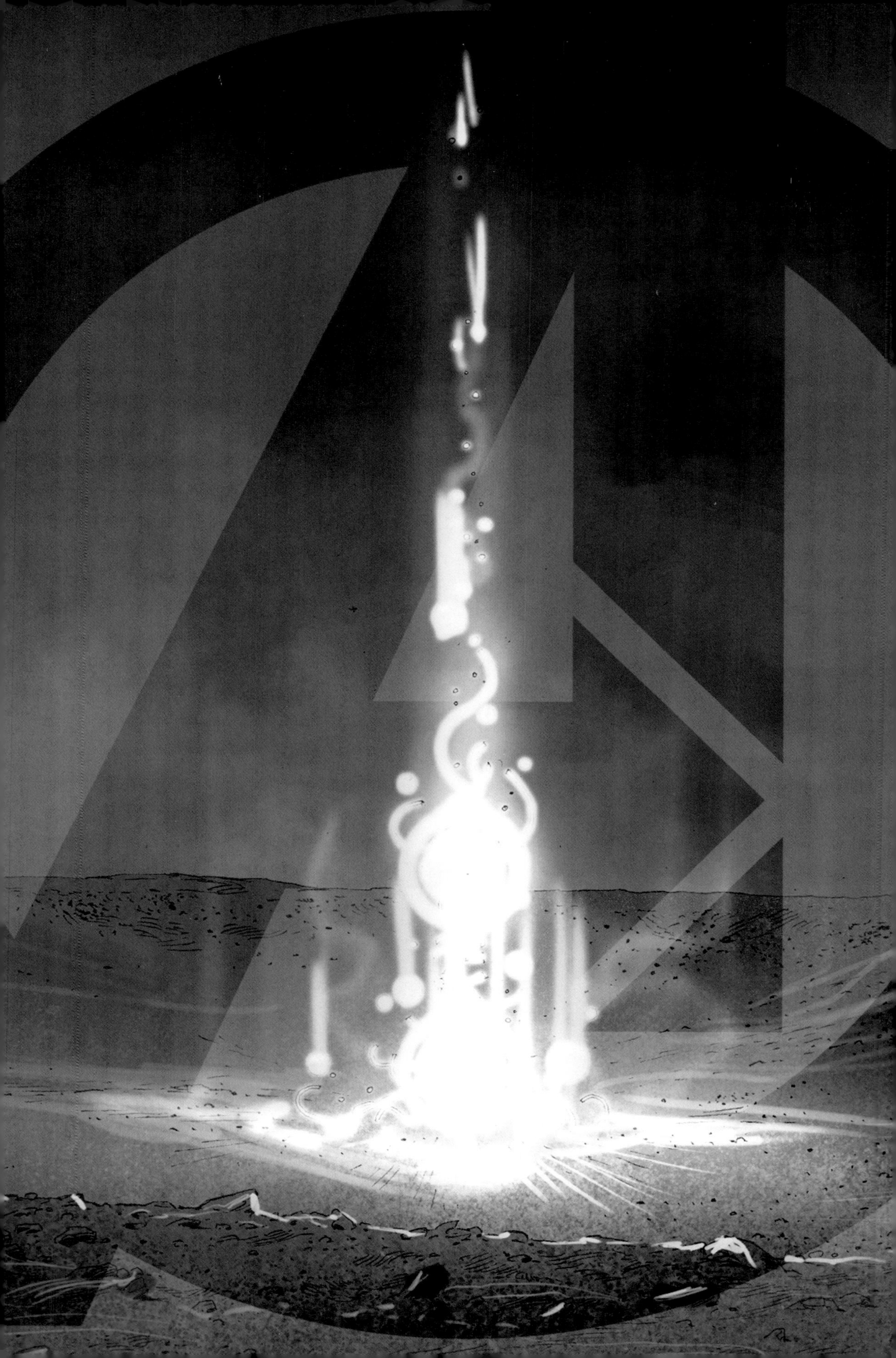

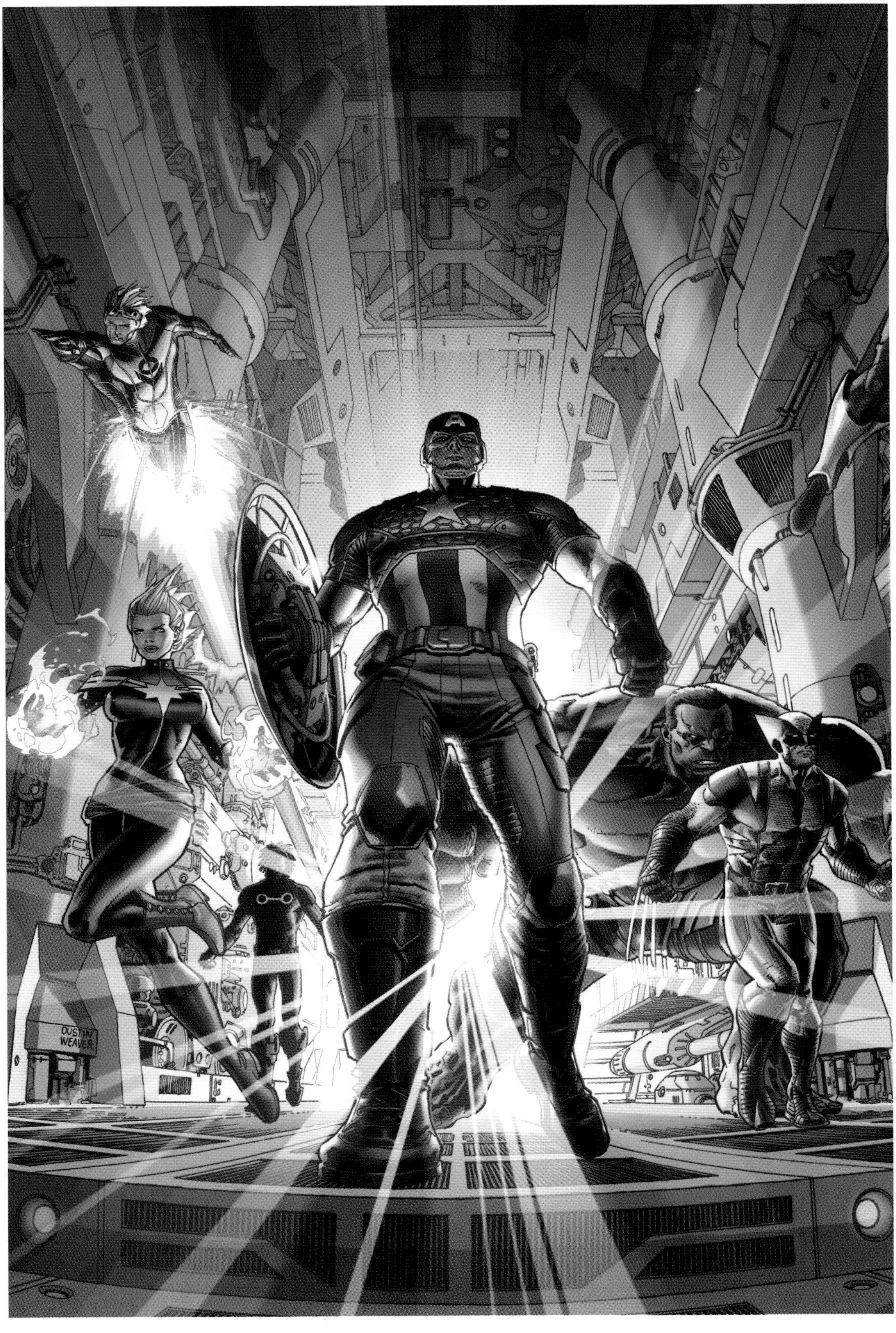
DUSTIN
WEAVER

PREVIOUSLY IN AVENGERS

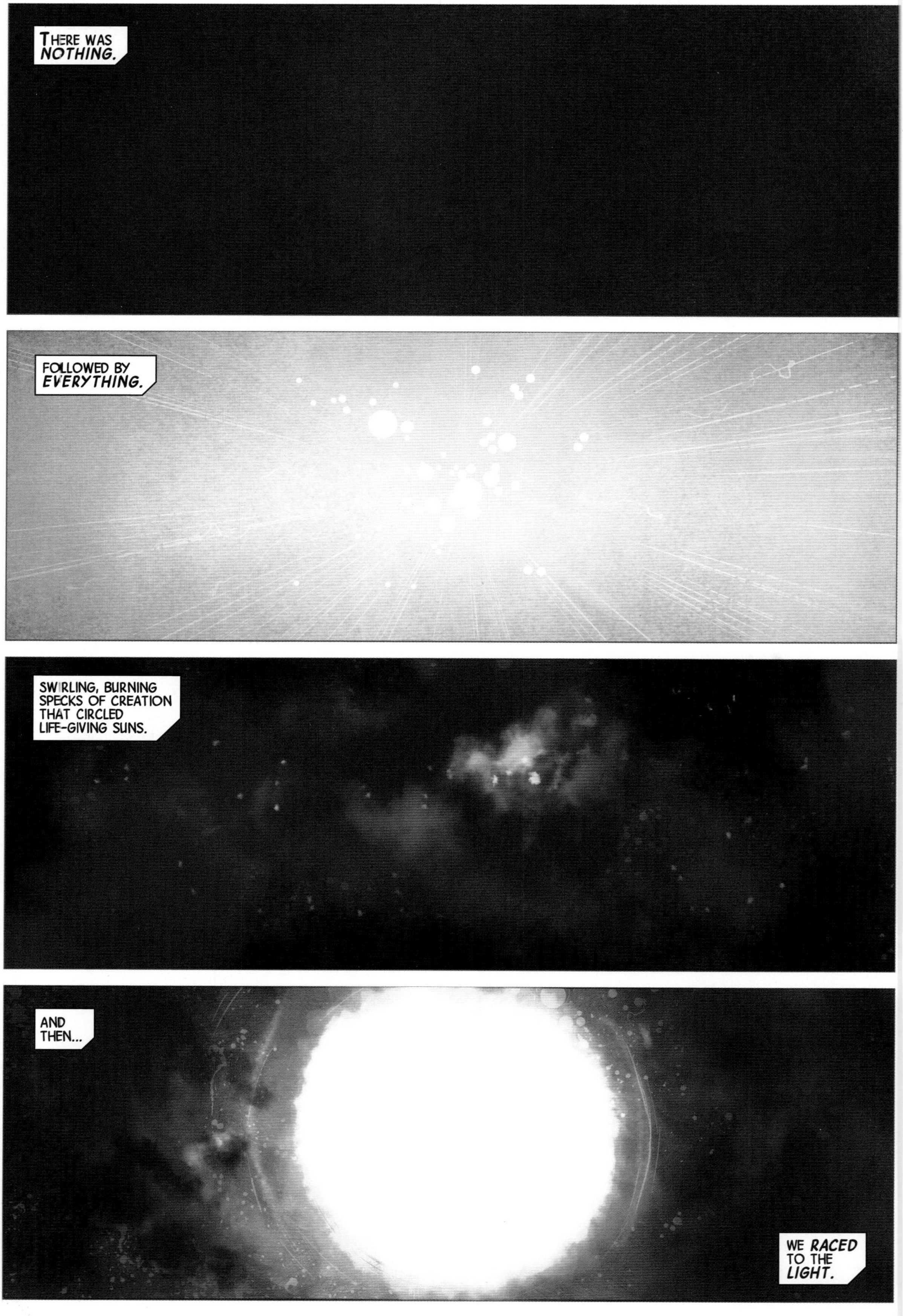
THERE WAS NOTHING.
FOLLOWED BY EVERYTHING.
SWIRLING, BURNING SPECKS OF CREATION THAT CIRCLED LIFE-GIVING SUNS.
AND THEN...
WE RACED TO THE LIGHT.

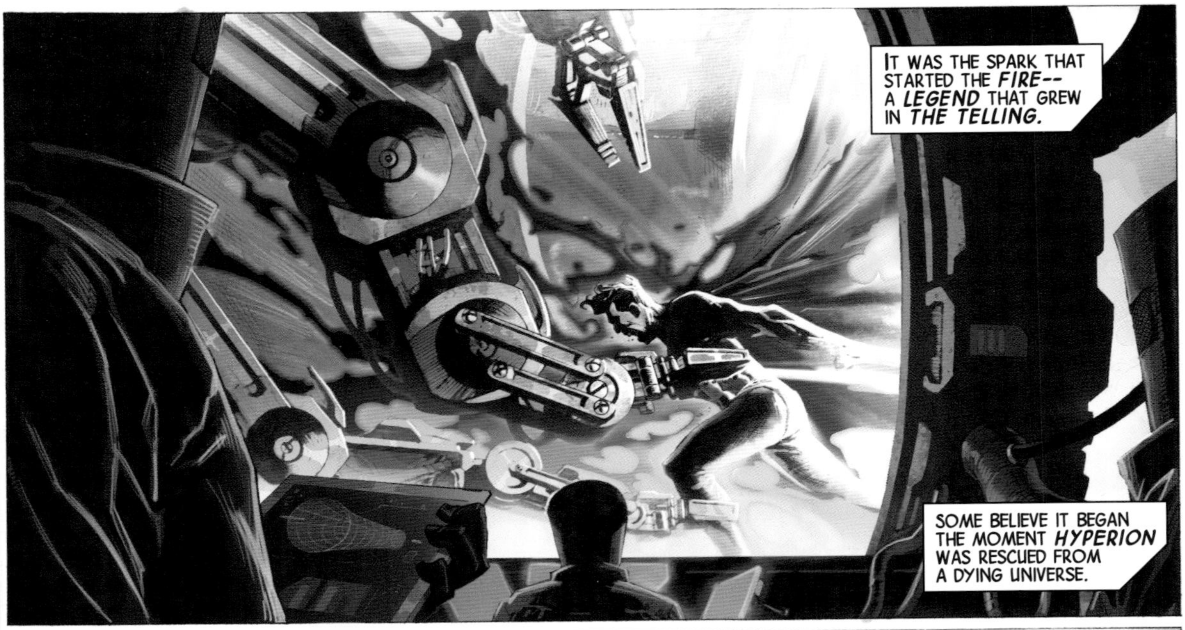
IT WAS THE SPARK THAT STARTED THE FIRE-- A LEGEND THAT GREW IN THE TELLING.
SOME BELIEVE IT BEGAN THE MOMENT HYPERION WAS RESCUED FROM A DYING UNIVERSE.

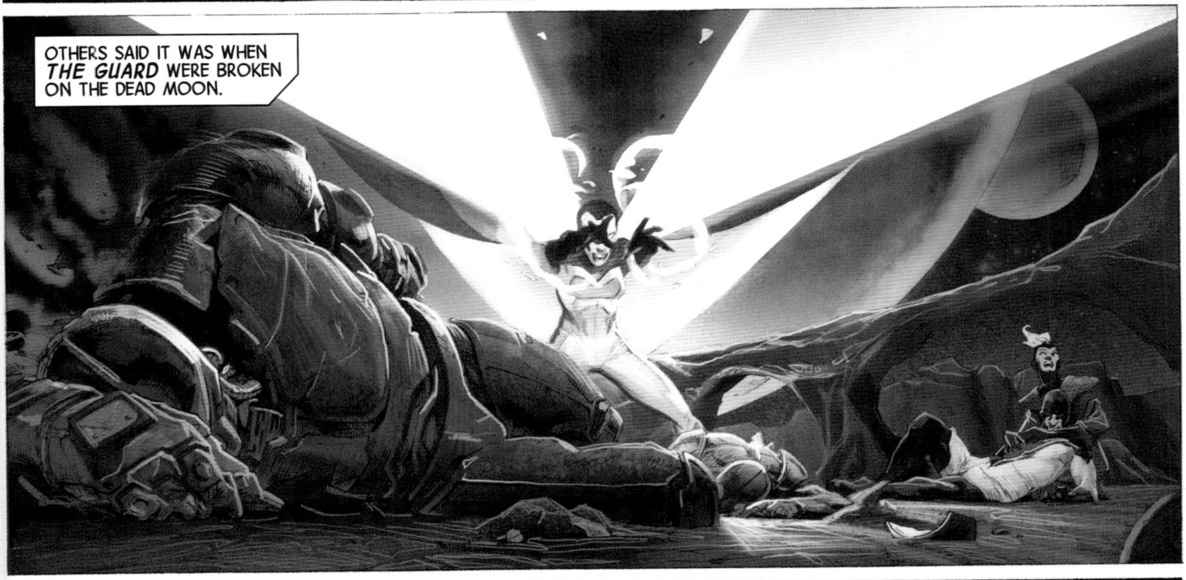
OTHERS SAID IT WAS WHEN THE GUARD WERE BROKEN ON THE DEAD MOON.

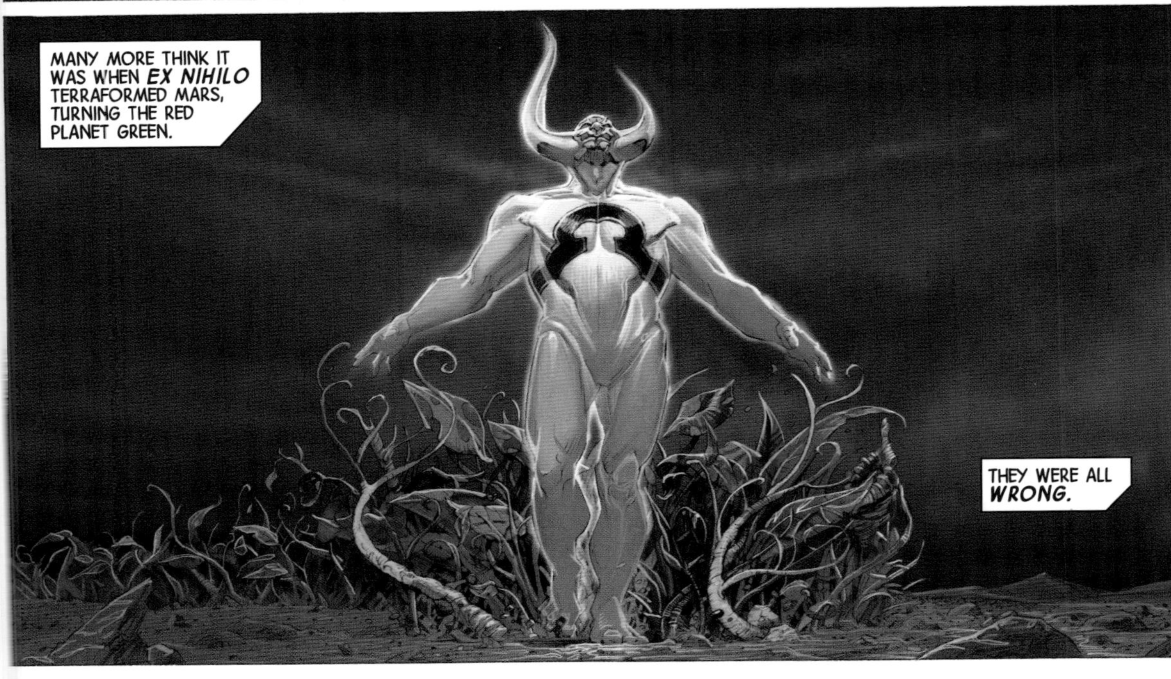
MANY MORE THINK IT WAS WHEN EX NIHILO TERRAFORMED MARS, TURNING THE RED PLANET GREEN.
THEY WERE ALL WRONG.

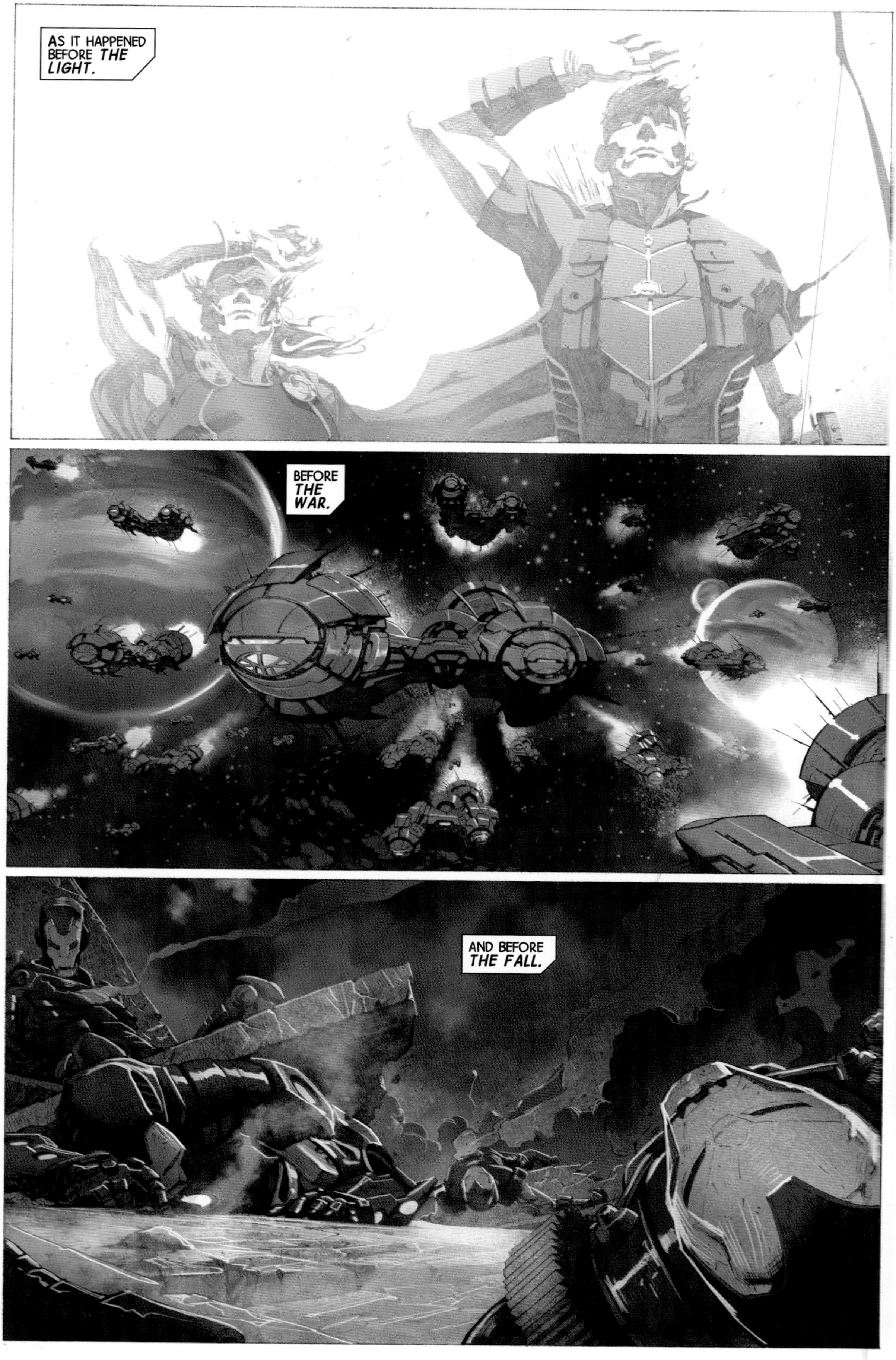
AS IT HAPPENED BEFORE *THE LIGHT.*
BEFORE *THE WAR.*
AND BEFORE *THE FALL.*

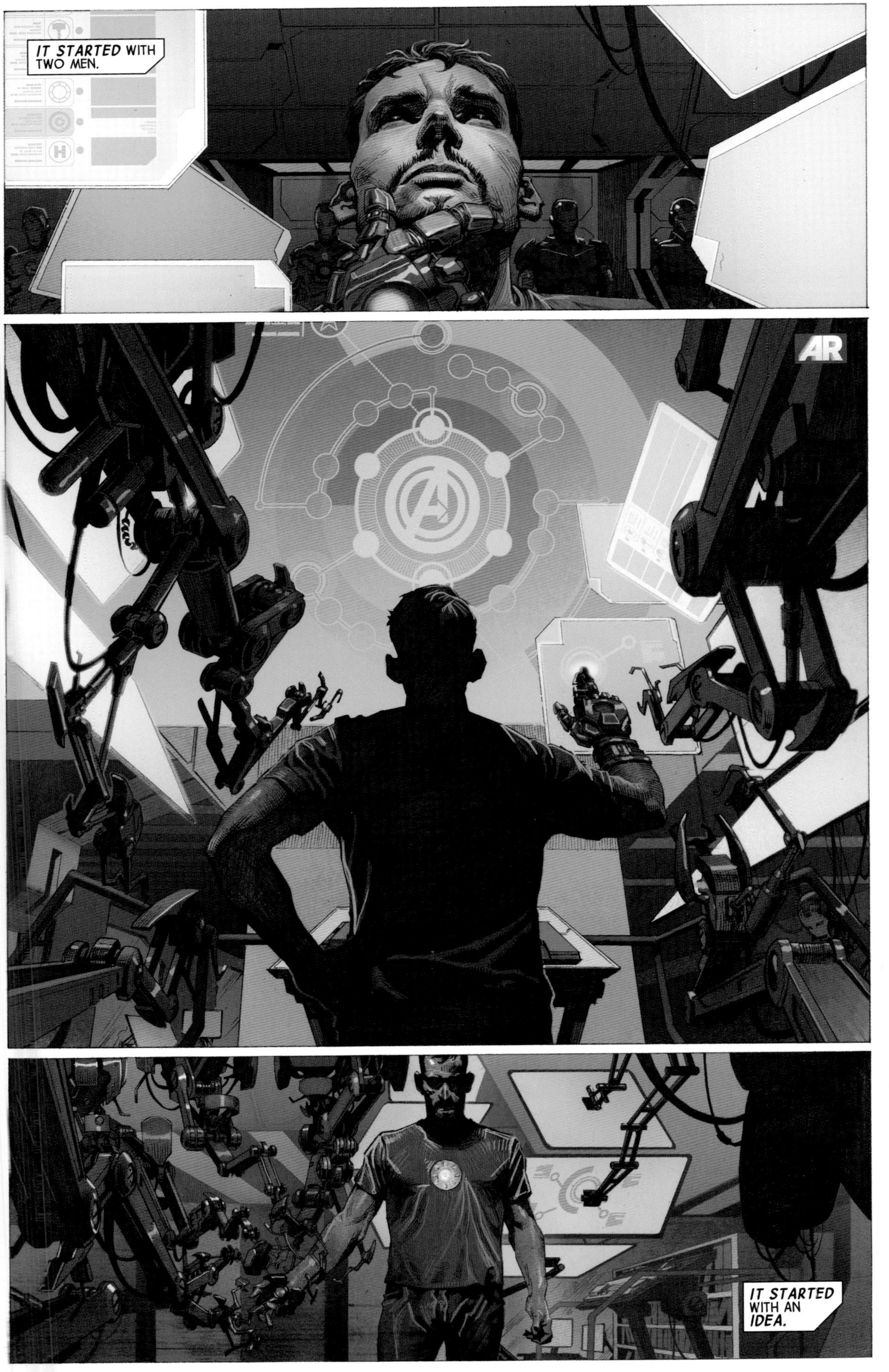
IT STARTED WITH TWO MEN.
IT STARTED WITH AN IDEA.

NHHMMM?

WAKE UP, OLD MAN.

I HAVEN'T BEEN ABLE TO SLEEP.

I COULDN'T STOP THINKING ABOUT SOMETHING YOU SAID, AND, WELL... *I'VE BEEN BUSY.*

I'M SORRY. I KNOW IT'S LATE.

IT'S FINE, TONY.

I'M GRATEFUL.

BAD DREAMS?

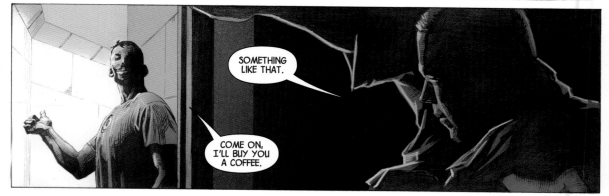

SOMETHING LIKE THAT.

COME ON, I'LL BUY YOU A COFFEE.

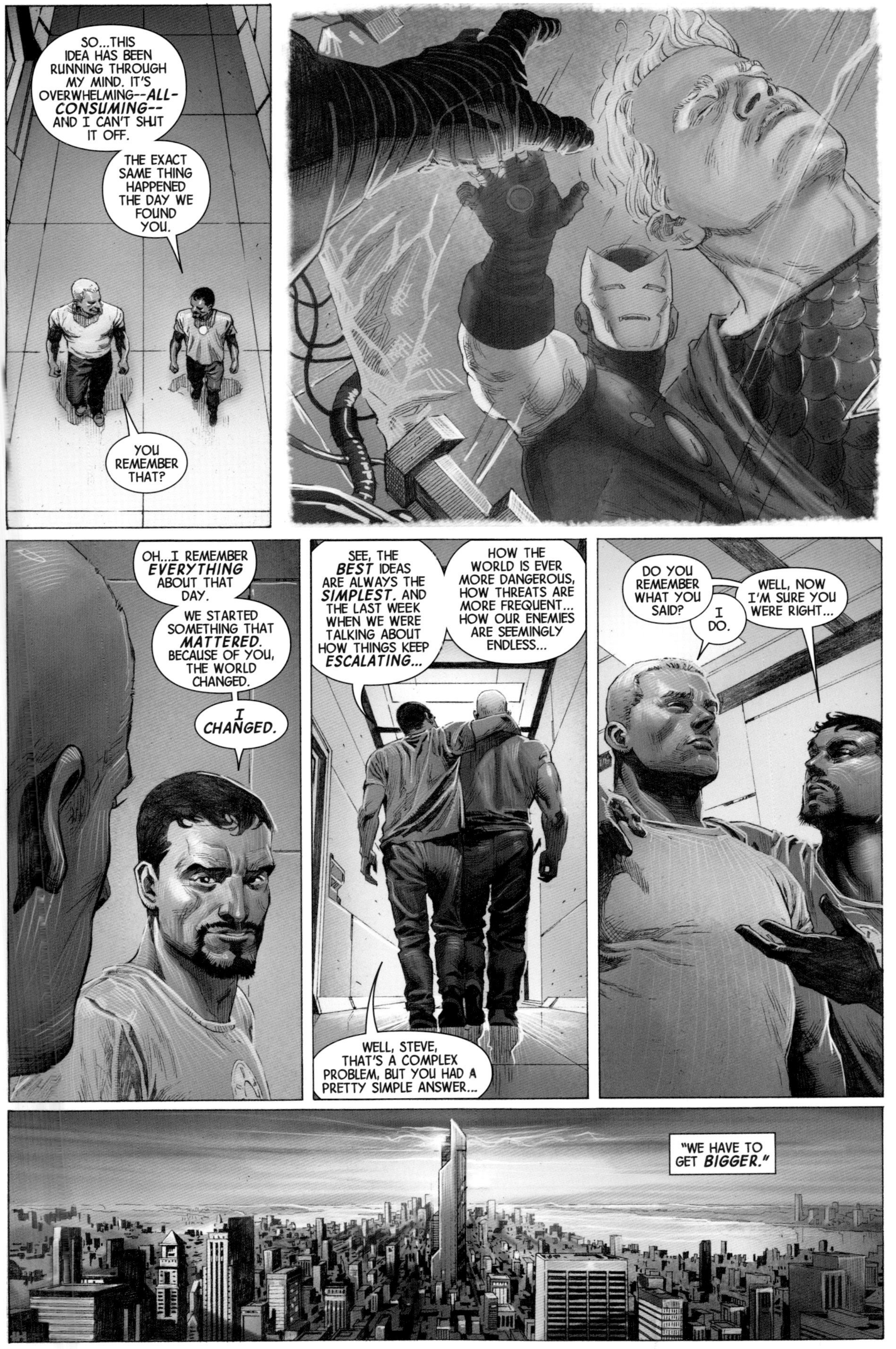
SO...THIS IDEA HAS BEEN RUNNING THROUGH MY MIND. IT'S OVERWHELMING--ALL-CONSUMING--AND I CAN'T SHUT IT OFF.
THE EXACT SAME THING HAPPENED THE DAY WE FOUND YOU.
YOU REMEMBER THAT?
OH...I REMEMBER EVERYTHING ABOUT THAT DAY.
WE STARTED SOMETHING THAT MATTERED. BECAUSE OF YOU, THE WORLD CHANGED.
I CHANGED.
SEE, THE BEST IDEAS ARE ALWAYS THE SIMPLEST. AND THE LAST WEEK WHEN WE WERE TALKING ABOUT HOW THINGS KEEP ESCALATING...
HOW THE WORLD IS EVER MORE DANGEROUS, HOW THREATS ARE MORE FREQUENT... HOW OUR ENEMIES ARE SEEMINGLY ENDLESS...
WELL, STEVE, THAT'S A COMPLEX PROBLEM, BUT YOU HAD A PRETTY SIMPLE ANSWER...
DO YOU REMEMBER WHAT YOU SAID?
I DO.
WELL, NOW I'M SURE YOU WERE RIGHT...
"WE HAVE TO GET BIGGER."

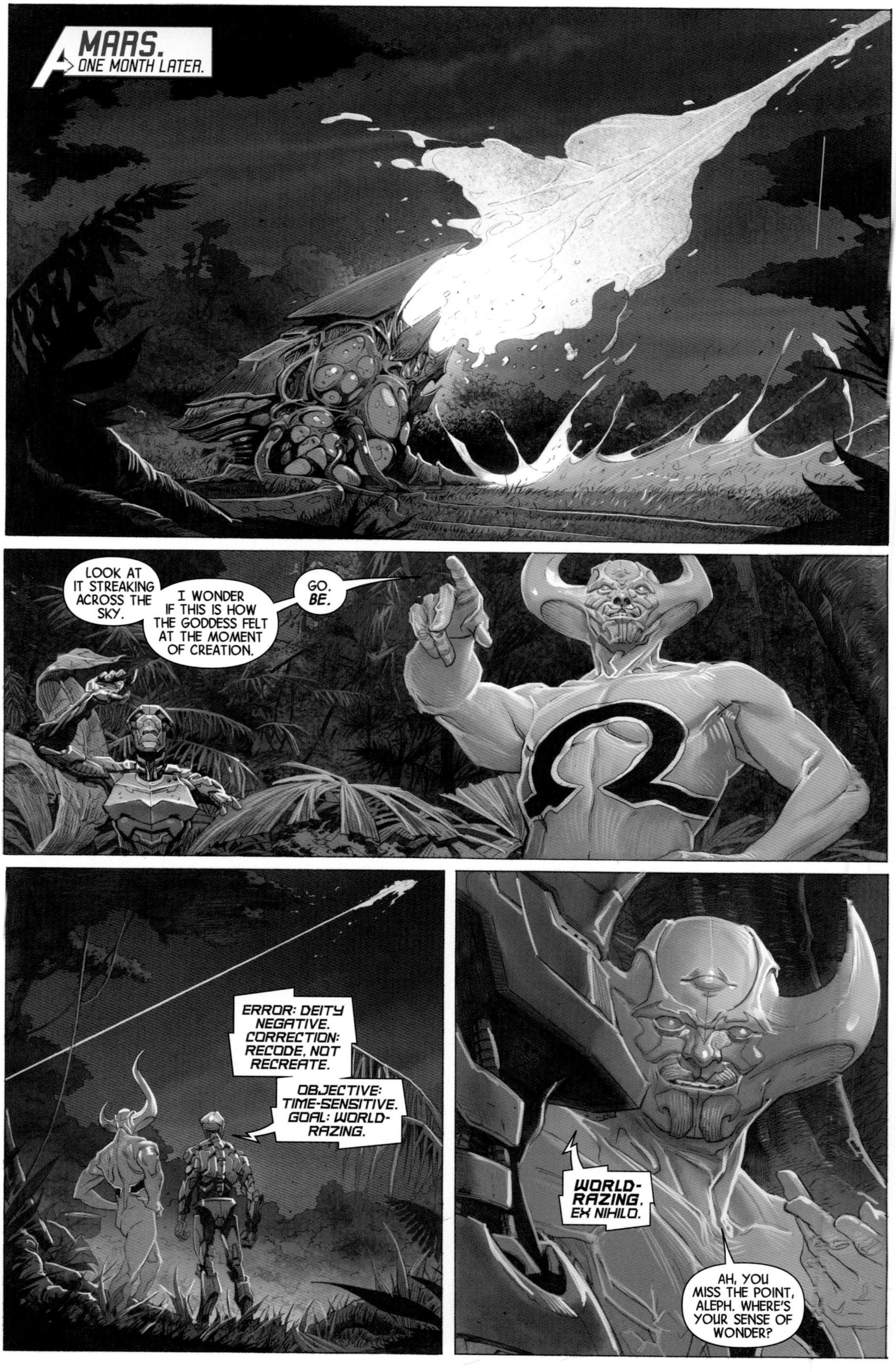
MARS. ONE MONTH LATER.
LOOK AT IT STREAKING ACROSS THE SKY.
I WONDER IF THIS IS HOW THE GODDESS FELT AT THE MOMENT OF CREATION.
GO. BE.
ERROR: DEITY NEGATIVE. CORRECTION: RECODE, NOT RECREATE.
OBJECTIVE: TIME-SENSITIVE. GOAL: WORLD-RAZING.
WORLD-RAZING, EX NIHILO.
AH, YOU MISS THE POINT, ALEPH. WHERE'S YOUR SENSE OF WONDER?

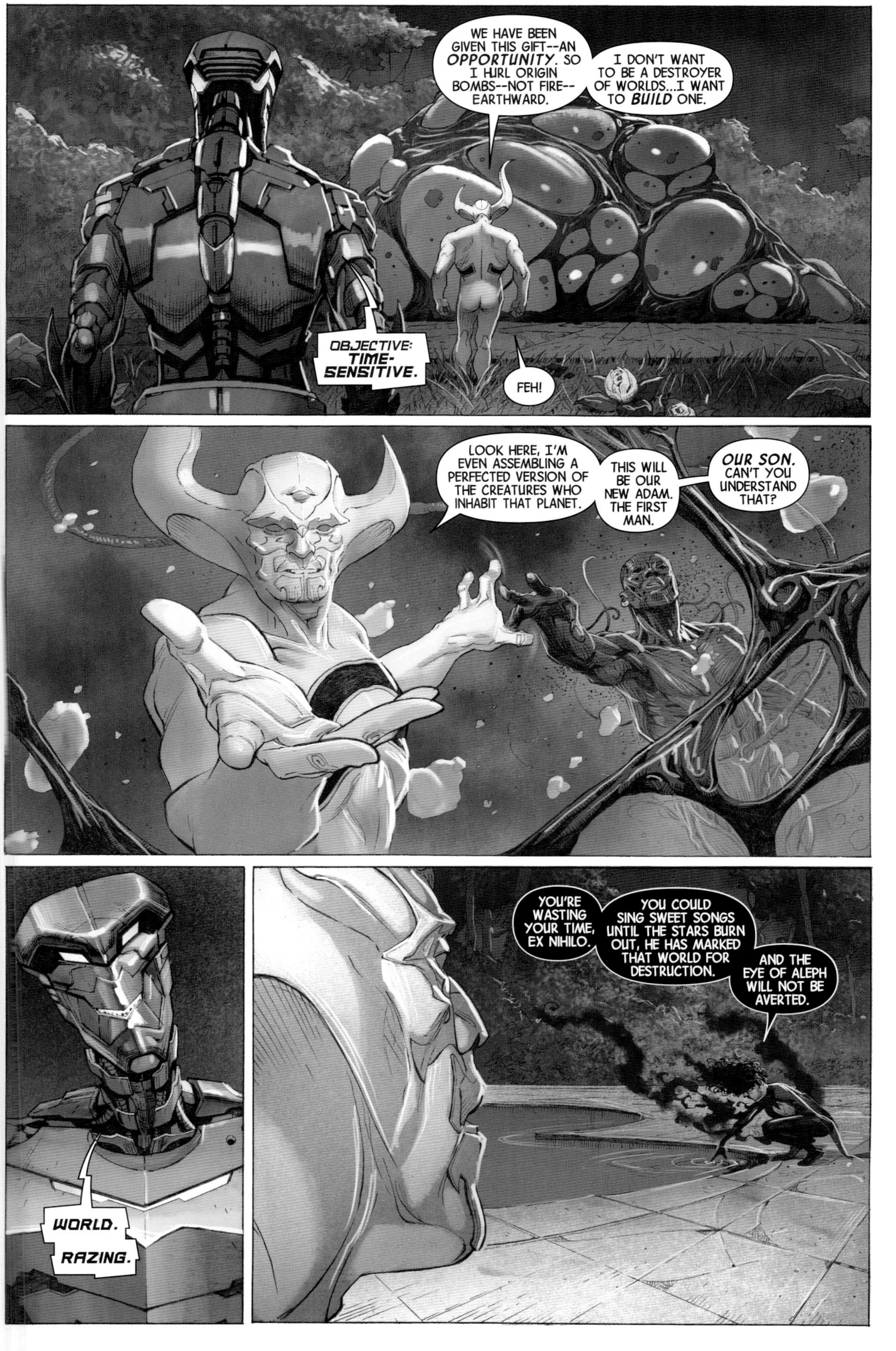
WE HAVE BEEN GIVEN THIS GIFT--AN OPPORTUNITY. SO I HURL ORIGIN BOMBS--NOT FIRE--EARTHWARD.
I DON'T WANT TO BE A DESTROYER OF WORLDS...I WANT TO BUILD ONE.
OBJECTIVE: TIME-SENSITIVE.
FEH!
LOOK HERE, I'M EVEN ASSEMBLING A PERFECTED VERSION OF THE CREATURES WHO INHABIT THAT PLANET.
THIS WILL BE OUR NEW ADAM. THE FIRST MAN.
OUR SON. CAN'T YOU UNDERSTAND THAT?
WORLD. RAZING.
YOU'RE WASTING YOUR TIME, EX NIHILO.
YOU COULD SING SWEET SONGS UNTIL THE STARS BURN OUT, HE HAS MARKED THAT WORLD FOR DESTRUCTION.
AND THE EYE OF ALEPH WILL NOT BE AVERTED.

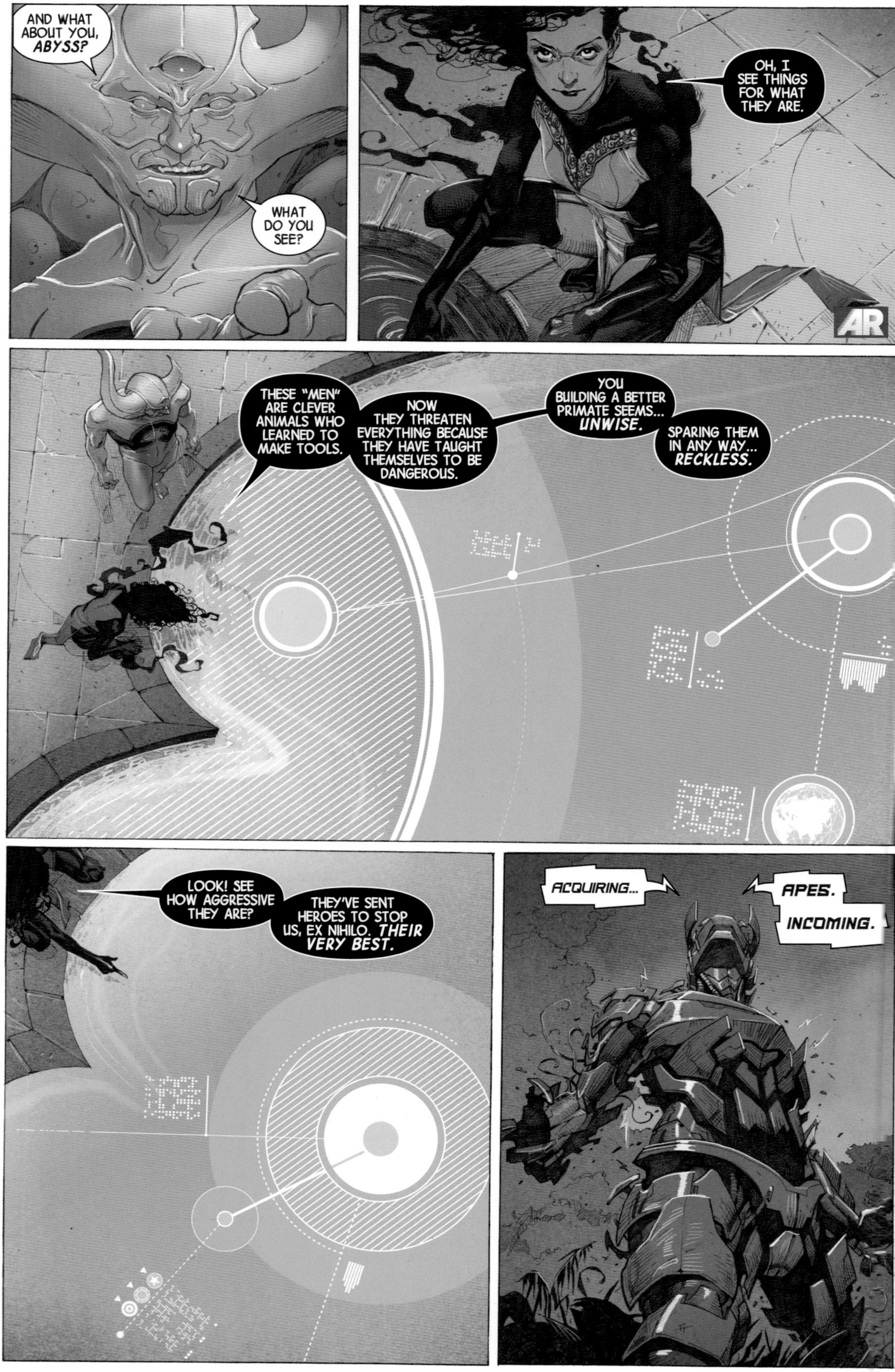
AND WHAT ABOUT YOU, *ABYSS?*
WHAT DO YOU SEE?
OH, I SEE THINGS FOR WHAT THEY ARE.
THESE "MEN" ARE CLEVER ANIMALS WHO LEARNED TO MAKE TOOLS.
NOW THEY THREATEN EVERYTHING BECAUSE THEY HAVE TAUGHT THEMSELVES TO BE DANGEROUS.
YOU BUILDING A BETTER PRIMATE SEEMS... *UNWISE.*
SPARING THEM IN ANY WAY... *RECKLESS.*
LOOK! SEE HOW AGGRESSIVE THEY ARE?
THEY'VE SENT HEROES TO STOP US, EX NIHILO. *THEIR VERY BEST.*
ACQUIRING...
APES.
INCOMING.

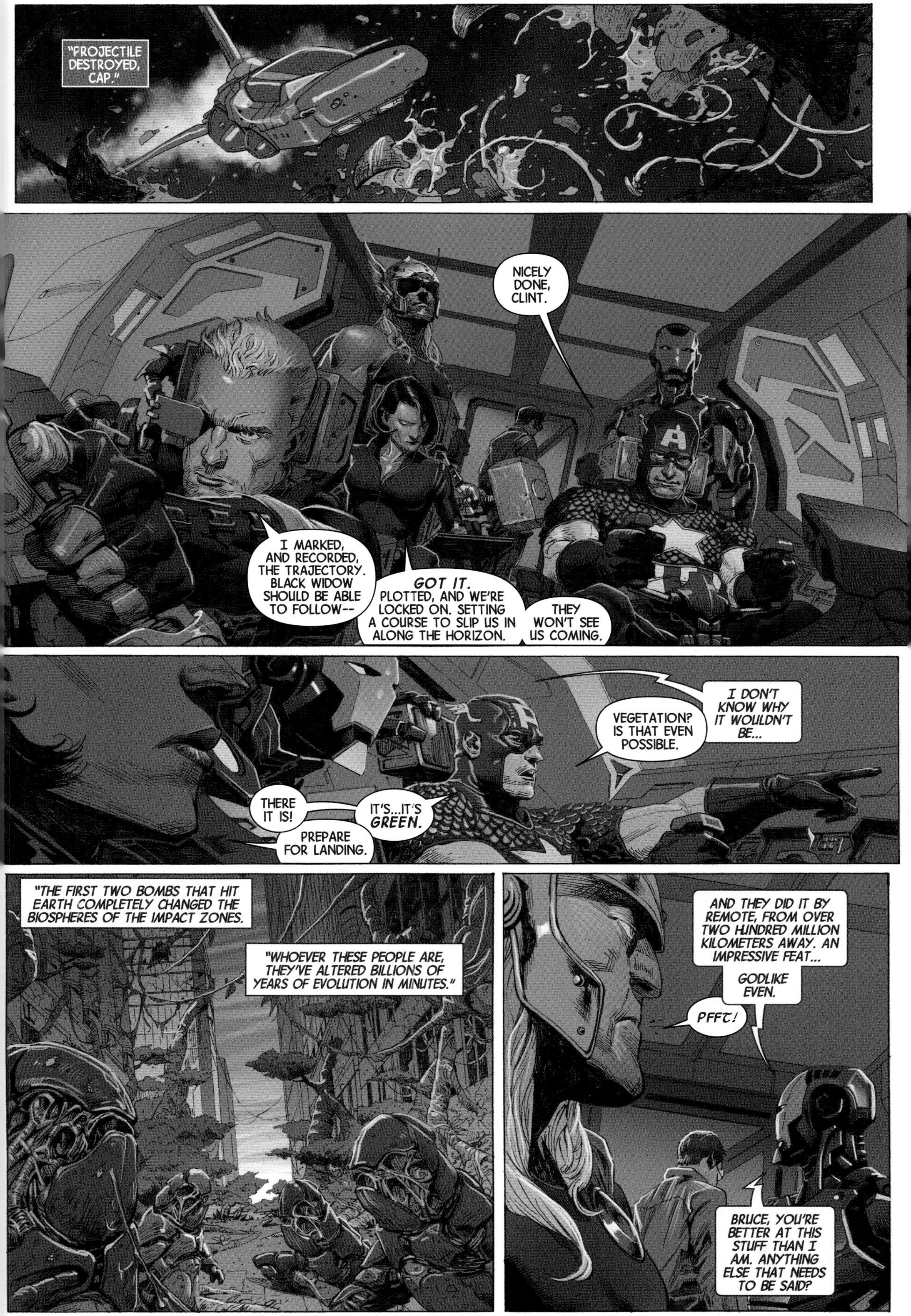
"PROJECTILE DESTROYED, CAP."
NICELY DONE, CLINT.
I MARKED, AND RECORDED, THE TRAJECTORY. BLACK WIDOW SHOULD BE ABLE TO FOLLOW--
GOT IT. PLOTTED, AND WE'RE LOCKED ON. SETTING A COURSE TO SLIP US IN ALONG THE HORIZON.
THEY WON'T SEE US COMING.
VEGETATION? IS THAT EVEN POSSIBLE.
I DON'T KNOW WHY IT WOULDN'T BE...
THERE IT IS!
IT'S...IT'S GREEN.
PREPARE FOR LANDING.
"THE FIRST TWO BOMBS THAT HIT EARTH COMPLETELY CHANGED THE BIOSPHERES OF THE IMPACT ZONES.
"WHOEVER THESE PEOPLE ARE, THEY'VE ALTERED BILLIONS OF YEARS OF EVOLUTION IN MINUTES."
AND THEY DID IT BY REMOTE, FROM OVER TWO HUNDRED MILLION KILOMETERS AWAY. AN IMPRESSIVE FEAT...
GODLIKE EVEN.
PFFT!
BRUCE, YOU'RE BETTER AT THIS STUFF THAN I AM. ANYTHING ELSE THAT NEEDS TO BE SAID?

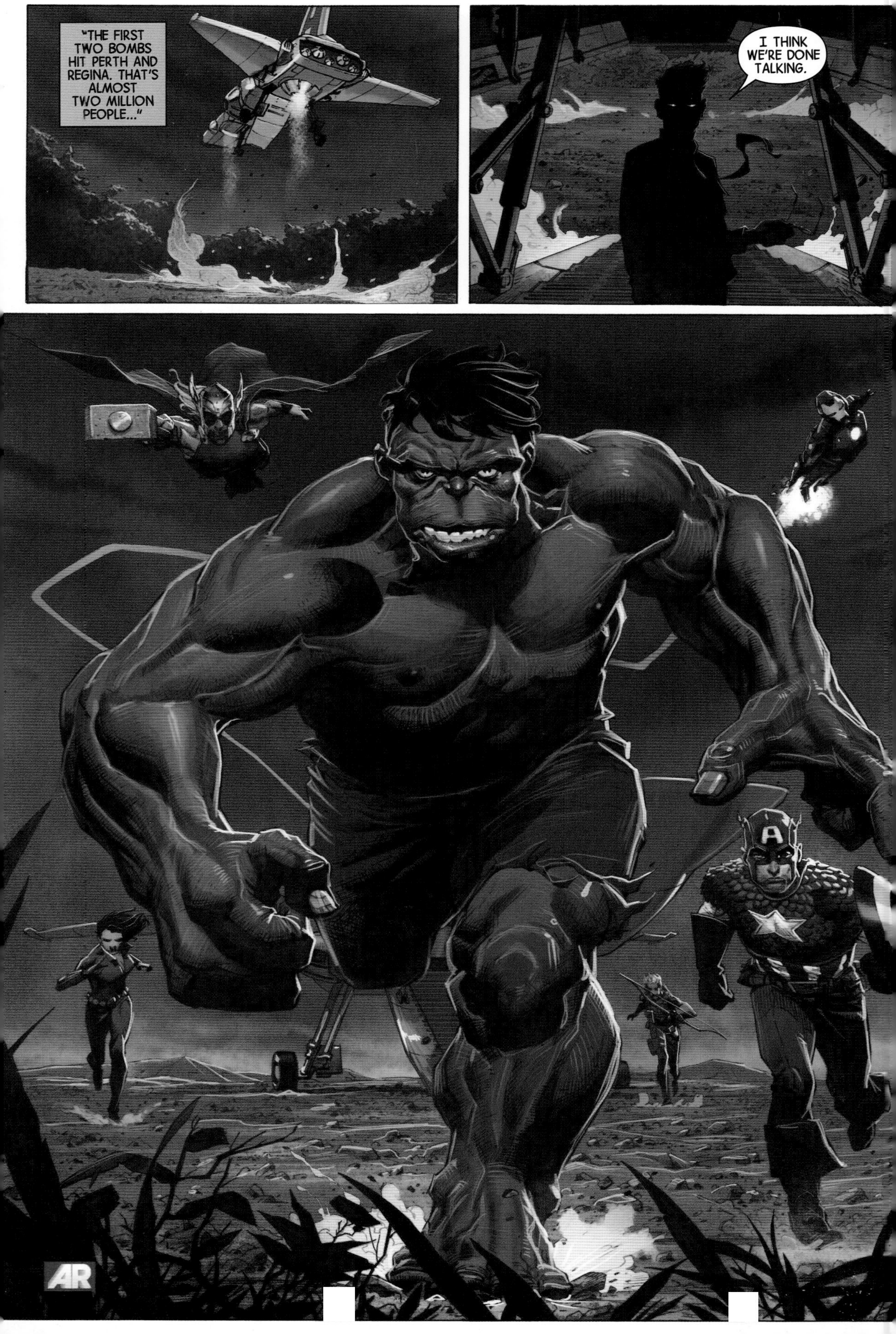
"THE FIRST TWO BOMBS HIT PERTH AND REGINA. THAT'S ALMOST TWO MILLION PEOPLE..."
I THINK WE'RE DONE TALKING.

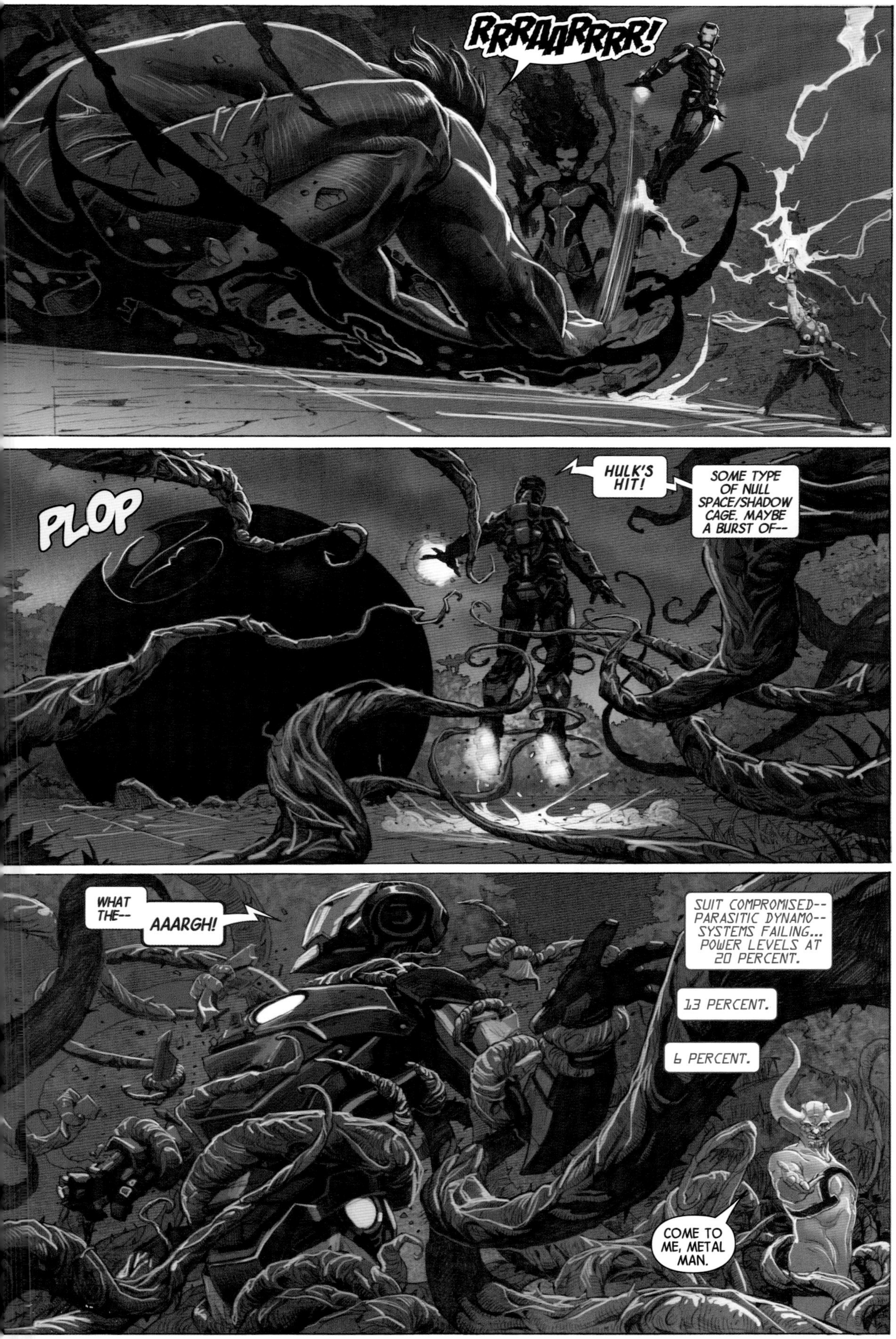
RRRAAARRRR!
PLOP
HULK'S HIT!
SOME TYPE OF NULL SPACE/SHADOW CAGE. MAYBE A BURST OF--
WHAT THE--
AAARGH!
SUIT COMPROMISED--PARASITIC DYNAMO--SYSTEMS FAILING... POWER LEVELS AT 20 PERCENT.
13 PERCENT.
6 PERCENT.
COME TO ME, METAL MAN.

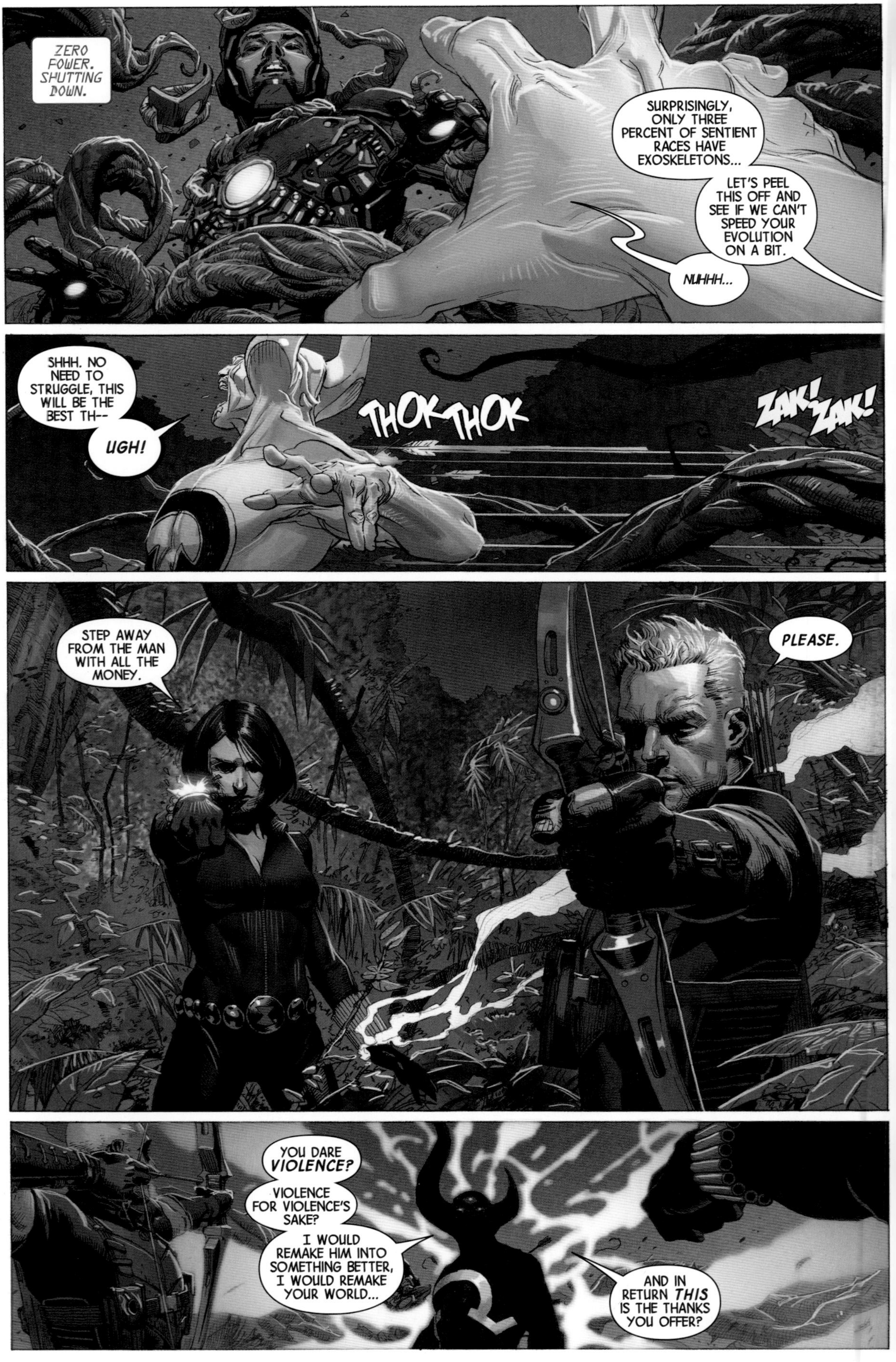

ZERO POWER. SHUTTING DOWN.
SURPRISINGLY, ONLY THREE PERCENT OF SENTIENT RACES HAVE EXOSKELETONS...
LET'S PEEL THIS OFF AND SEE IF WE CAN'T SPEED YOUR EVOLUTION ON A BIT.
NUHHH...
SHHH. NO NEED TO STRUGGLE, THIS WILL BE THE BEST TH--
UGH!
THOK THOK
ZAK! ZAK!
STEP AWAY FROM THE MAN WITH ALL THE MONEY.
PLEASE.
YOU DARE VIOLENCE?
VIOLENCE FOR VIOLENCE'S SAKE?
I WOULD REMAKE HIM INTO SOMETHING BETTER, I WOULD REMAKE YOUR WORLD...
AND IN RETURN THIS IS THE THANKS YOU OFFER?

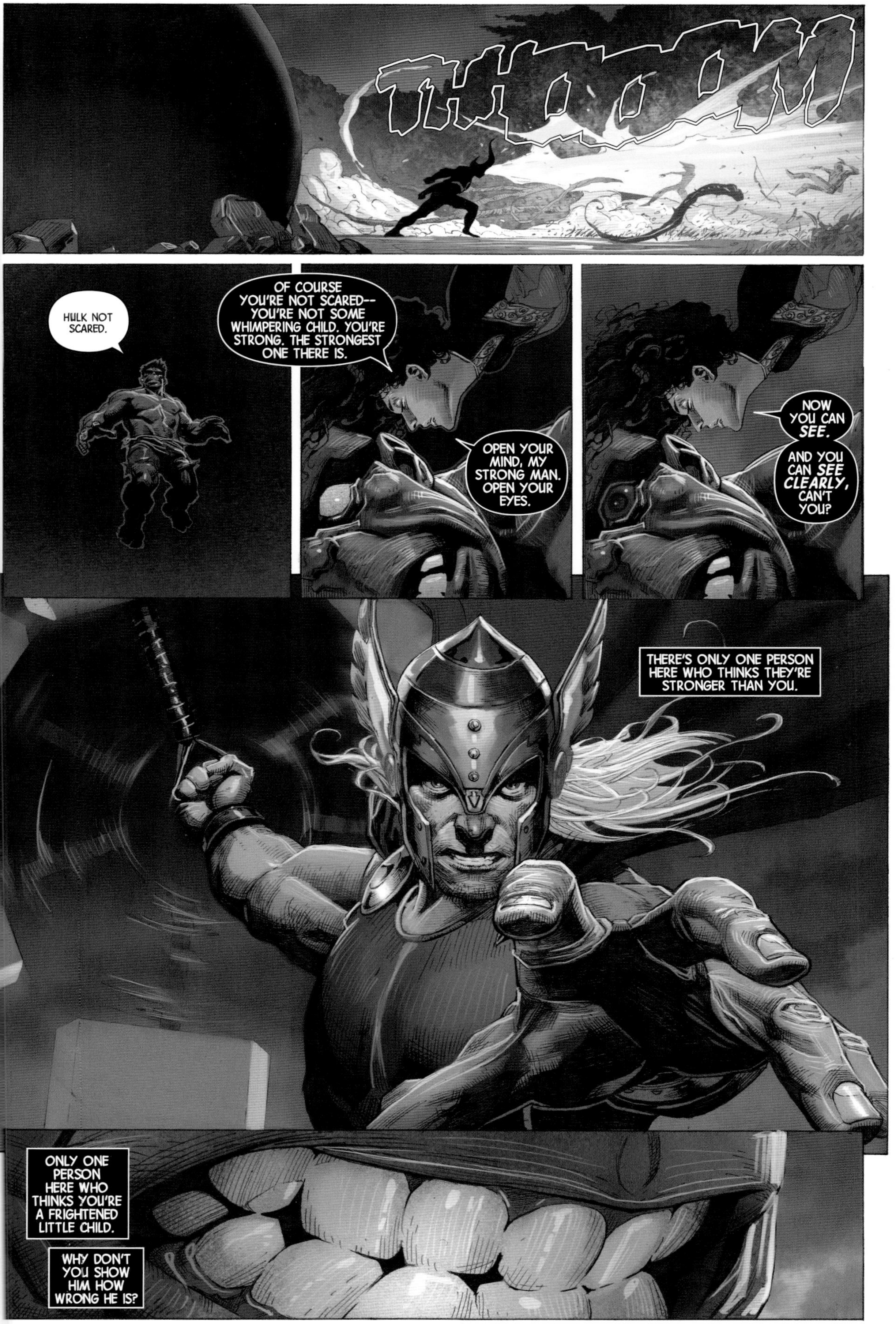
THOOOM
HULK NOT SCARED.
OF COURSE YOU'RE NOT SCARED-- YOU'RE NOT SOME WHIMPERING CHILD. YOU'RE STRONG. THE STRONGEST ONE THERE IS.
OPEN YOUR MIND, MY STRONG MAN. OPEN YOUR EYES.
NOW YOU CAN SEE.
AND YOU CAN SEE CLEARLY, CAN'T YOU?
THERE'S ONLY ONE PERSON HERE WHO THINKS THEY'RE STRONGER THAN YOU.
ONLY ONE PERSON HERE WHO THINKS YOU'RE A FRIGHTENED LITTLE CHILD.
WHY DON'T YOU SHOW HIM HOW WRONG HE IS?

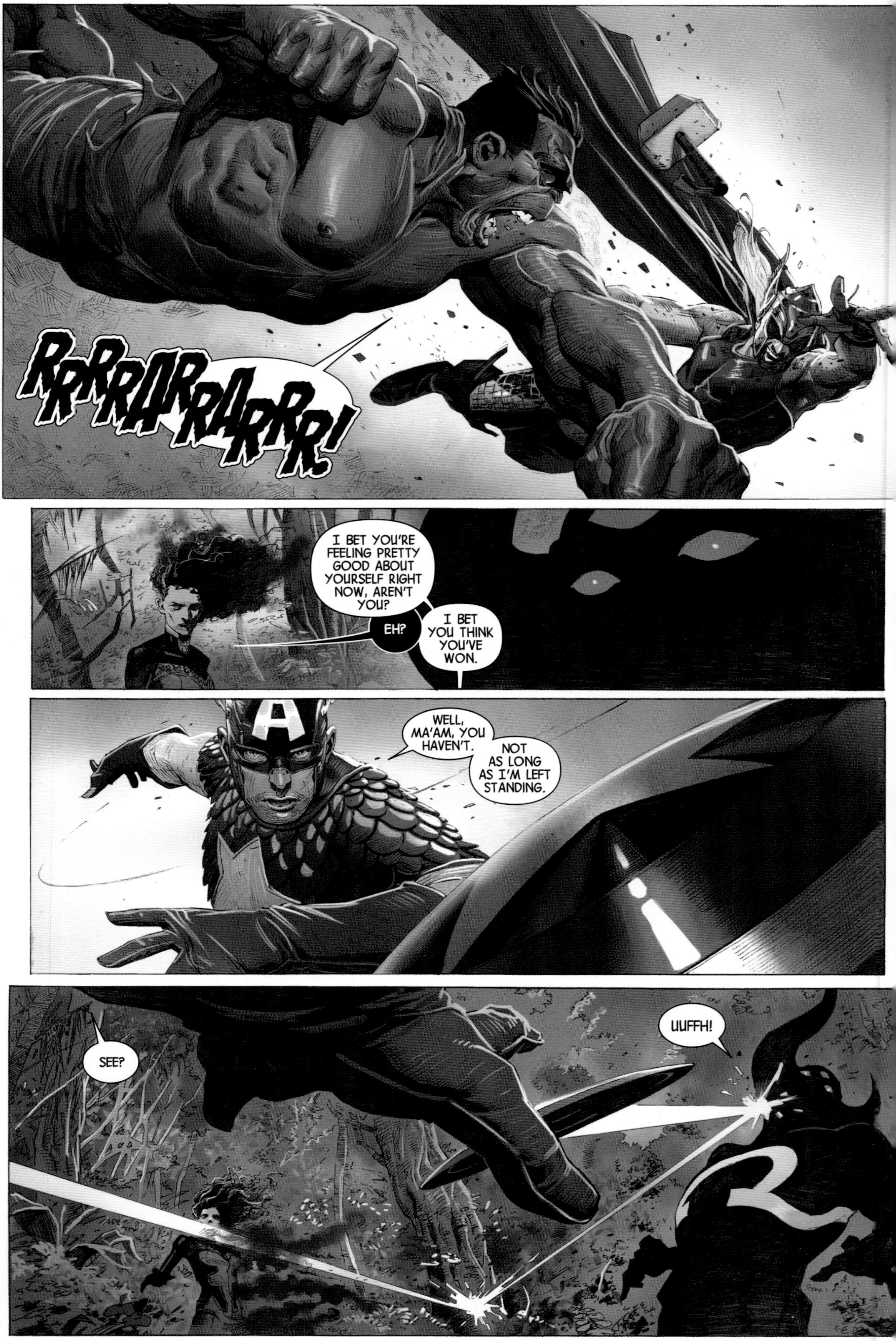
RRRRARRRARRR!
I BET YOU'RE FEELING PRETTY GOOD ABOUT YOURSELF RIGHT NOW, AREN'T YOU?
EH?
I BET YOU THINK YOU'VE WON.
WELL, MA'AM, YOU HAVEN'T.
NOT AS LONG AS I'M LEFT STANDING.
SEE?
UUFFH!

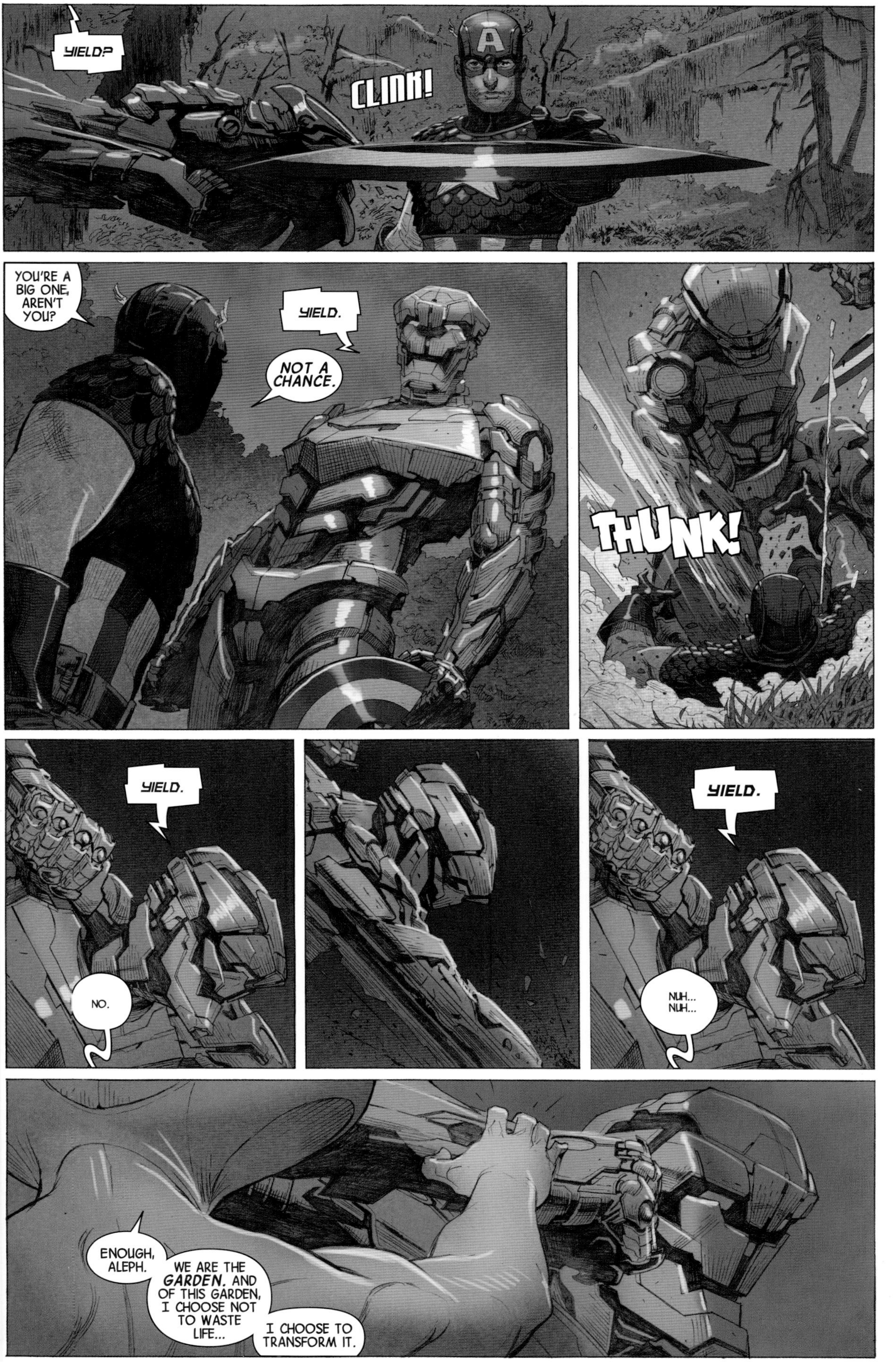
YIELD?
CLINK!
YOU'RE A BIG ONE, AREN'T YOU?
YIELD.
NOT A CHANCE.
THUNK!
YIELD.
NO.
YIELD.
NUH... NUH...
ENOUGH, ALEPH.
WE ARE THE GARDEN. AND OF THIS GARDEN, I CHOOSE NOT TO WASTE LIFE...
I CHOOSE TO TRANSFORM IT.

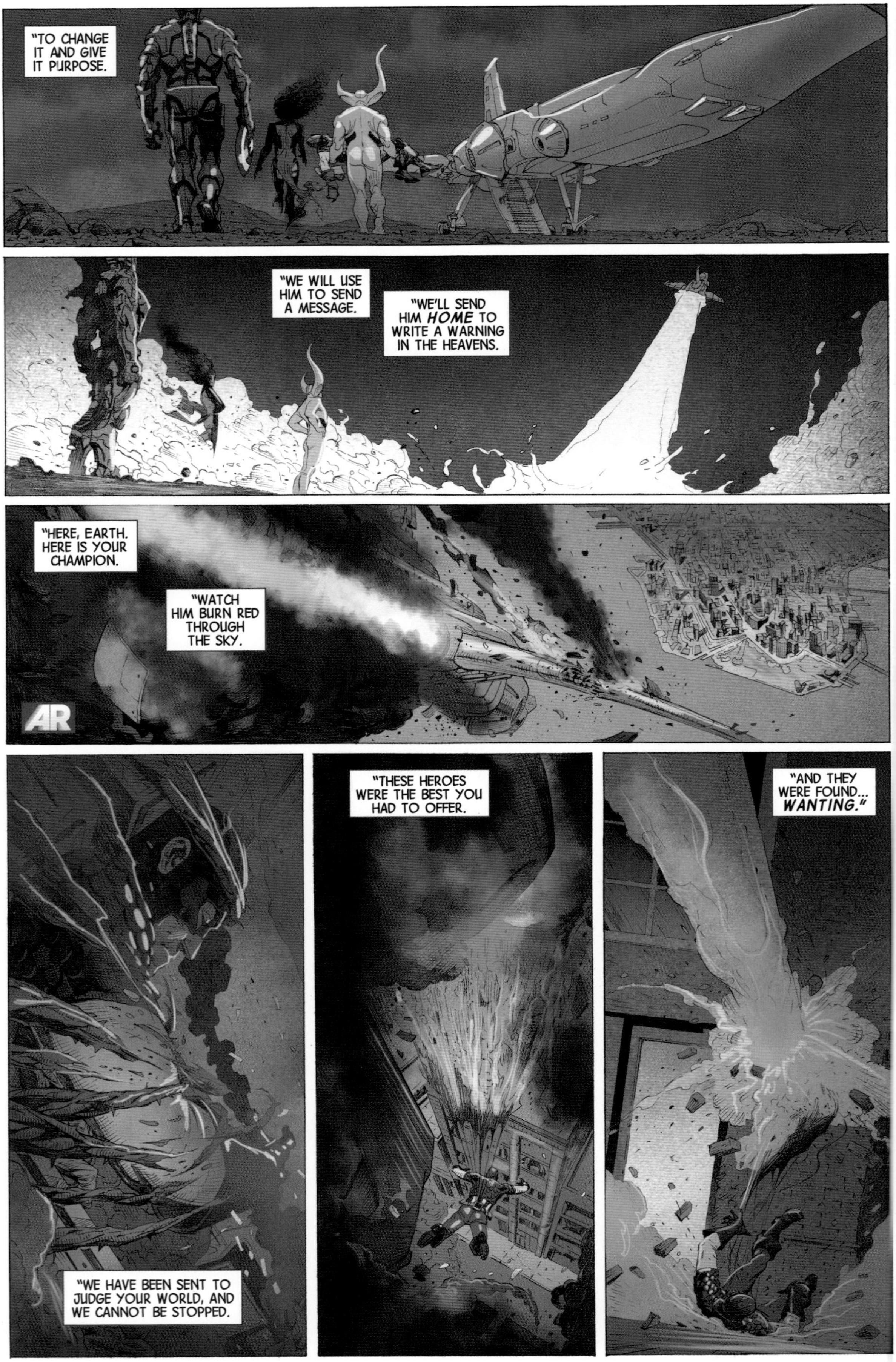
"TO CHANGE IT AND GIVE IT PURPOSE.
"WE WILL USE HIM TO SEND A MESSAGE.
"WE'LL SEND HIM HOME TO WRITE A WARNING IN THE HEAVENS.
"HERE, EARTH. HERE IS YOUR CHAMPION.
"WATCH HIM BURN RED THROUGH THE SKY.
AR
"WE HAVE BEEN SENT TO JUDGE YOUR WORLD, AND WE CANNOT BE STOPPED.
"THESE HEROES WERE THE BEST YOU HAD TO OFFER.
"AND THEY WERE FOUND... WANTING."

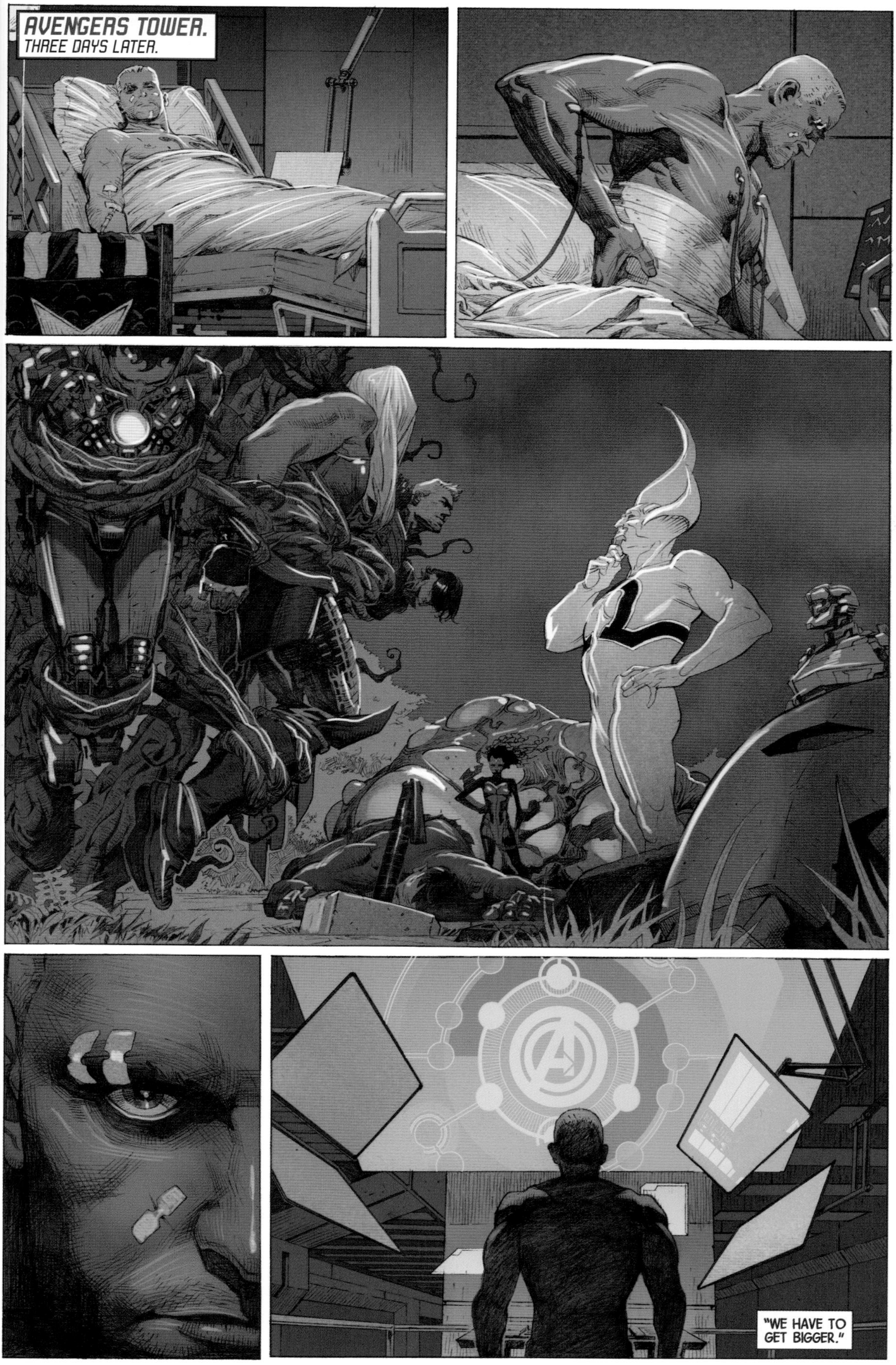
AVENGERS TOWER.
THREE DAYS LATER.
"WE HAVE TO GET BIGGER."

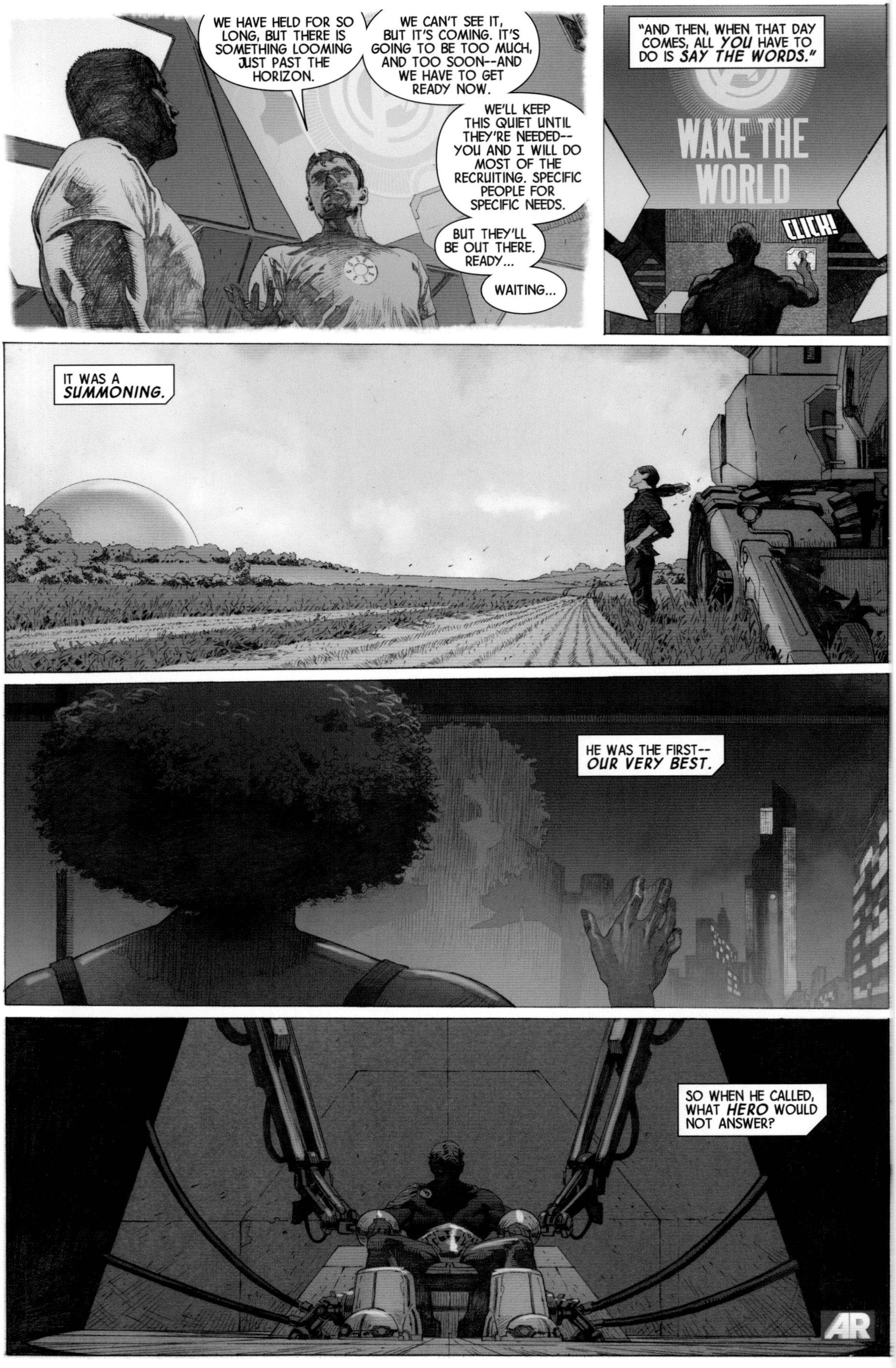

WE HAVE HELD FOR SO LONG, BUT THERE IS SOMETHING LOOMING JUST PAST THE HORIZON.
WE CAN'T SEE IT, BUT IT'S COMING. IT'S GOING TO BE TOO MUCH, AND TOO SOON--AND WE HAVE TO GET READY NOW.
WE'LL KEEP THIS QUIET UNTIL THEY'RE NEEDED--YOU AND I WILL DO MOST OF THE RECRUITING. SPECIFIC PEOPLE FOR SPECIFIC NEEDS.
BUT THEY'LL BE OUT THERE. READY...
WAITING...
"AND THEN, WHEN THAT DAY COMES, ALL *YOU* HAVE TO DO IS *SAY THE WORDS.*"
WAKE THE WORLD
CLICK!
IT WAS A *SUMMONING.*
HE WAS THE FIRST--*OUR VERY BEST.*
SO WHEN HE CALLED, WHAT *HERO* WOULD NOT ANSWER?

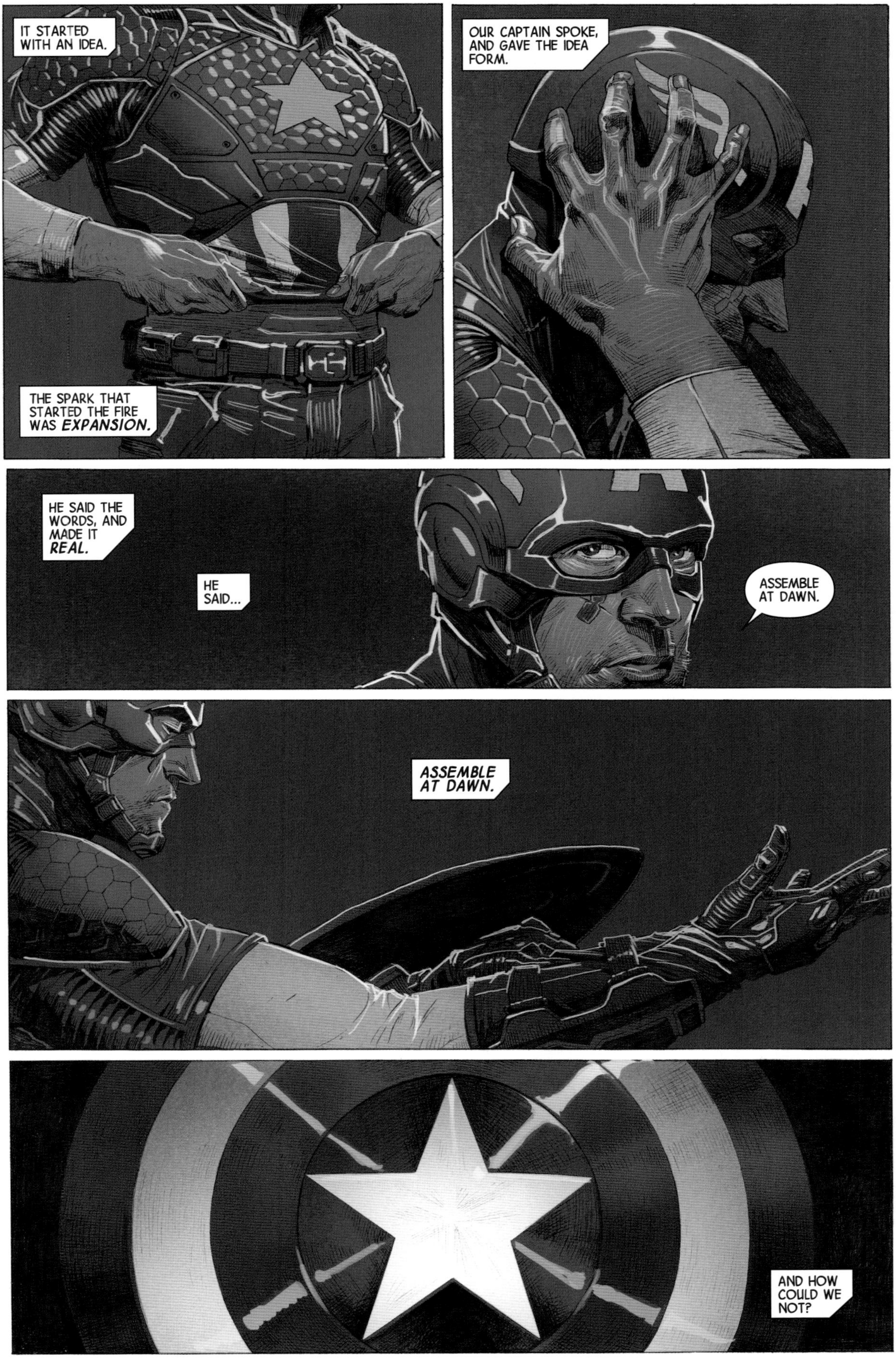
IT STARTED WITH AN IDEA.
THE SPARK THAT STARTED THE FIRE WAS *EXPANSION.*
OUR CAPTAIN SPOKE, AND GAVE THE IDEA FORM.
HE SAID THE WORDS, AND MADE IT *REAL.*
HE SAID...
ASSEMBLE AT DAWN.
ASSEMBLE AT DAWN.
AND HOW COULD WE NOT?

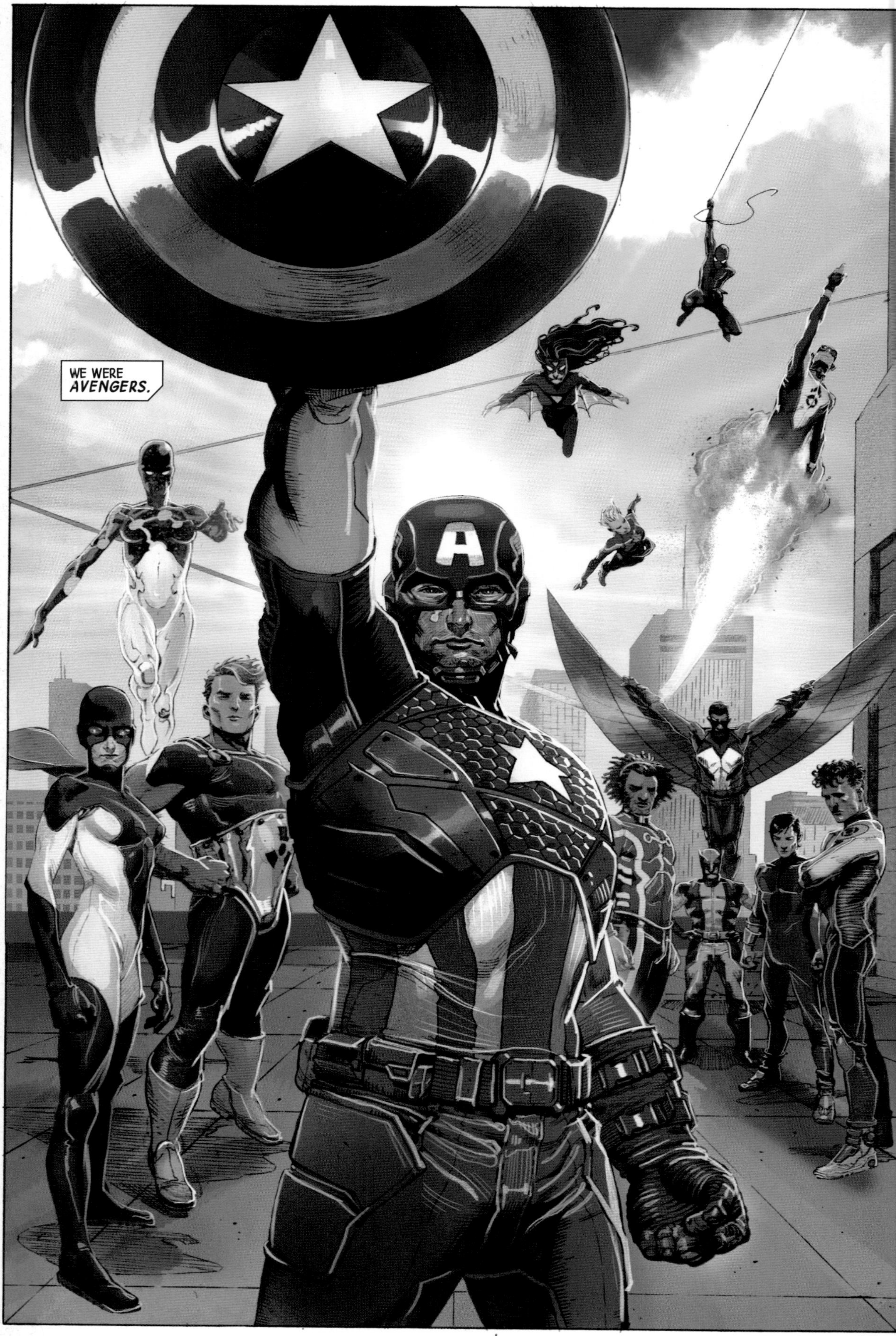
WE WERE AVENGERS.

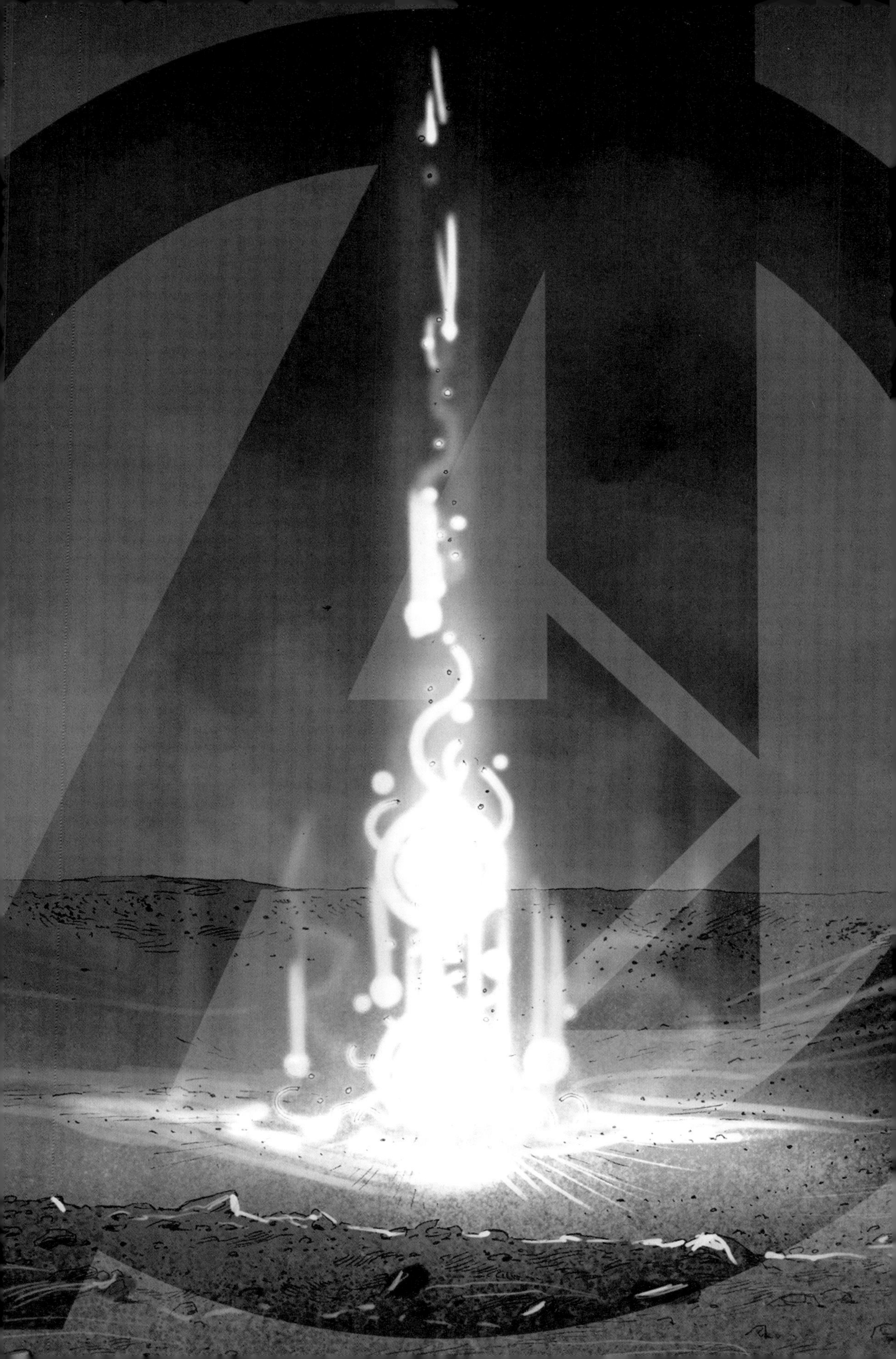

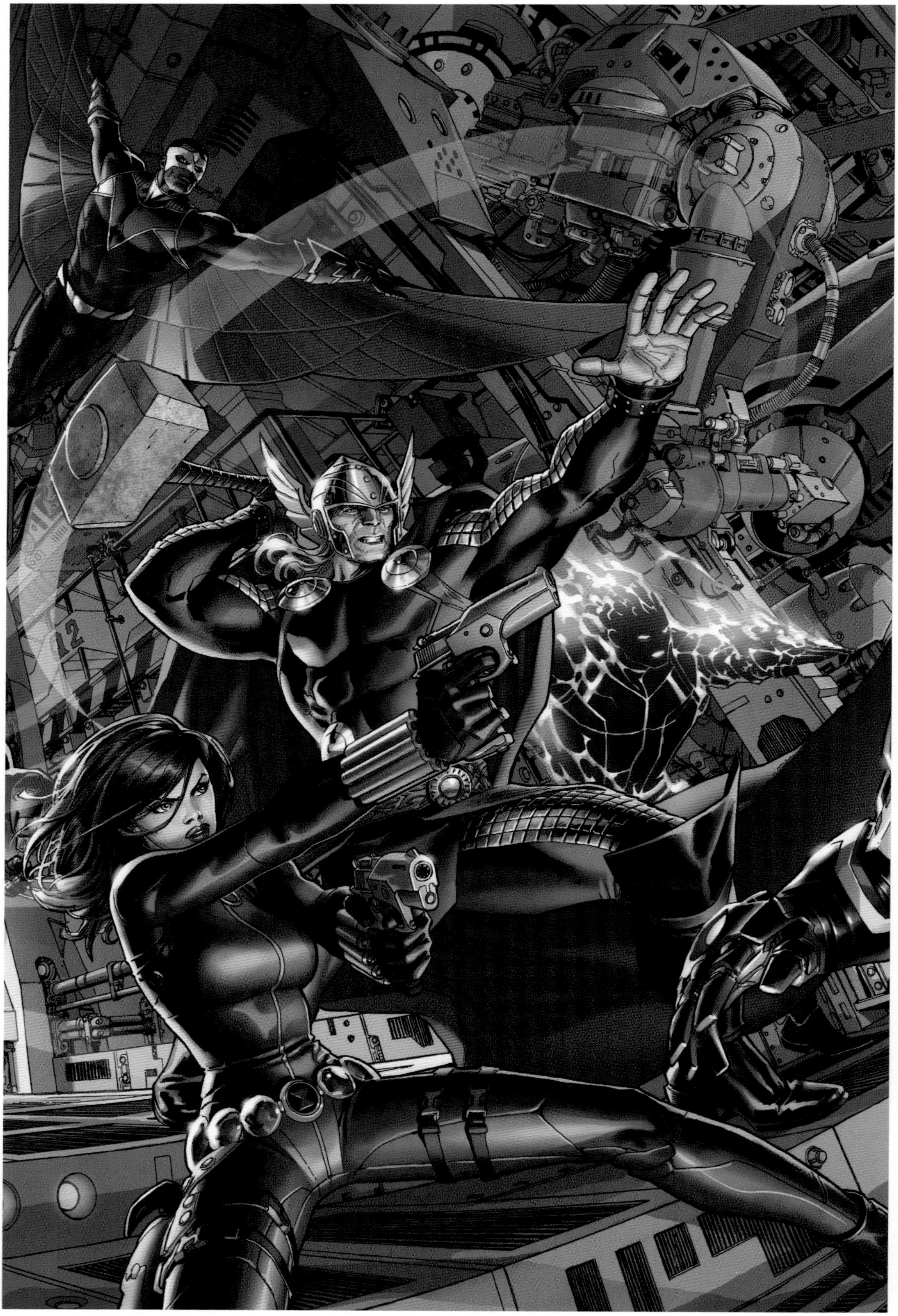

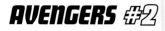

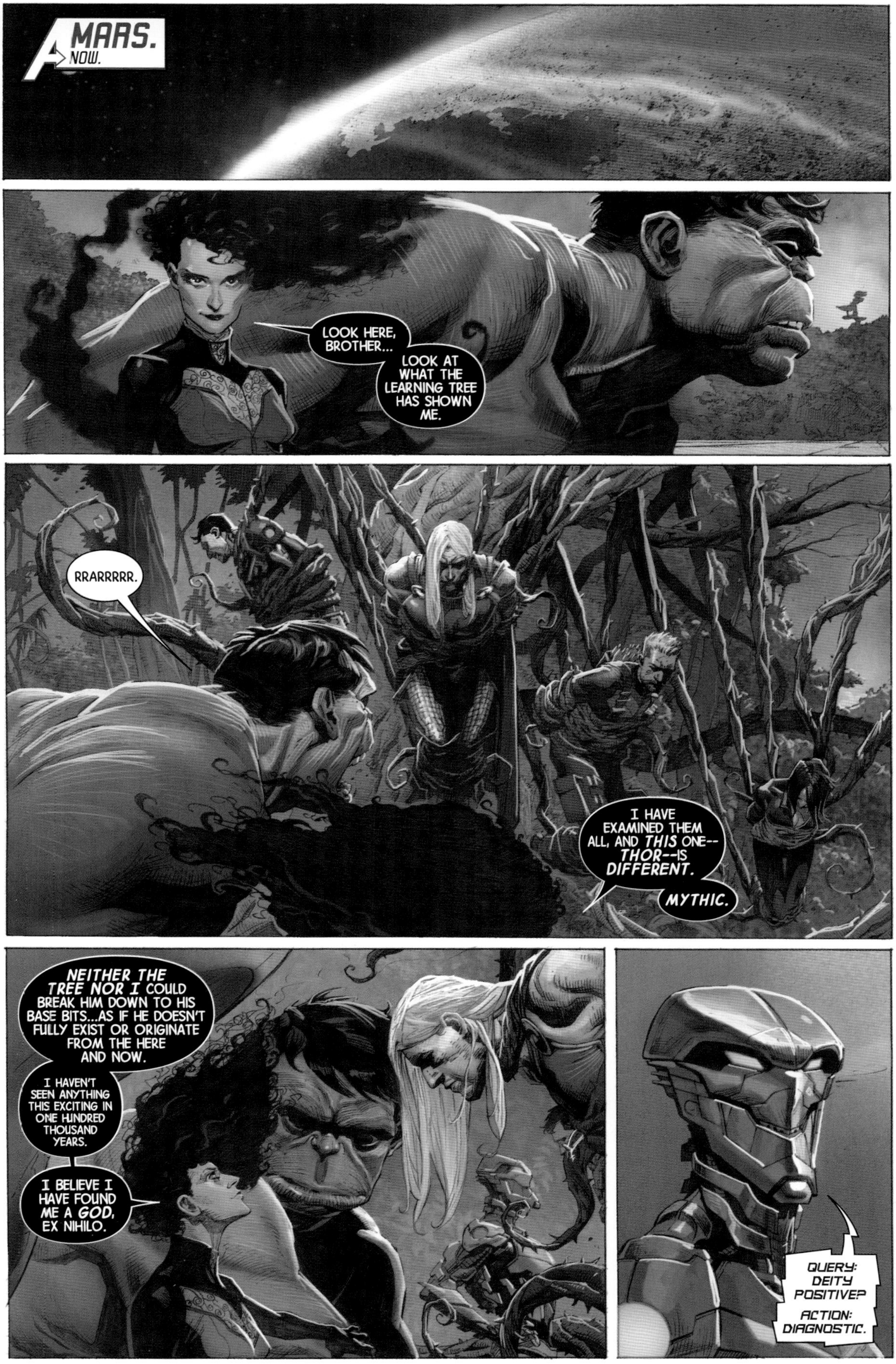
MARS. NOW.
LOOK HERE, BROTHER...
LOOK AT WHAT THE LEARNING TREE HAS SHOWN ME.
RRARRRRR.
I HAVE EXAMINED THEM ALL, AND THIS ONE--THOR--IS DIFFERENT.
MYTHIC.
NEITHER THE TREE NOR I COULD BREAK HIM DOWN TO HIS BASE BITS...AS IF HE DOESN'T FULLY EXIST OR ORIGINATE FROM THE HERE AND NOW.
I HAVEN'T SEEN ANYTHING THIS EXCITING IN ONE HUNDRED THOUSAND YEARS.
I BELIEVE I HAVE FOUND ME A GOD, EX NIHILO.
QUERY: DEITY POSITIVE?
ACTION: DIAGNOSTIC.

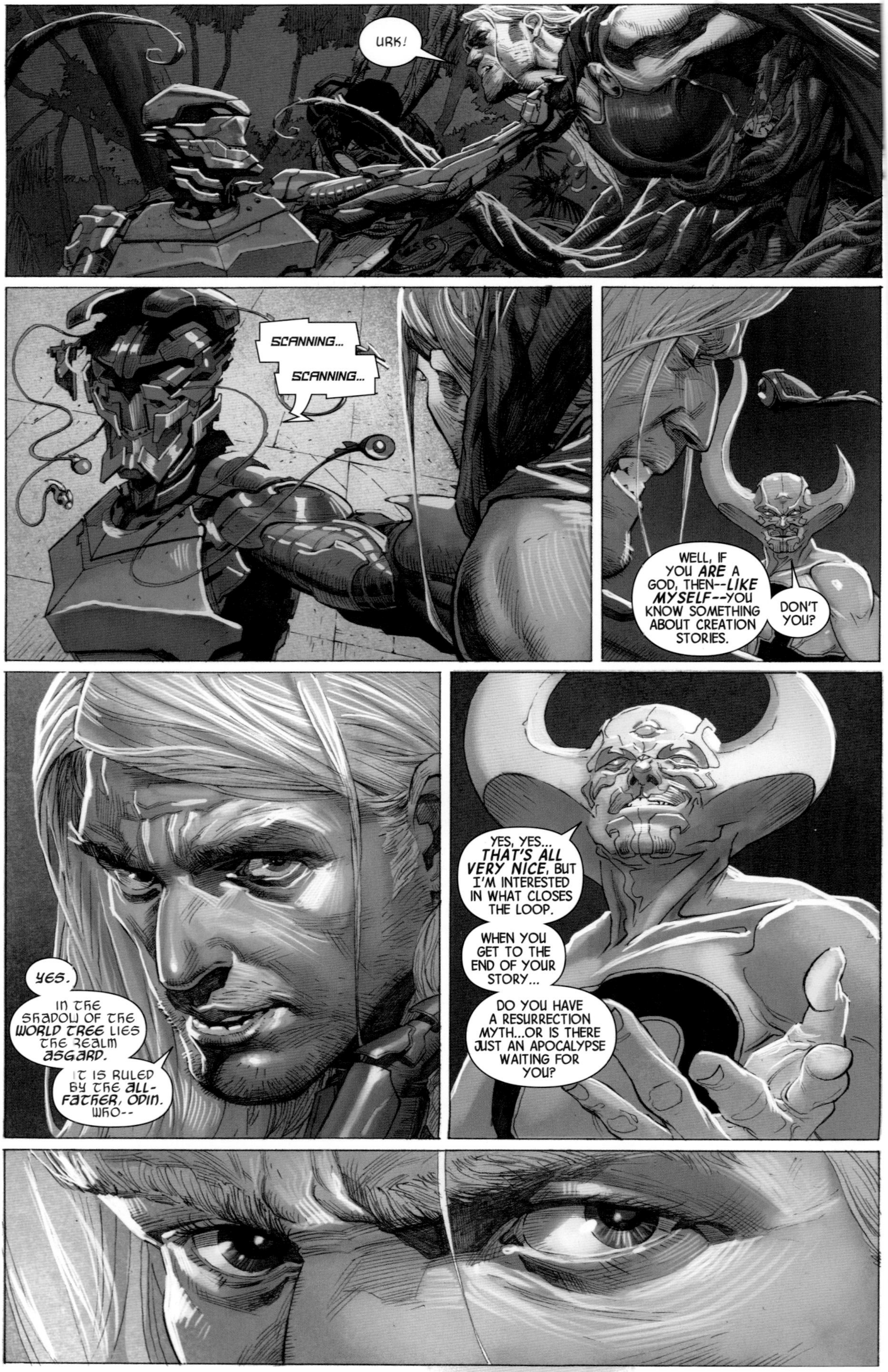
URK!
SCANNING...
SCANNING...
WELL, IF YOU ARE A GOD, THEN--LIKE MYSELF--YOU KNOW SOMETHING ABOUT CREATION STORIES.
DON'T YOU?
YES.
IN THE SHADOW OF THE WORLD TREE LIES THE REALM ASGARD.
IT IS RULED BY THE ALL-FATHER, ODIN. WHO--
YES, YES... THAT'S ALL VERY NICE, BUT I'M INTERESTED IN WHAT CLOSES THE LOOP.
WHEN YOU GET TO THE END OF YOUR STORY...
DO YOU HAVE A RESURRECTION MYTH...OR IS THERE JUST AN APOCALYPSE WAITING FOR YOU?

LISTEN CLOSELY, *GOD.*

THIS IS THE TRUE BEGINNING...

AND THIS IS HOW IT ALL ENDS FOR YOUR WORLD.

"AT THE DAWN OF EVERYTHING WERE THE *BUILDERS.* THEY WERE THE FIRST RACE, THE OLDEST LIVING THINGS IN THE COSMOS.

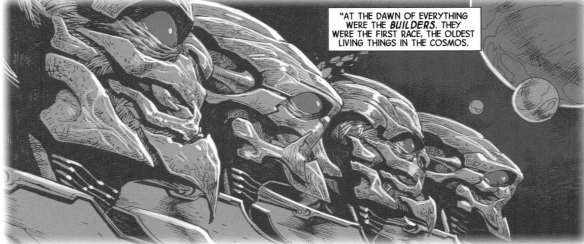

"THEY WERE A PERFECT PEOPLE--AND FOR A GREAT WHILE THEY WORSHIPPED THE GODDESS, THE MOTHER-MAKER HERSELF, *THE UNIVERSE.*

"EVENTUALLY, THEY GREW BEYOND THIS-- ABANDONING THE OLD WAYS OF REVERENCE FOR THE NEW PATH OF RELEVANCE.

"AS EXPANSION AND EVOLUTION OCCURRED, THE *BUILDERS* CREATED AGGRESSIVE *SYSTEMS* TO DIRECT, SHAPE AND CONTROL THE VERY STRUCTURE OF SPACE AND TIME.

"THE FIRST OF THESE SYSTEMS WERE *GARDENERS-- ALEPHS* SENT OUT INTO THE WILD TO PURGE SPECIES UNFIT, AND UNSUITABLE, FOR THEIR *NEW UNIVERSE.*

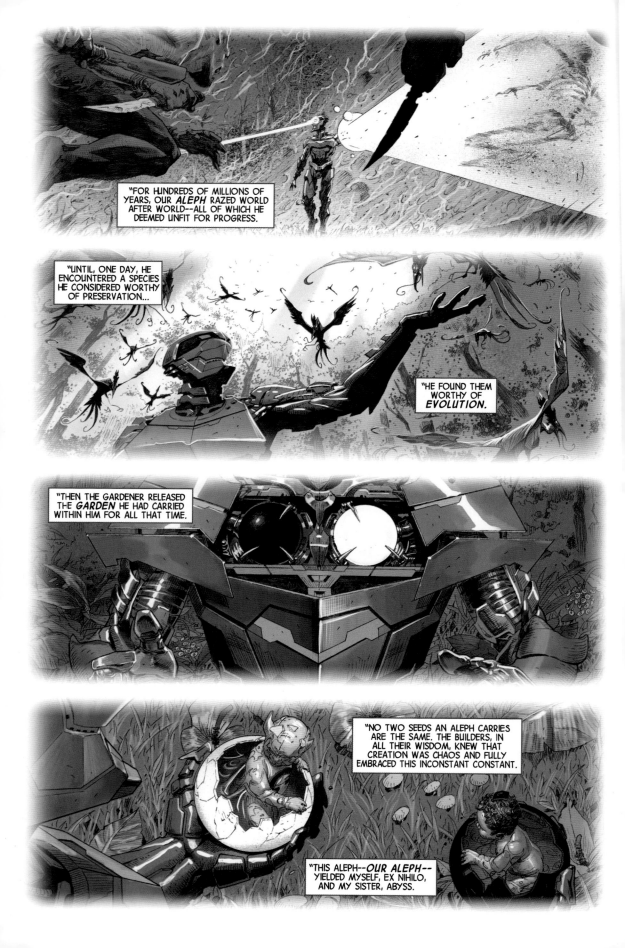

"FOR HUNDREDS OF MILLIONS OF YEARS, OUR *ALEPH* RAZED WORLD AFTER WORLD--ALL OF WHICH HE DEEMED UNFIT FOR PROGRESS.

"UNTIL, ONE DAY, HE ENCOUNTERED A SPECIES HE CONSIDERED WORTHY OF PRESERVATION...

"HE FOUND THEM WORTHY OF *EVOLUTION.*

"THEN THE GARDENER RELEASED THE *GARDEN* HE HAD CARRIED WITHIN HIM FOR ALL THAT TIME.

"NO TWO SEEDS AN ALEPH CARRIES ARE THE SAME. THE BUILDERS, IN ALL THEIR WISDOM, KNEW THAT CREATION WAS CHAOS AND FULLY EMBRACED THIS INCONSTANT CONSTANT.

"THIS ALEPH--*OUR ALEPH*-- YIELDED MYSELF, EX NIHILO, AND MY SISTER, ABYSS.

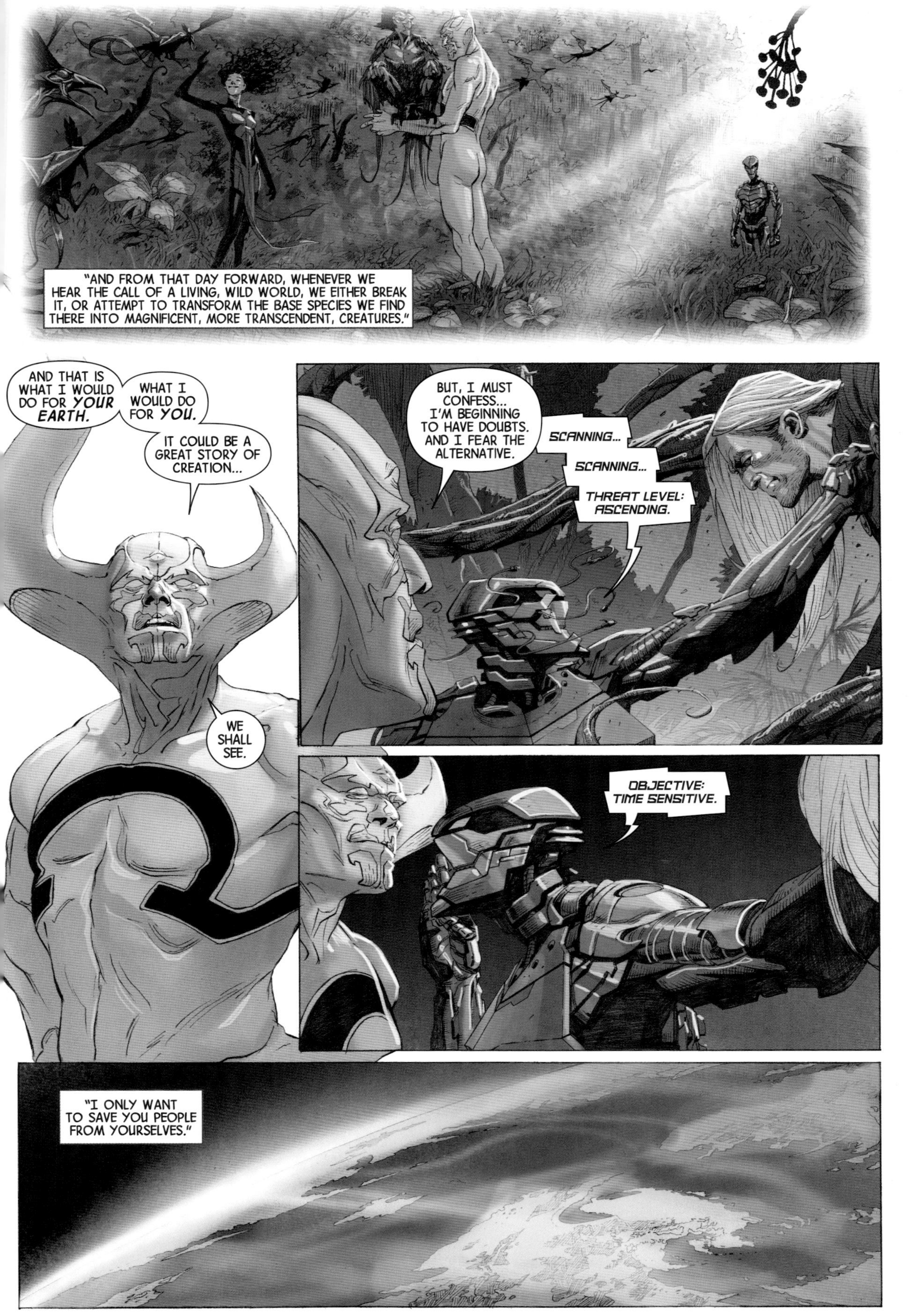
"AND FROM THAT DAY FORWARD, WHENEVER WE HEAR THE CALL OF A LIVING, WILD WORLD, WE EITHER BREAK IT, OR ATTEMPT TO TRANSFORM THE BASE SPECIES WE FIND THERE INTO MAGNIFICENT, MORE TRANSCENDENT, CREATURES."
AND THAT IS WHAT I WOULD DO FOR *YOUR EARTH.*
WHAT I WOULD DO FOR *YOU.*
IT COULD BE A GREAT STORY OF CREATION...
BUT, I MUST CONFESS... I'M BEGINNING TO HAVE DOUBTS. AND I FEAR THE ALTERNATIVE.
SCANNING...
SCANNING...
THREAT LEVEL: ASCENDING.
WE SHALL SEE.
OBJECTIVE: TIME SENSITIVE.
"I ONLY WANT TO SAVE YOU PEOPLE FROM YOURSELVES."

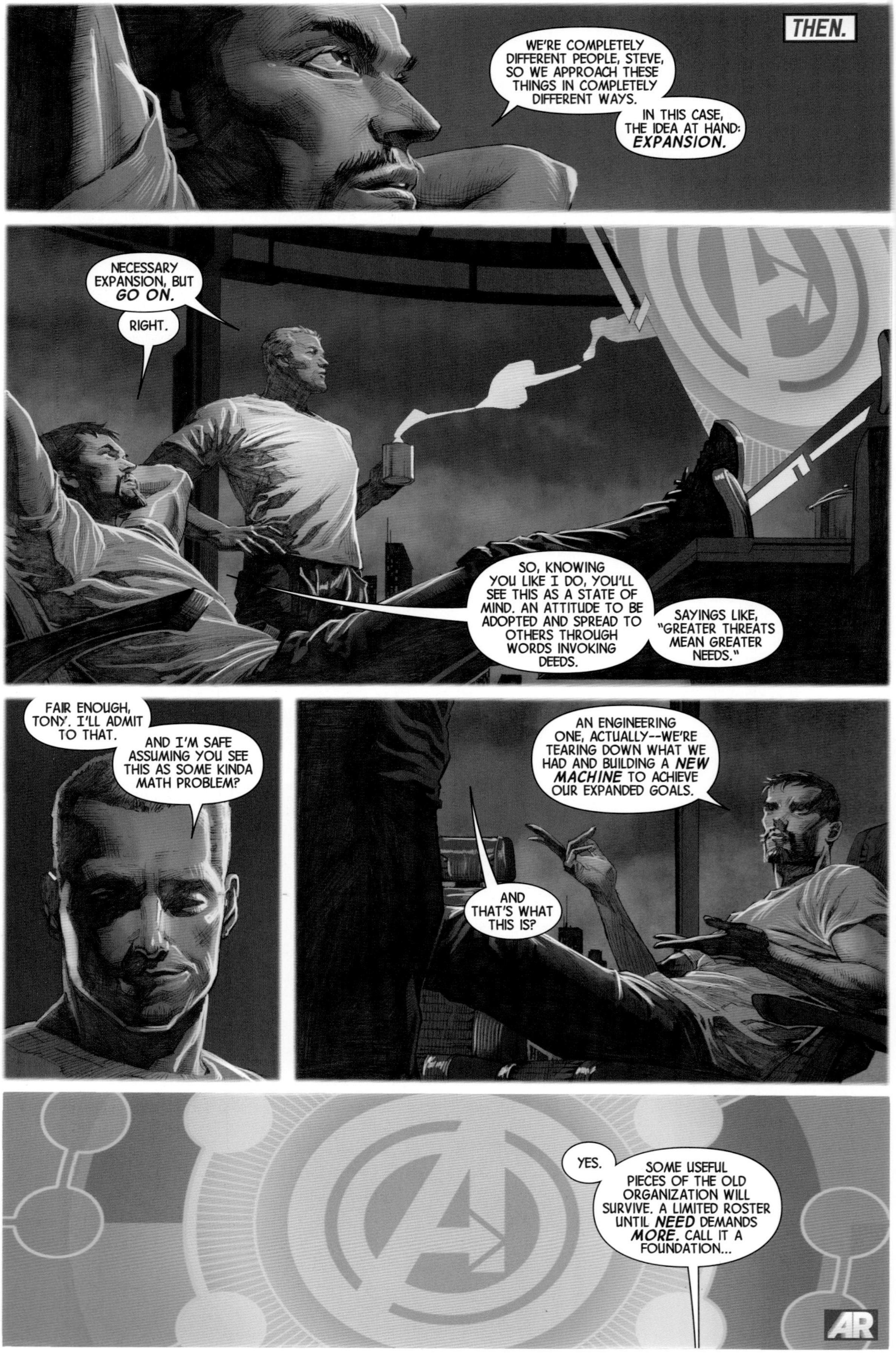
THEN.
WE'RE COMPLETELY DIFFERENT PEOPLE, STEVE, SO WE APPROACH THESE THINGS IN COMPLETELY DIFFERENT WAYS.
IN THIS CASE, THE IDEA AT HAND: EXPANSION.
NECESSARY EXPANSION, BUT GO ON.
RIGHT.
SO, KNOWING YOU LIKE I DO, YOU'LL SEE THIS AS A STATE OF MIND. AN ATTITUDE TO BE ADOPTED AND SPREAD TO OTHERS THROUGH WORDS INVOKING DEEDS.
SAYINGS LIKE, "GREATER THREATS MEAN GREATER NEEDS."
FAIR ENOUGH, TONY. I'LL ADMIT TO THAT.
AND I'M SAFE ASSUMING YOU SEE THIS AS SOME KINDA MATH PROBLEM?
AN ENGINEERING ONE, ACTUALLY--WE'RE TEARING DOWN WHAT WE HAD AND BUILDING A NEW MACHINE TO ACHIEVE OUR EXPANDED GOALS.
AND THAT'S WHAT THIS IS?
YES.
SOME USEFUL PIECES OF THE OLD ORGANIZATION WILL SURVIVE. A LIMITED ROSTER UNTIL NEED DEMANDS MORE. CALL IT A FOUNDATION...
AR

UH-HUH. THE TWO OF US... PLUS THOR, *OF COURSE.*

WE'LL WANT HAWKEYE AND BLACK WIDOW.

AGREED. ALSO, BANNER.

BANNER?

REALLY?

IN TIJUANA. OR A MONASTERY. MAYBE SPACE CAMP.

JOKE ALL YOU WANT, BUT WHEN WE SEND OUT THE CALL TO EXPAND, WE'LL WANT A SUPPORT STRUCTURE WITHIN THIS LARGER GROUP--PEOPLE WHO UNDERSTAND OUR *TRADITION* AND OUR *PURPOSE.*

YOU KNOW HOW THAT ALWAYS ENDS.

AH, YOU MEAN FORMER MEMBERS TO GO ALONG WITH ANY NEWER ONES.

UH-HUH.

CAPTAIN UNIVERSE

HYPERION

ESPECIALLY IF WE'RE TALKING ABOUT PUSHING THE BOUNDARIES AS FAR AS WE CAN.

SMASHER

ALREADY THERE.

I'VE DONE THE INITIAL VETTING OF EVERYONE ON THIS LIST. WE'LL WANT TO GET INTO IT A BIT MORE...

BUT FOR NOW, I THINK WE'RE FINE USING THIS AS A LAUNCHING POINT.

ALL RIGHT...

CLICK

• WAN... ...MOFF
• PI... ...IMO...
• HE...
• MARC SPECTOR
• ...ONITA JUÁR...
...S RHODE...
...ETT
...ORR
...A JONES
...ARRETT
...ROVIK
... AQUE...
...LL
...YDS
...RM
...MM
...ARA BAR...
00 099
...ICA RAMB...
...ER WALT...
DANVERS
...EL WILSON
...ON WILLIA...
PA...IA WA...
• BRIAN B...DD...
MATTH...
DAISY...
JAMES BAR...

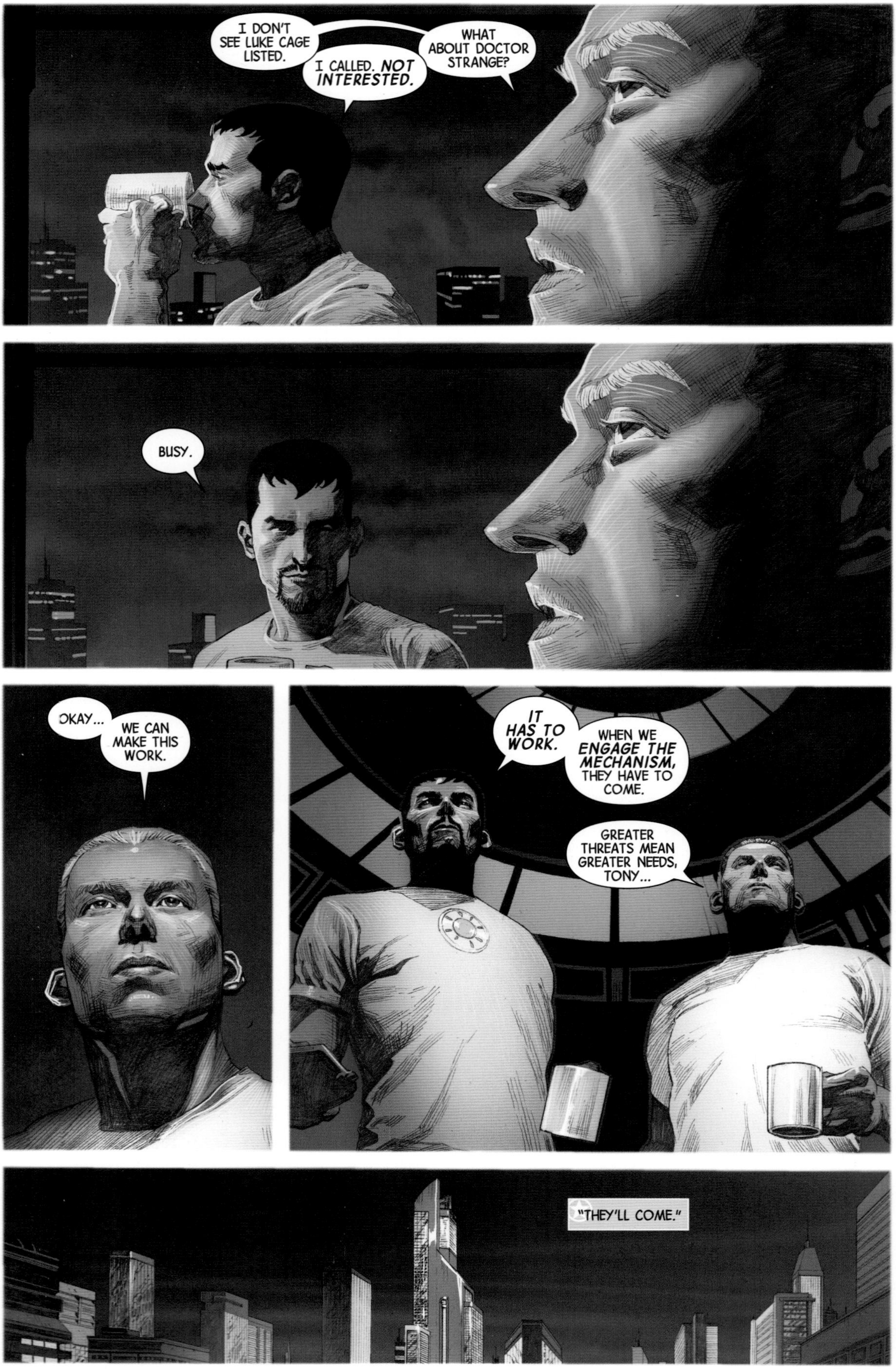
I DON'T SEE LUKE CAGE LISTED.
I CALLED. NOT INTERESTED.
WHAT ABOUT DOCTOR STRANGE?
BUSY.
OKAY...
WE CAN MAKE THIS WORK.
IT HAS TO WORK.
WHEN WE ENGAGE THE MECHANISM, THEY HAVE TO COME.
GREATER THREATS MEAN GREATER NEEDS, TONY...
"THEY'LL COME."

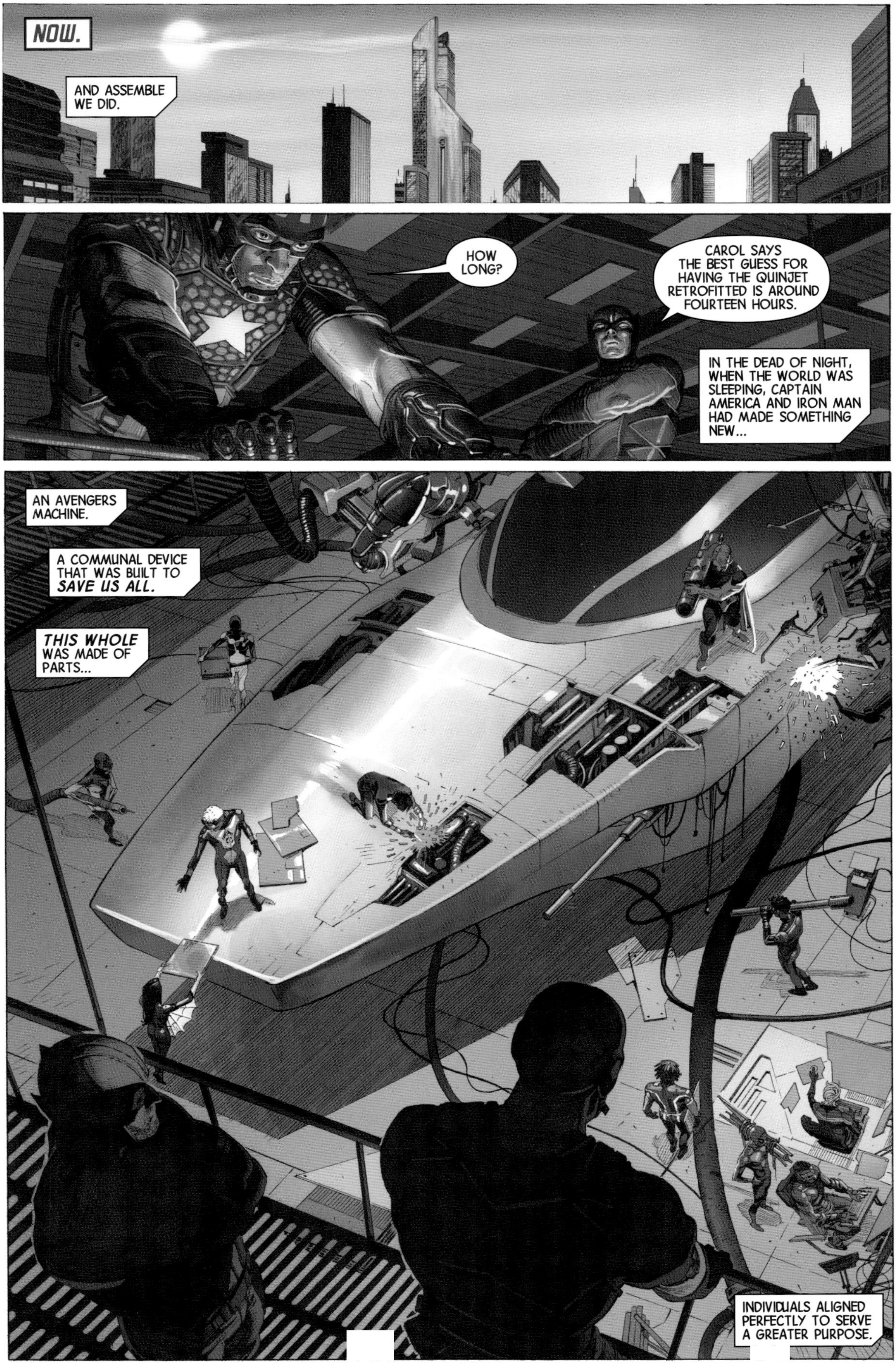
NOW.
AND ASSEMBLE WE DID.
HOW LONG?
CAROL SAYS THE BEST GUESS FOR HAVING THE QUINJET RETROFITTED IS AROUND FOURTEEN HOURS.
IN THE DEAD OF NIGHT, WHEN THE WORLD WAS SLEEPING, CAPTAIN AMERICA AND IRON MAN HAD MADE SOMETHING NEW...
AN AVENGERS MACHINE.
A COMMUNAL DEVICE THAT WAS BUILT TO *SAVE US ALL.*
THIS WHOLE WAS MADE OF PARTS...
INDIVIDUALS ALIGNED PERFECTLY TO SERVE A GREATER PURPOSE.

WHEN CALLED, THEY EACH CAME FOR DIFFERENT REASONS.

WE HAVE BEER.

SOLD.

WOLVERINE.

WE HAVE MONEY.

OH, THANK GOD.

SPIDER-MAN.

I DUNNO... BIRDSEED?

PHSST.

THIS IS ME ASKING, SAM.

THEN YOU ALREADY KNOW.

GOOD. KEEP YOUR PHONE ON.

THE FALCON.

SOME OF US WANTED A NEW CHALLENGE.

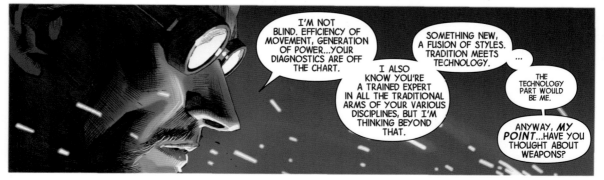

I'M NOT BLIND. EFFICIENCY OF MOVEMENT, GENERATION OF POWER...YOUR DIAGNOSTICS ARE OFF THE CHART.

I ALSO KNOW YOU'RE A TRAINED EXPERT IN ALL THE TRADITIONAL ARMS OF YOUR VARIOUS DISCIPLINES, BUT I'M THINKING BEYOND THAT.

SOMETHING NEW, A FUSION OF STYLES. TRADITION MEETS TECHNOLOGY.

...

THE TECHNOLOGY PART WOULD BE ME.

ANYWAY, MY POINT...HAVE YOU THOUGHT ABOUT WEAPONS?

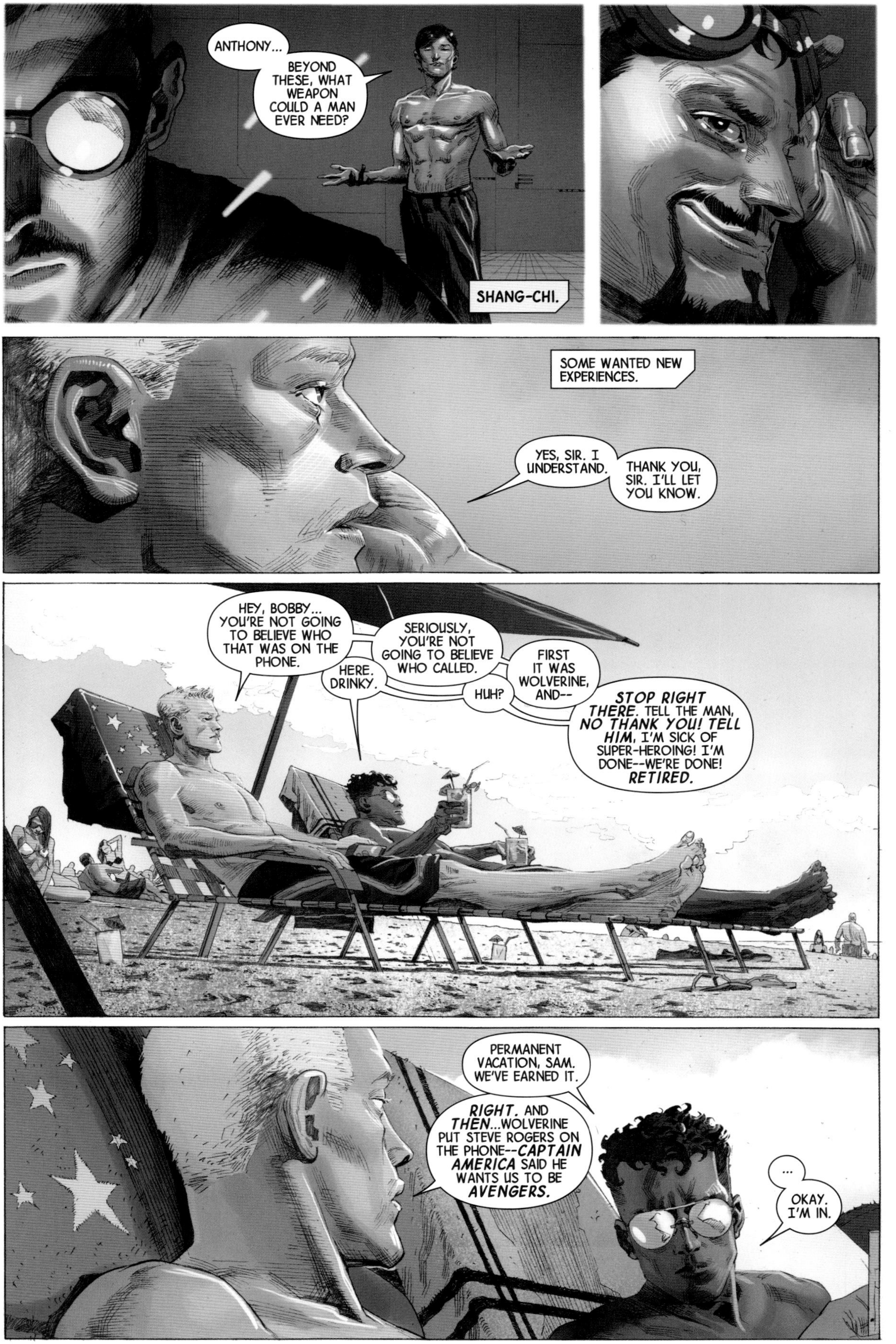
ANTHONY...
BEYOND THESE, WHAT WEAPON COULD A MAN EVER NEED?
SHANG-CHI.
SOME WANTED NEW EXPERIENCES.
YES, SIR. I UNDERSTAND.
THANK YOU, SIR. I'LL LET YOU KNOW.
HEY, BOBBY... YOU'RE NOT GOING TO BELIEVE WHO THAT WAS ON THE PHONE.
SERIOUSLY, YOU'RE NOT GOING TO BELIEVE WHO CALLED.
HERE. DRINKY.
HUH?
FIRST IT WAS WOLVERINE, AND--
STOP RIGHT THERE. TELL THE MAN, NO THANK YOU! TELL HIM, I'M SICK OF SUPER-HEROING! I'M DONE--WE'RE DONE! RETIRED.
PERMANENT VACATION, SAM. WE'VE EARNED IT.
RIGHT. AND THEN...WOLVERINE PUT STEVE ROGERS ON THE PHONE--CAPTAIN AMERICA SAID HE WANTS US TO BE AVENGERS.
...
OKAY. I'M IN.

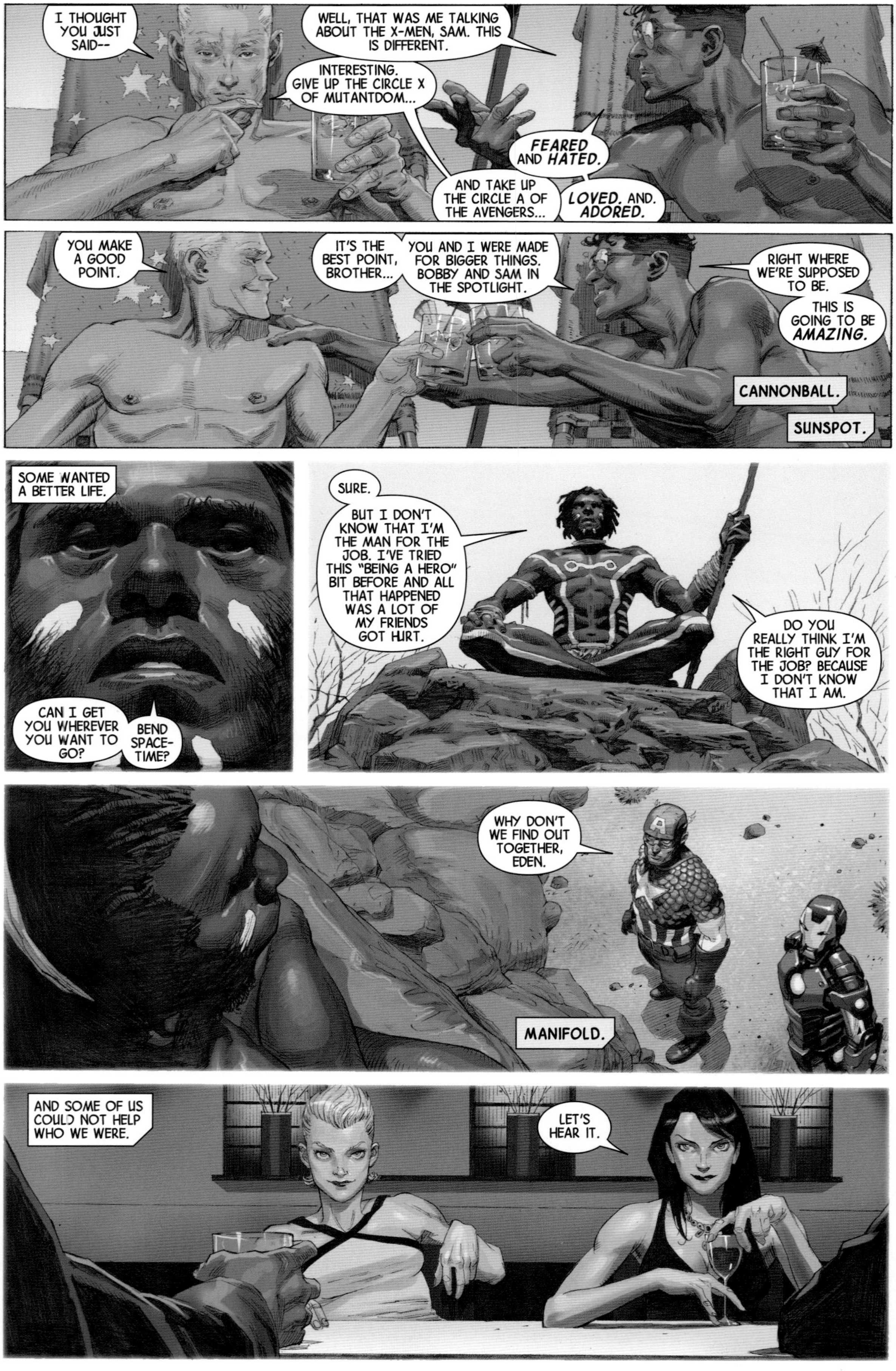
I THOUGHT YOU JUST SAID--
WELL, THAT WAS ME TALKING ABOUT THE X-MEN, SAM. THIS IS DIFFERENT.
INTERESTING. GIVE UP THE CIRCLE X OF MUTANTDOM...
AND TAKE UP THE CIRCLE A OF THE AVENGERS...
FEARED AND HATED.
LOVED. AND. ADORED.
YOU MAKE A GOOD POINT.
IT'S THE BEST POINT, BROTHER...
YOU AND I WERE MADE FOR BIGGER THINGS. BOBBY AND SAM IN THE SPOTLIGHT.
RIGHT WHERE WE'RE SUPPOSED TO BE.
THIS IS GOING TO BE AMAZING.
CANNONBALL.
SUNSPOT.
SOME WANTED A BETTER LIFE.
CAN I GET YOU WHEREVER YOU WANT TO GO?
BEND SPACE-TIME?
SURE.
BUT I DON'T KNOW THAT I'M THE MAN FOR THE JOB. I'VE TRIED THIS "BEING A HERO" BIT BEFORE AND ALL THAT HAPPENED WAS A LOT OF MY FRIENDS GOT HURT.
DO YOU REALLY THINK I'M THE RIGHT GUY FOR THE JOB? BECAUSE I DON'T KNOW THAT I AM.
WHY DON'T WE FIND OUT TOGETHER, EDEN.
MANIFOLD.
AND SOME OF US COULD NOT HELP WHO WE WERE.
LET'S HEAR IT.

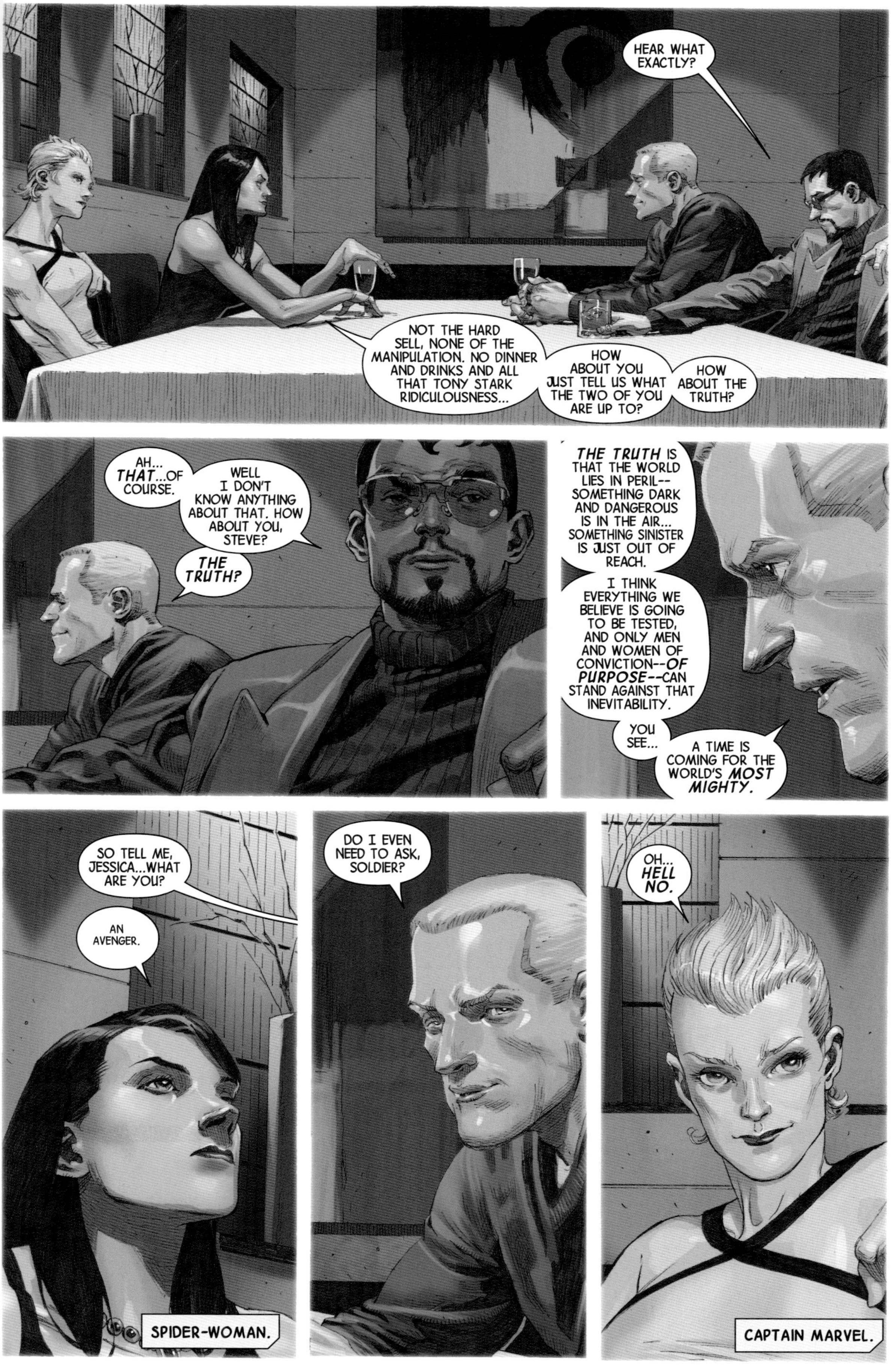
HEAR WHAT EXACTLY?
NOT THE HARD SELL, NONE OF THE MANIPULATION. NO DINNER AND DRINKS AND ALL THAT TONY STARK RIDICULOUSNESS...
HOW ABOUT YOU JUST TELL US WHAT THE TWO OF YOU ARE UP TO?
HOW ABOUT THE TRUTH?
AH... THAT...OF COURSE.
WELL I DON'T KNOW ANYTHING ABOUT THAT. HOW ABOUT YOU, STEVE?
THE TRUTH?
THE TRUTH IS THAT THE WORLD LIES IN PERIL-- SOMETHING DARK AND DANGEROUS IS IN THE AIR... SOMETHING SINISTER IS JUST OUT OF REACH.
I THINK EVERYTHING WE BELIEVE IS GOING TO BE TESTED, AND ONLY MEN AND WOMEN OF CONVICTION--OF PURPOSE--CAN STAND AGAINST THAT INEVITABILITY.
YOU SEE...
A TIME IS COMING FOR THE WORLD'S MOST MIGHTY.
SO TELL ME, JESSICA...WHAT ARE YOU?
AN AVENGER.
SPIDER-WOMAN.
DO I EVEN NEED TO ASK, SOLDIER?
OH... HELL NO.
CAPTAIN MARVEL.

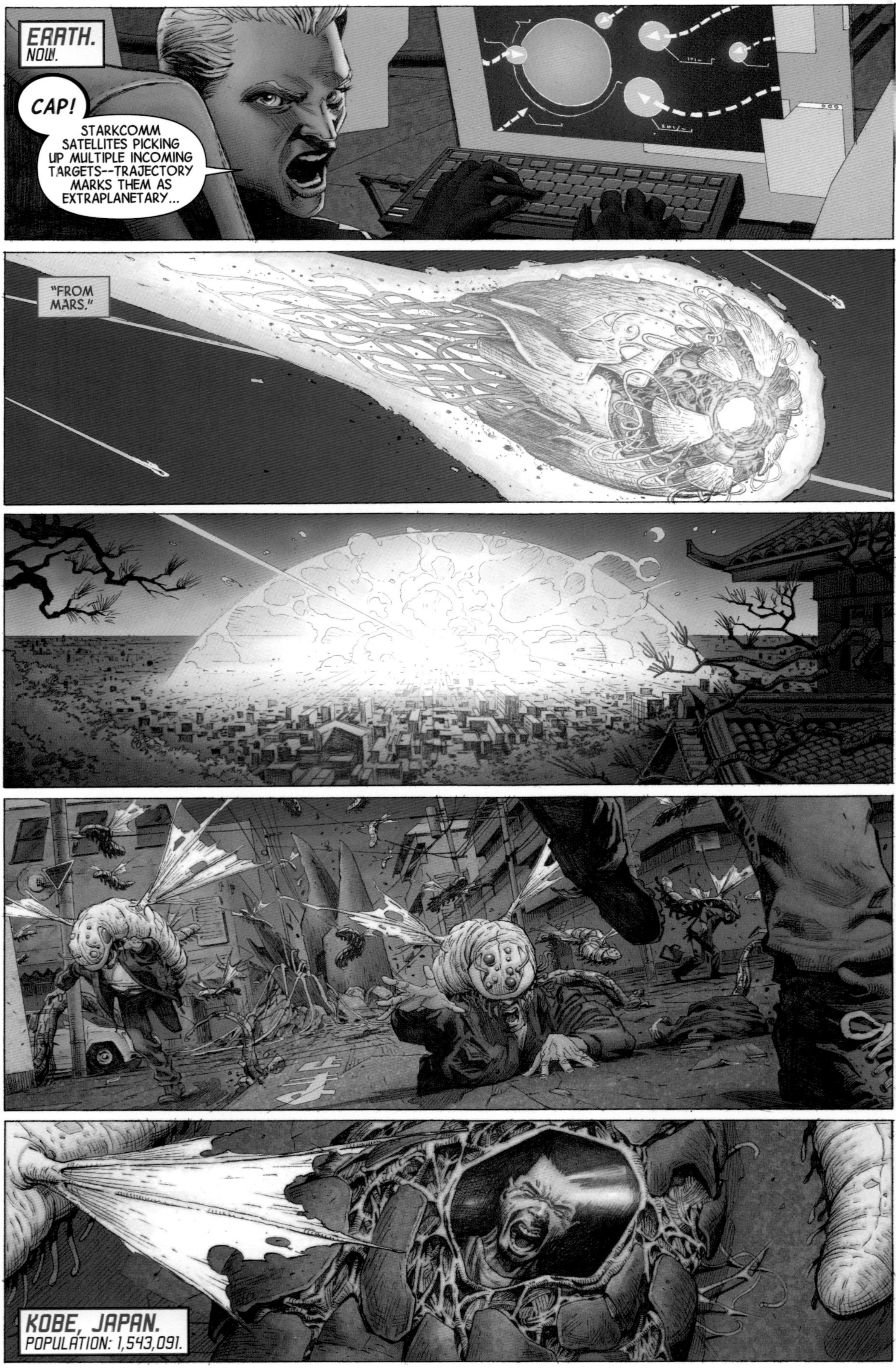
EARTH.
NOW.
CAP!
STARKCOMM SATELLITES PICKING UP MULTIPLE INCOMING TARGETS--TRAJECTORY MARKS THEM AS EXTRAPLANETARY...
"FROM MARS."
KOBE, JAPAN.
POPULATION: 1,543,091.

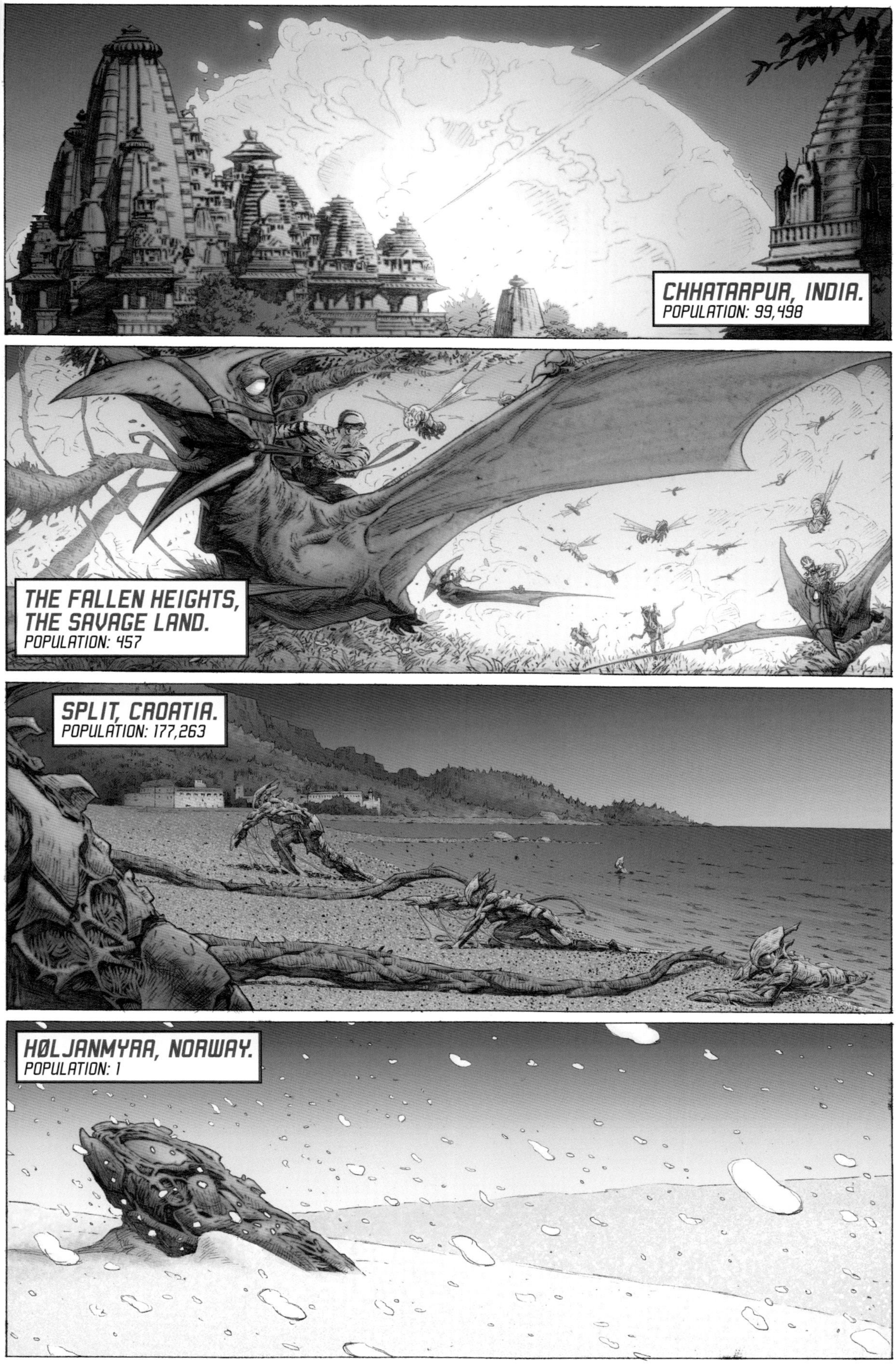
CHHATARPUR, INDIA.
POPULATION: 99,498
THE FALLEN HEIGHTS, THE SAVAGE LAND.
POPULATION: 457
SPLIT, CROATIA.
POPULATION: 177,263
HØLJANMYRA, NORWAY.
POPULATION: 1

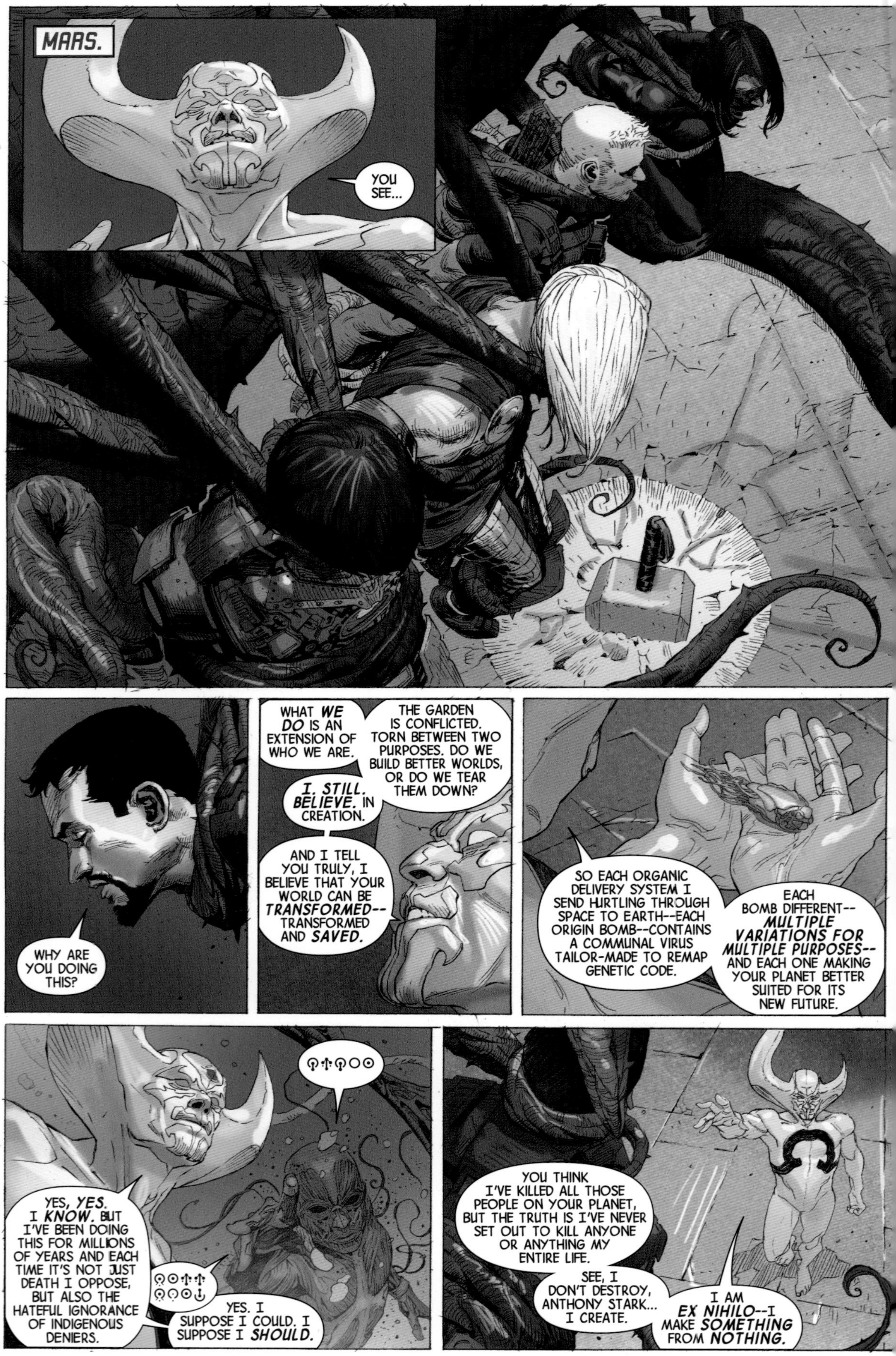
MARS.
YOU SEE...
WHY ARE YOU DOING THIS?
WHAT WE DO IS AN EXTENSION OF WHO WE ARE.
THE GARDEN IS CONFLICTED. TORN BETWEEN TWO PURPOSES. DO WE BUILD BETTER WORLDS, OR DO WE TEAR THEM DOWN?
I. STILL. BELIEVE. IN CREATION.
AND I TELL YOU TRULY, I BELIEVE THAT YOUR WORLD CAN BE TRANSFORMED-- TRANSFORMED AND SAVED.
SO EACH ORGANIC DELIVERY SYSTEM I SEND HURTLING THROUGH SPACE TO EARTH--EACH ORIGIN BOMB--CONTAINS A COMMUNAL VIRUS TAILOR-MADE TO REMAP GENETIC CODE.
EACH BOMB DIFFERENT-- MULTIPLE VARIATIONS FOR MULTIPLE PURPOSES-- AND EACH ONE MAKING YOUR PLANET BETTER SUITED FOR ITS NEW FUTURE.
YES, YES. I KNOW. BUT I'VE BEEN DOING THIS FOR MILLIONS OF YEARS AND EACH TIME IT'S NOT JUST DEATH I OPPOSE, BUT ALSO THE HATEFUL IGNORANCE OF INDIGENOUS DENIERS.
YES. I SUPPOSE I COULD. I SUPPOSE I SHOULD.
YOU THINK I'VE KILLED ALL THOSE PEOPLE ON YOUR PLANET, BUT THE TRUTH IS I'VE NEVER SET OUT TO KILL ANYONE OR ANYTHING MY ENTIRE LIFE.
SEE, I DON'T DESTROY, ANTHONY STARK... I CREATE.
I AM EX NIHILO--I MAKE SOMETHING FROM NOTHING.

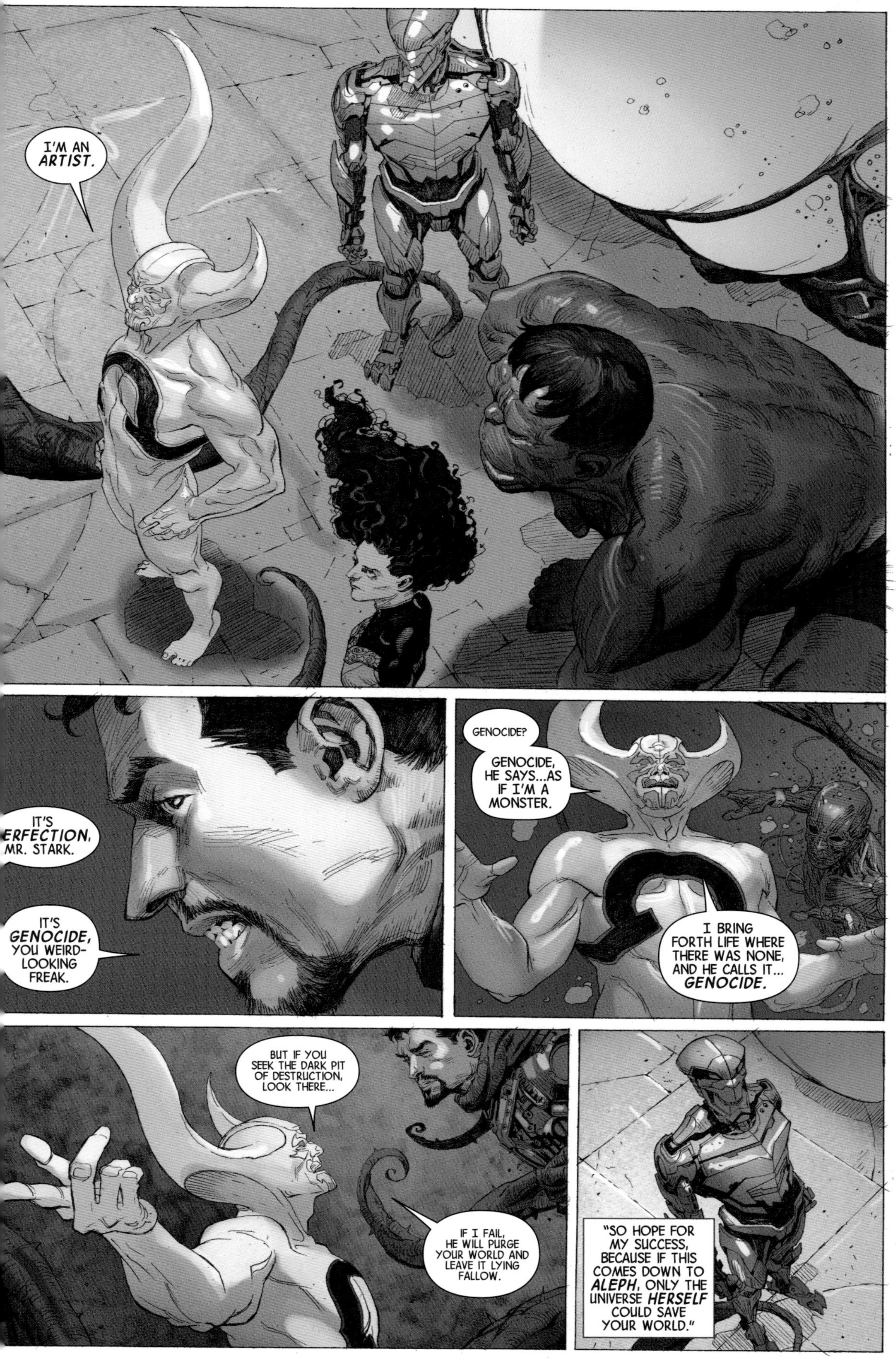

I'M AN ARTIST.
IT'S ERFECTION, MR. STARK.
IT'S GENOCIDE, YOU WEIRD-LOOKING FREAK.
GENOCIDE?
GENOCIDE, HE SAYS...AS IF I'M A MONSTER.
I BRING FORTH LIFE WHERE THERE WAS NONE, AND HE CALLS IT... GENOCIDE.
BUT IF YOU SEEK THE DARK PIT OF DESTRUCTION, LOOK THERE...
IF I FAIL, HE WILL PURGE YOUR WORLD AND LEAVE IT LYING FALLOW.
"SO HOPE FOR MY SUCCESS, BECAUSE IF THIS COMES DOWN TO ALEPH, ONLY THE UNIVERSE HERSELF COULD SAVE YOUR WORLD."

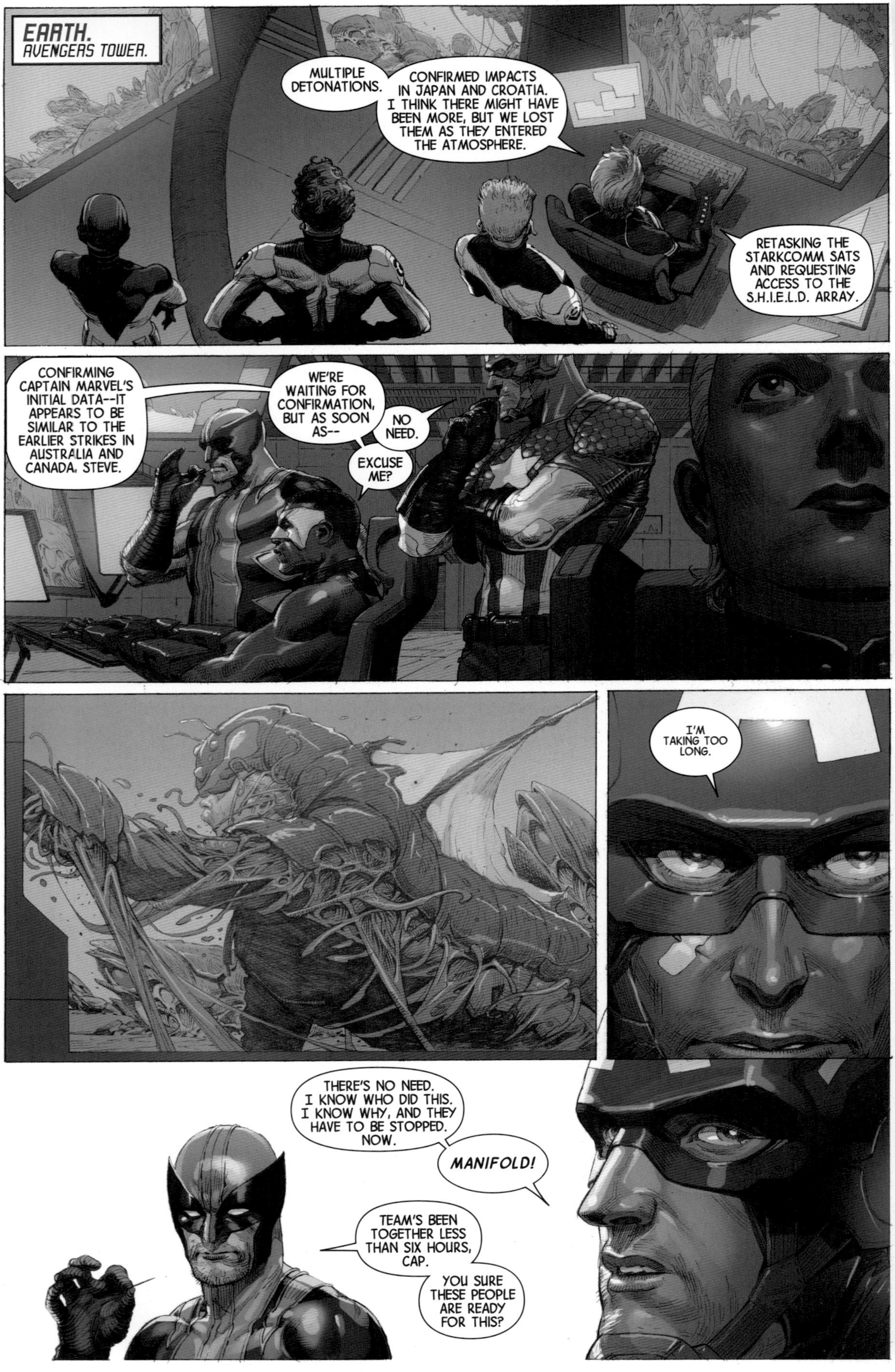
EARTH.
AVENGERS TOWER.
MULTIPLE DETONATIONS.
CONFIRMED IMPACTS IN JAPAN AND CROATIA. I THINK THERE MIGHT HAVE BEEN MORE, BUT WE LOST THEM AS THEY ENTERED THE ATMOSPHERE.
RETASKING THE STARKCOMM SATS AND REQUESTING ACCESS TO THE S.H.I.E.L.D. ARRAY.
CONFIRMING CAPTAIN MARVEL'S INITIAL DATA--IT APPEARS TO BE SIMILAR TO THE EARLIER STRIKES IN AUSTRALIA AND CANADA, STEVE.
WE'RE WAITING FOR CONFIRMATION, BUT AS SOON AS--
NO NEED.
EXCUSE ME?
I'M TAKING TOO LONG.
THERE'S NO NEED. I KNOW WHO DID THIS. I KNOW WHY, AND THEY HAVE TO BE STOPPED. NOW.
MANIFOLD!
TEAM'S BEEN TOGETHER LESS THAN SIX HOURS, CAP.
YOU SURE THESE PEOPLE ARE READY FOR THIS?

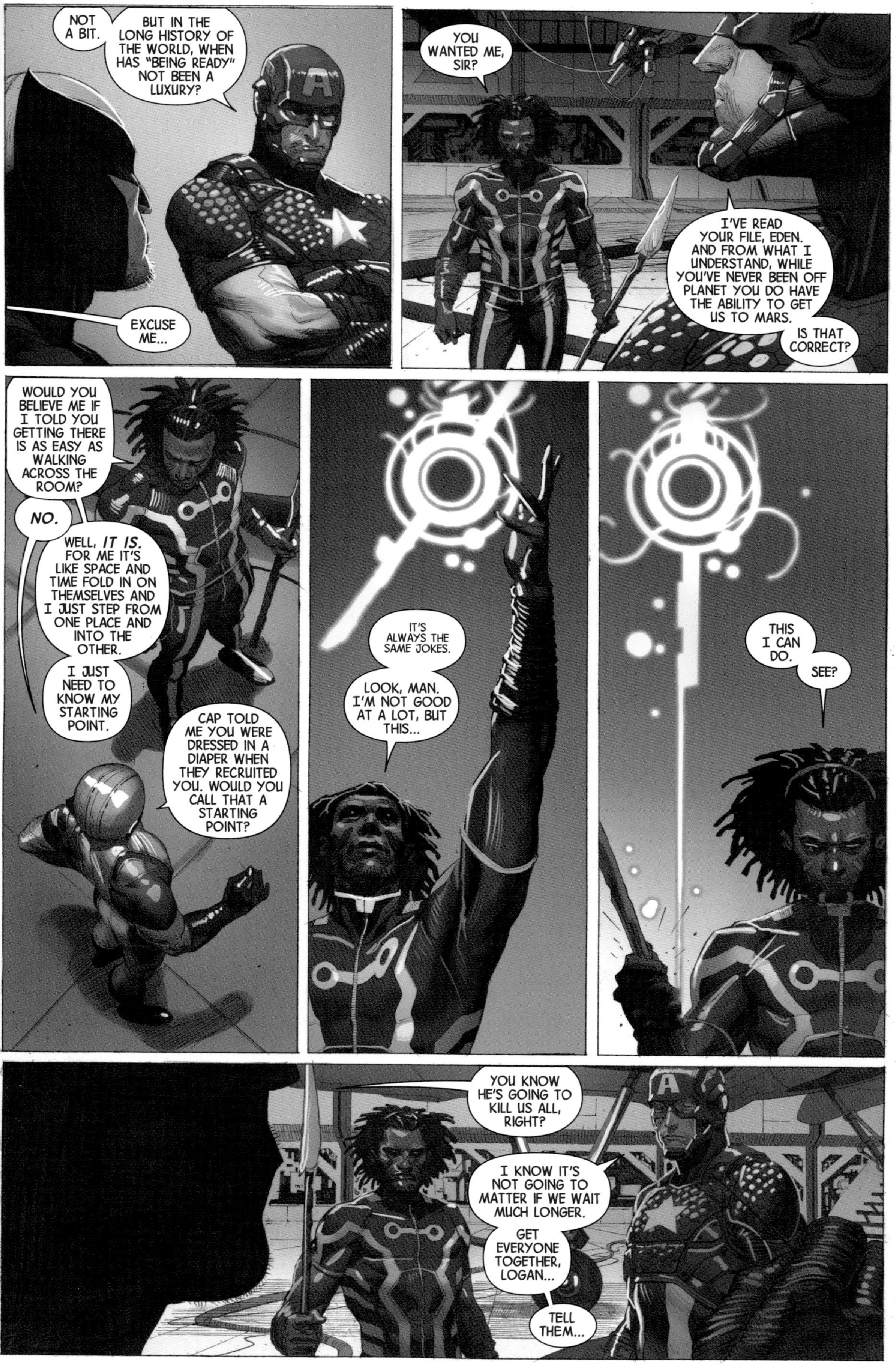
NOT A BIT.
BUT IN THE LONG HISTORY OF THE WORLD, WHEN HAS "BEING READY" NOT BEEN A LUXURY?
EXCUSE ME...
YOU WANTED ME, SIR?
I'VE READ YOUR FILE, EDEN. AND FROM WHAT I UNDERSTAND, WHILE YOU'VE NEVER BEEN OFF PLANET YOU DO HAVE THE ABILITY TO GET US TO MARS.
IS THAT CORRECT?
WOULD YOU BELIEVE ME IF I TOLD YOU GETTING THERE IS AS EASY AS WALKING ACROSS THE ROOM?
NO.
WELL, IT IS. FOR ME IT'S LIKE SPACE AND TIME FOLD IN ON THEMSELVES AND I JUST STEP FROM ONE PLACE AND INTO THE OTHER.
I JUST NEED TO KNOW MY STARTING POINT.
CAP TOLD ME YOU WERE DRESSED IN A DIAPER WHEN THEY RECRUITED YOU. WOULD YOU CALL THAT A STARTING POINT?
IT'S ALWAYS THE SAME JOKES.
LOOK, MAN. I'M NOT GOOD AT A LOT, BUT THIS...
THIS I CAN DO.
SEE?
YOU KNOW HE'S GOING TO KILL US ALL, RIGHT?
I KNOW IT'S NOT GOING TO MATTER IF WE WAIT MUCH LONGER.
GET EVERYONE TOGETHER, LOGAN...
TELL THEM...

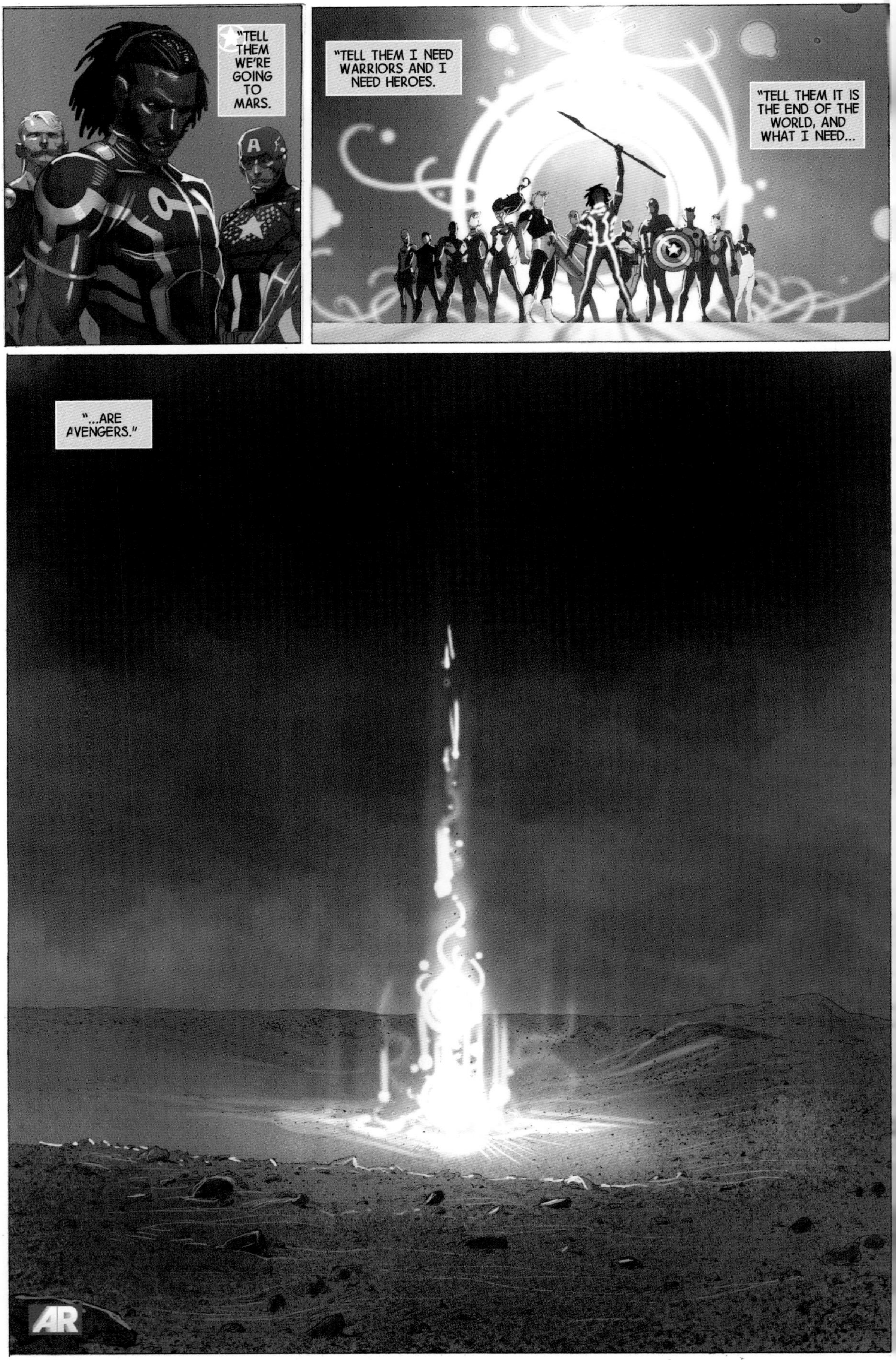
"TELL THEM WE'RE GOING TO MARS.
"TELL THEM I NEED WARRIORS AND I NEED HEROES.
"TELL THEM IT IS THE END OF THE WORLD, AND WHAT I NEED...
"...ARE AVENGERS."
AR

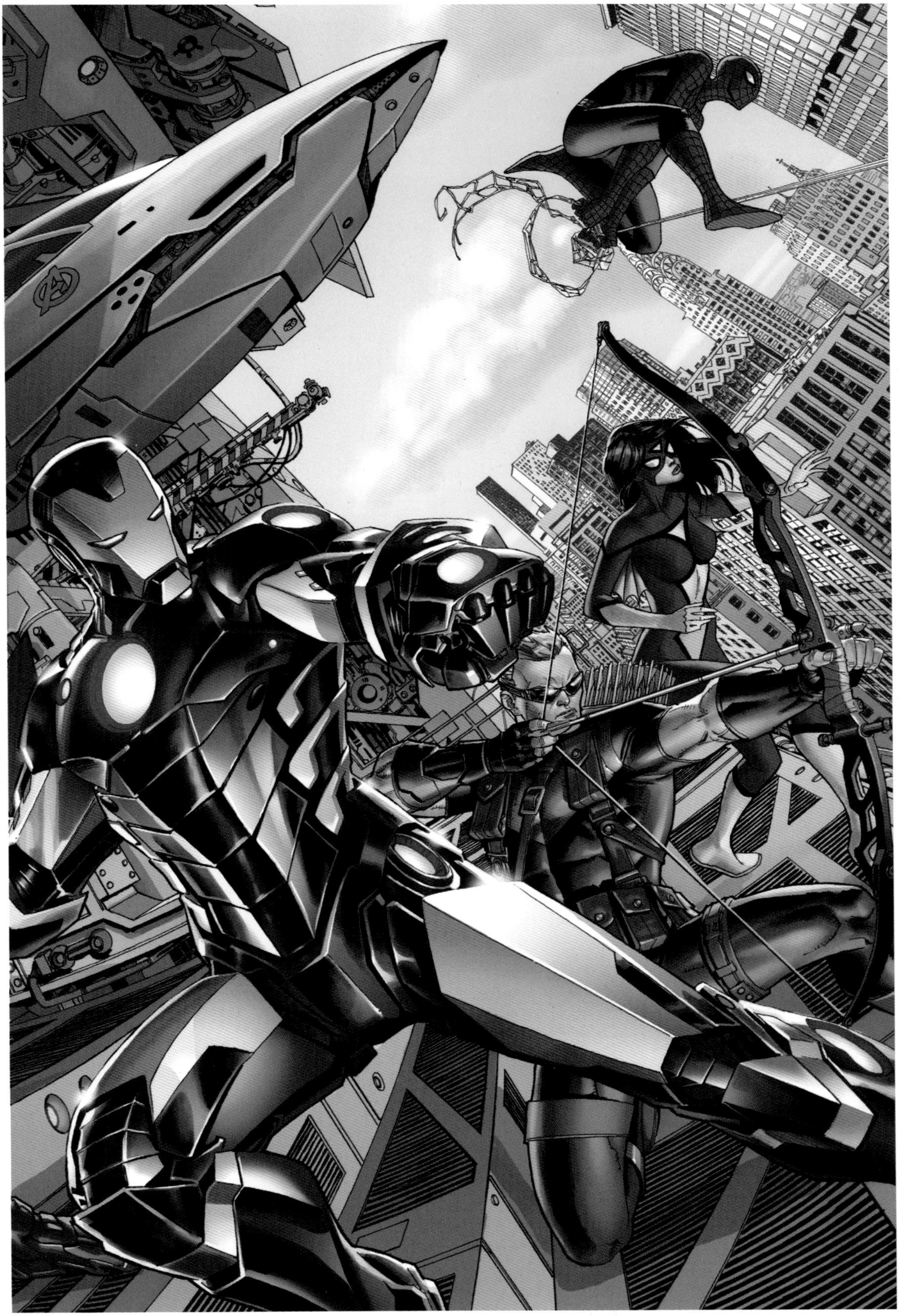

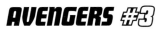

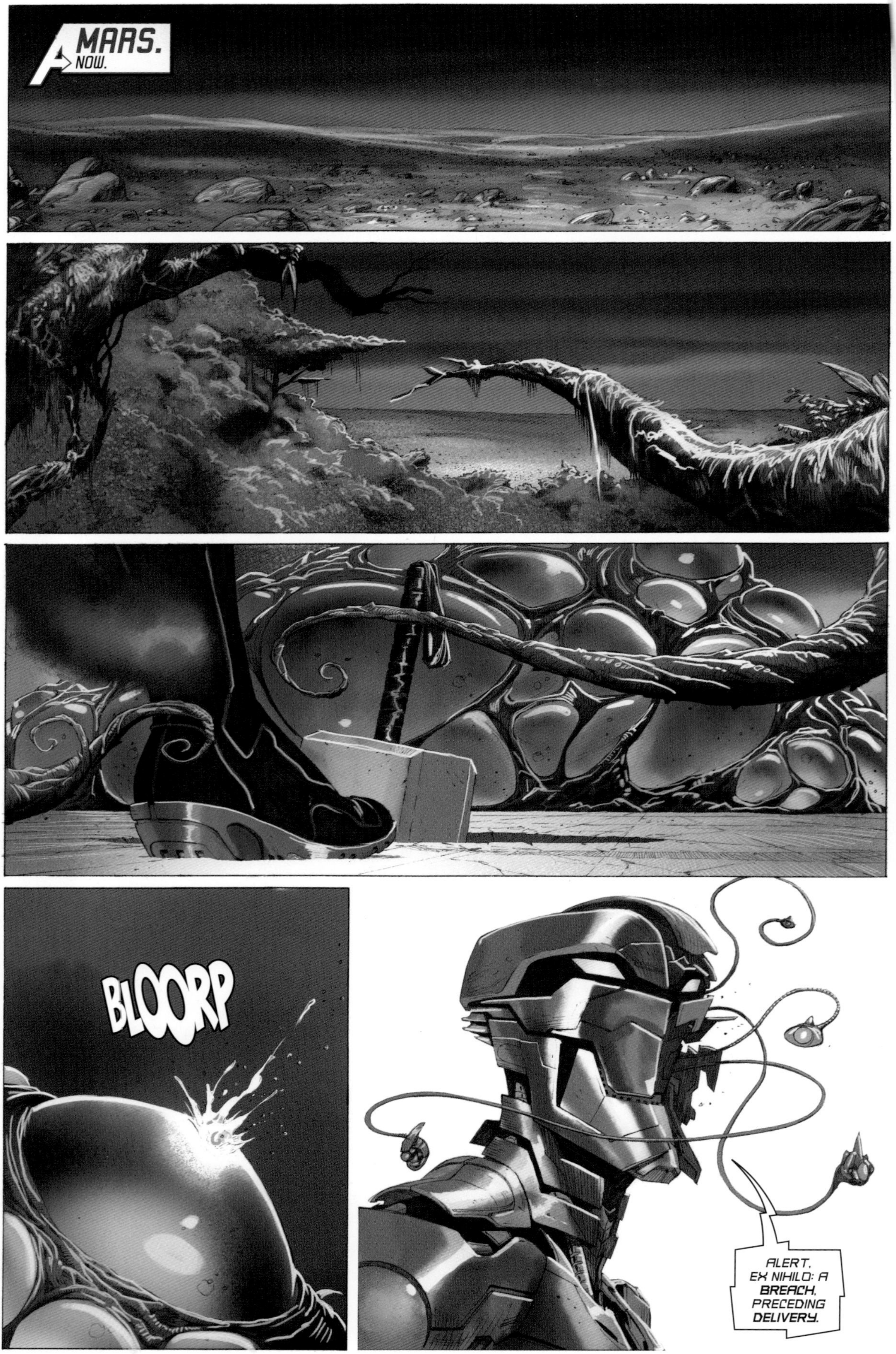
MARS.
NOW.
BLOORP
ALERT, EX NIHILO: A BREACH, PRECEDING DELIVERY.

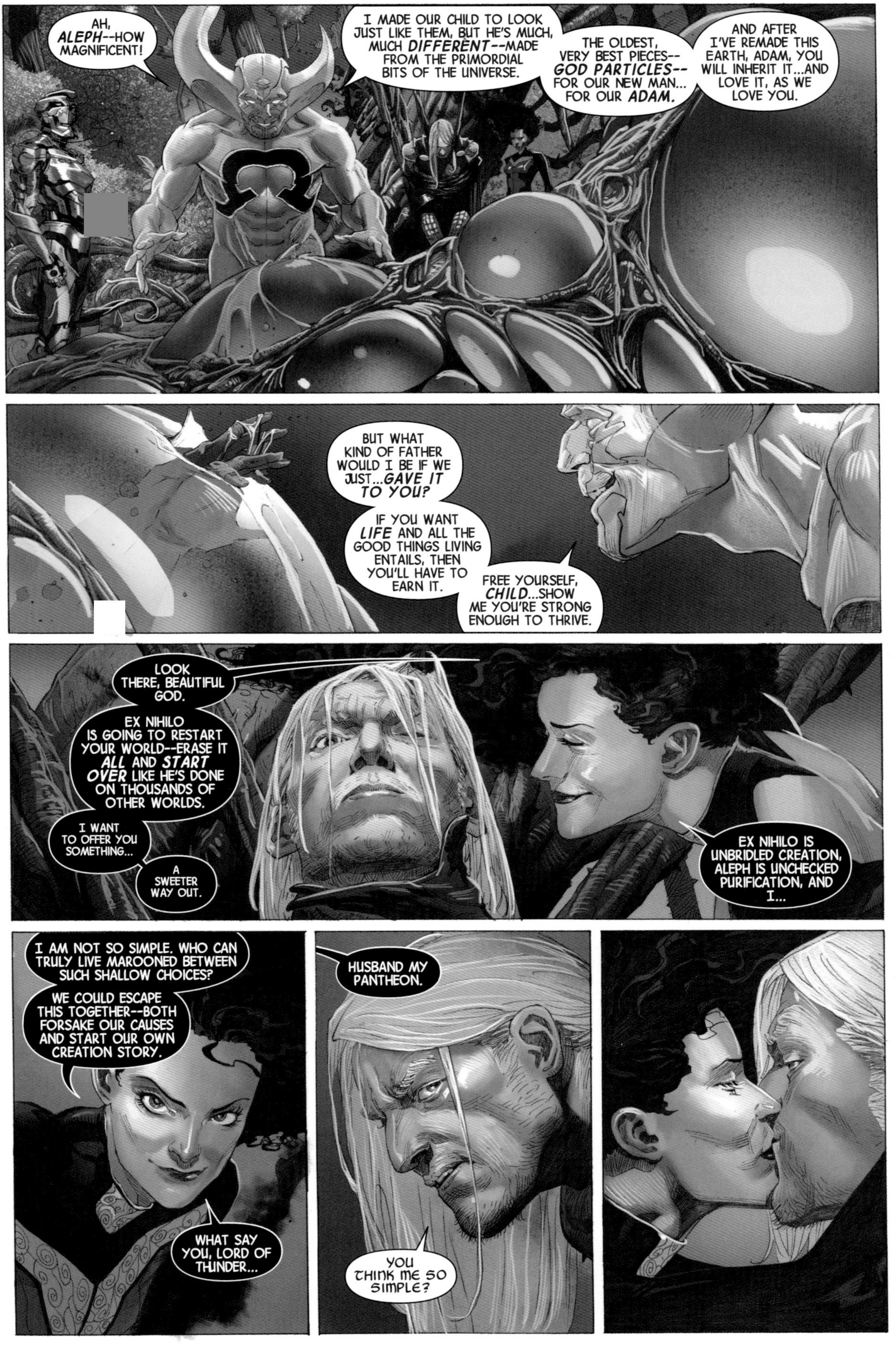
AH, ALEPH--HOW MAGNIFICENT!
I MADE OUR CHILD TO LOOK JUST LIKE THEM, BUT HE'S MUCH, MUCH DIFFERENT--MADE FROM THE PRIMORDIAL BITS OF THE UNIVERSE.
THE OLDEST, VERY BEST PIECES--GOD PARTICLES--FOR OUR NEW MAN... FOR OUR ADAM.
AND AFTER I'VE REMADE THIS EARTH, ADAM, YOU WILL INHERIT IT...AND LOVE IT, AS WE LOVE YOU.
BUT WHAT KIND OF FATHER WOULD I BE IF WE JUST...GAVE IT TO YOU?
IF YOU WANT LIFE AND ALL THE GOOD THINGS LIVING ENTAILS, THEN YOU'LL HAVE TO EARN IT.
FREE YOURSELF, CHILD...SHOW ME YOU'RE STRONG ENOUGH TO THRIVE.
LOOK THERE, BEAUTIFUL GOD.
EX NIHILO IS GOING TO RESTART YOUR WORLD--ERASE IT ALL AND START OVER LIKE HE'S DONE ON THOUSANDS OF OTHER WORLDS.
I WANT TO OFFER YOU SOMETHING...
A SWEETER WAY OUT.
EX NIHILO IS UNBRIDLED CREATION, ALEPH IS UNCHECKED PURIFICATION, AND I...
I AM NOT SO SIMPLE. WHO CAN TRULY LIVE MAROONED BETWEEN SUCH SHALLOW CHOICES?
WE COULD ESCAPE THIS TOGETHER--BOTH FORSAKE OUR CAUSES AND START OUR OWN CREATION STORY.
WHAT SAY YOU, LORD OF THUNDER...
HUSBAND MY PANTHEON.
YOU THINK ME SO SIMPLE?

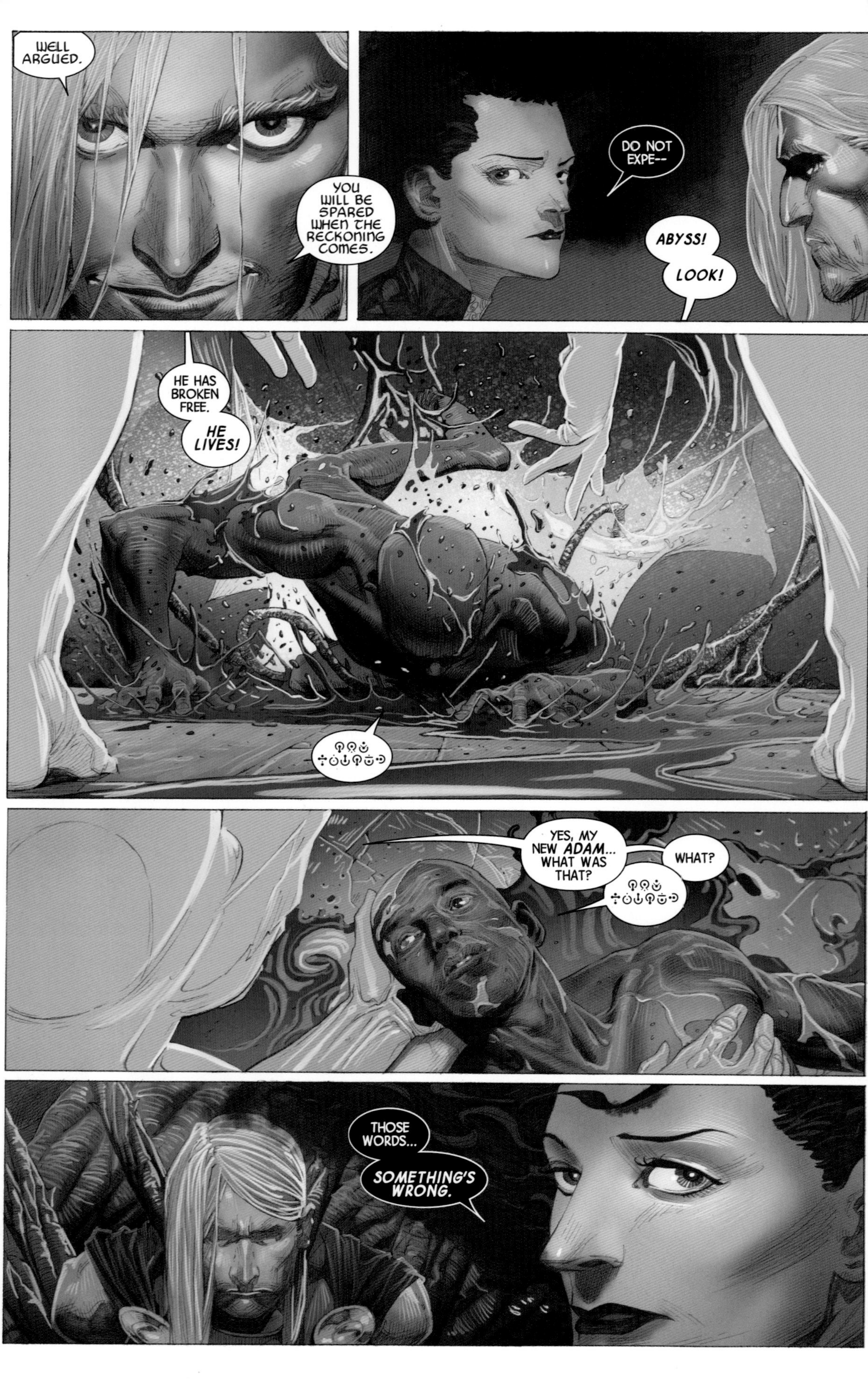
WELL ARGUED.
YOU WILL BE SPARED WHEN THE RECKONING COMES.
DO NOT EXPE--
ABYSS!
LOOK!
HE HAS BROKEN FREE.
HE LIVES!
YES, MY NEW ADAM... WHAT WAS THAT?
WHAT?
THOSE WORDS...
SOMETHING'S WRONG.

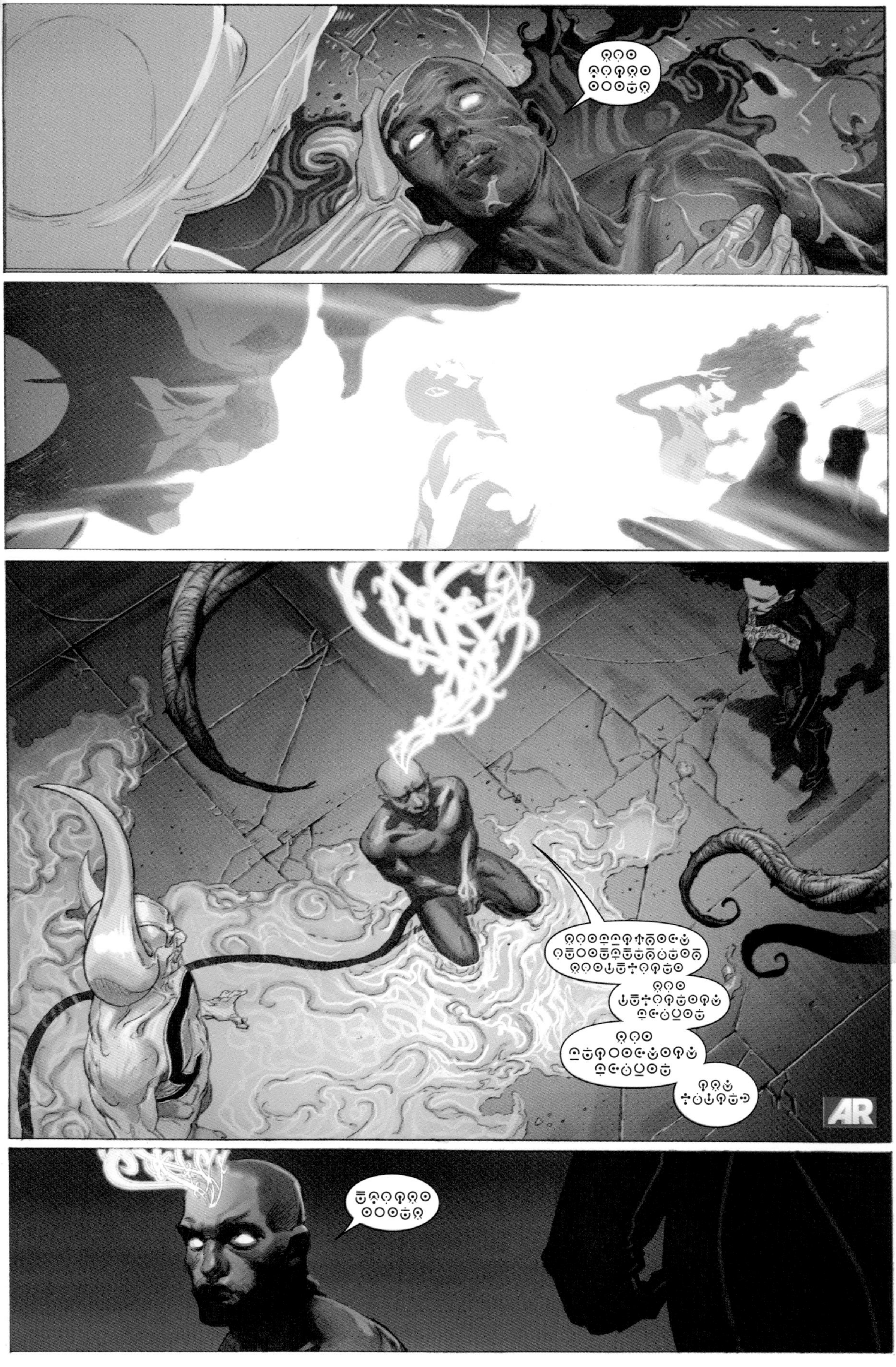

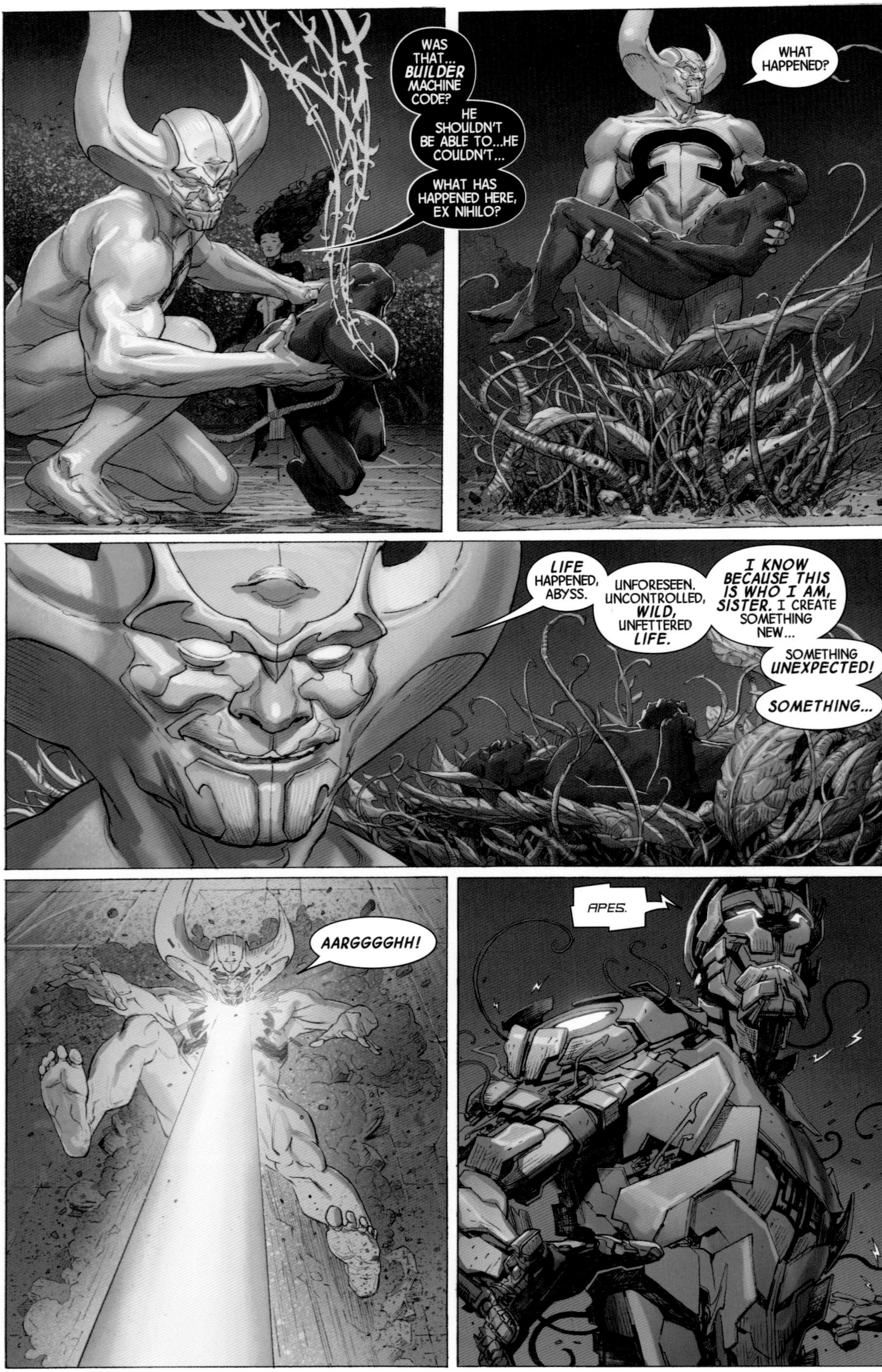
WAS THAT... BUILDER MACHINE CODE?
HE SHOULDN'T BE ABLE TO...HE COULDN'T...
WHAT HAS HAPPENED HERE, EX NIHILO?
WHAT HAPPENED?
LIFE HAPPENED, ABYSS.
UNFORESEEN. UNCONTROLLED, WILD, UNFETTERED LIFE.
I KNOW BECAUSE THIS IS WHO I AM, SISTER. I CREATE SOMETHING NEW...
SOMETHING UNEXPECTED!
SOMETHING...
AARGGGGHH!
APES.

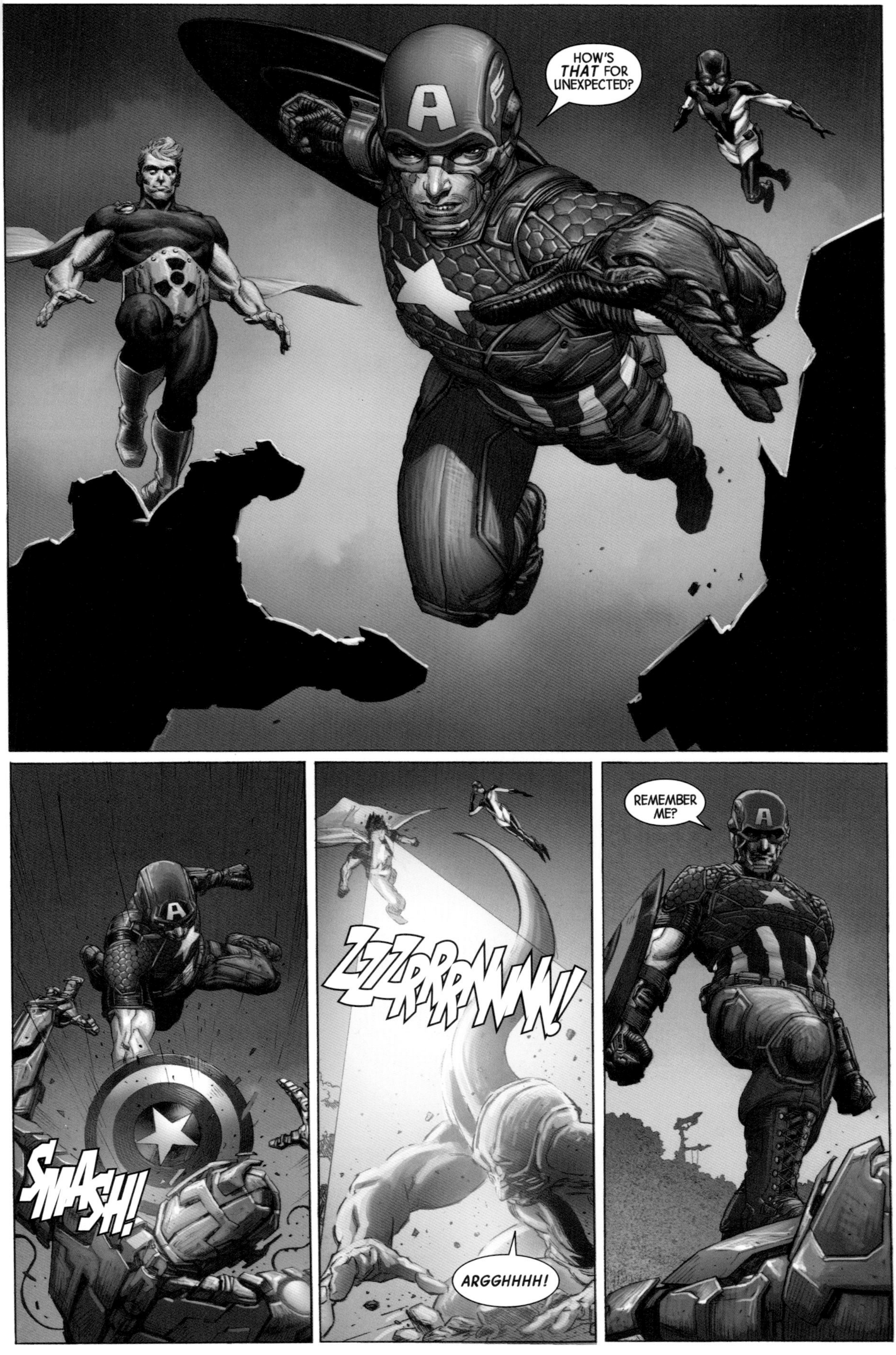
HOW'S THAT FOR UNEXPECTED?
SMASH!
ZZZRRRNNN!
ARGGHHHH!
REMEMBER ME?

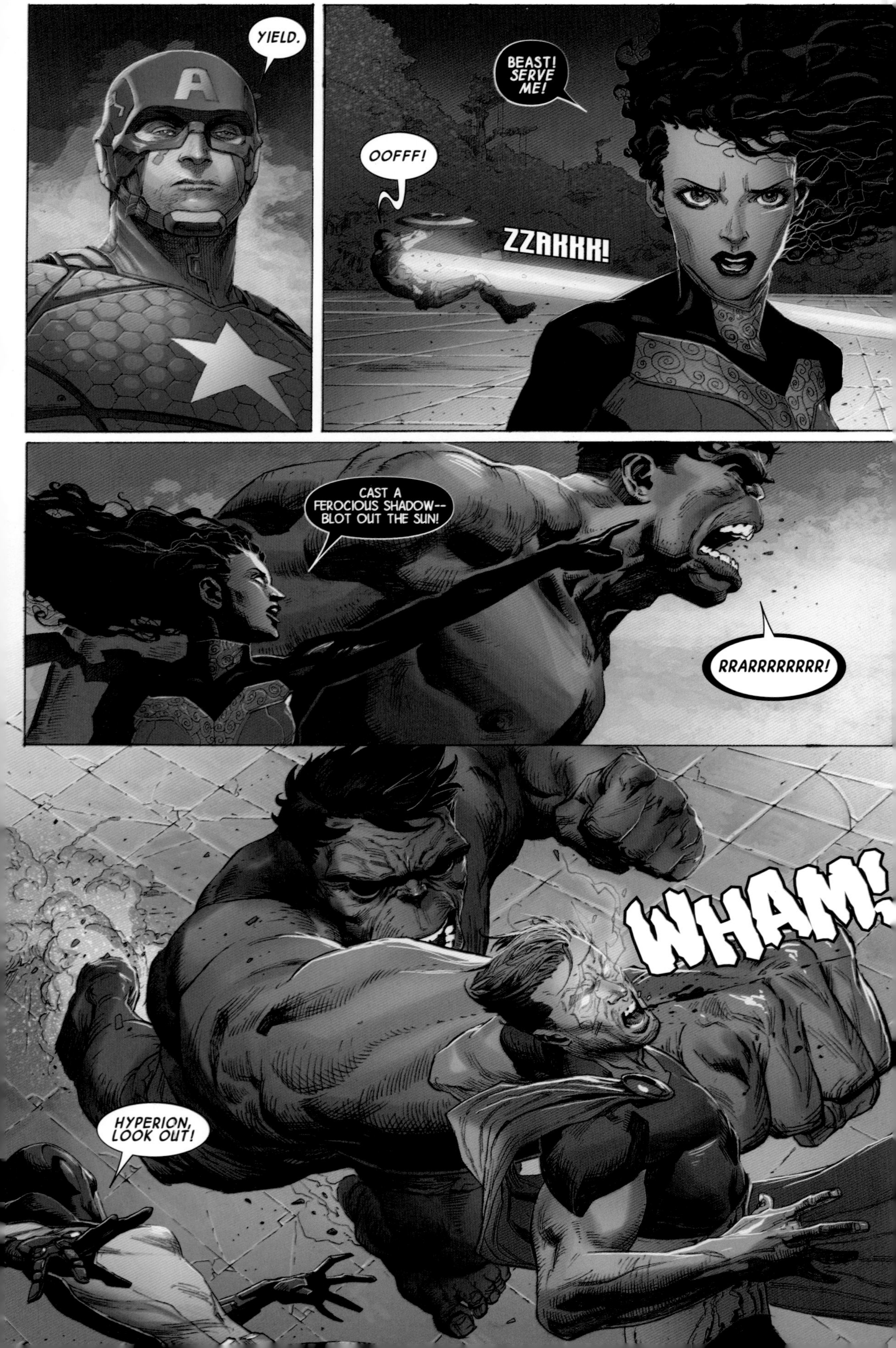
YIELD.
BEAST! SERVE ME!
OOFFF!
ZZAKKK!
CAST A FEROCIOUS SHADOW-- BLOT OUT THE SUN!
RRARRRRRRRR!
WHAM!
HYPERION, LOOK OUT!

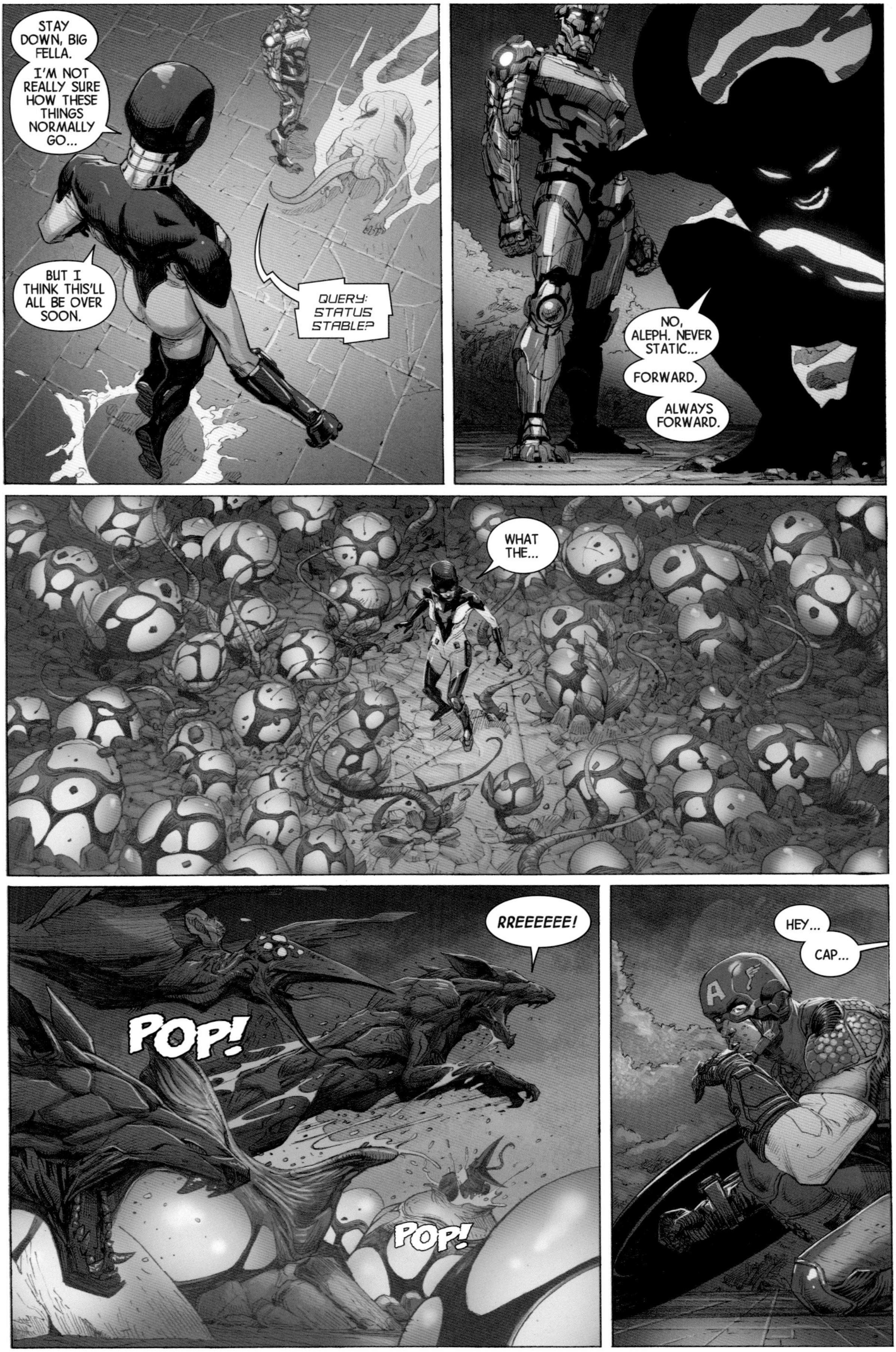
STAY DOWN, BIG FELLA.
I'M NOT REALLY SURE HOW THESE THINGS NORMALLY GO...
BUT I THINK THIS'LL ALL BE OVER SOON.
QUERY: STATUS STABLE?
NO, ALEPH. NEVER STATIC...
FORWARD.
ALWAYS FORWARD.
WHAT THE...
RREEEEEE!
POP!
POP!
HEY...
CAP...

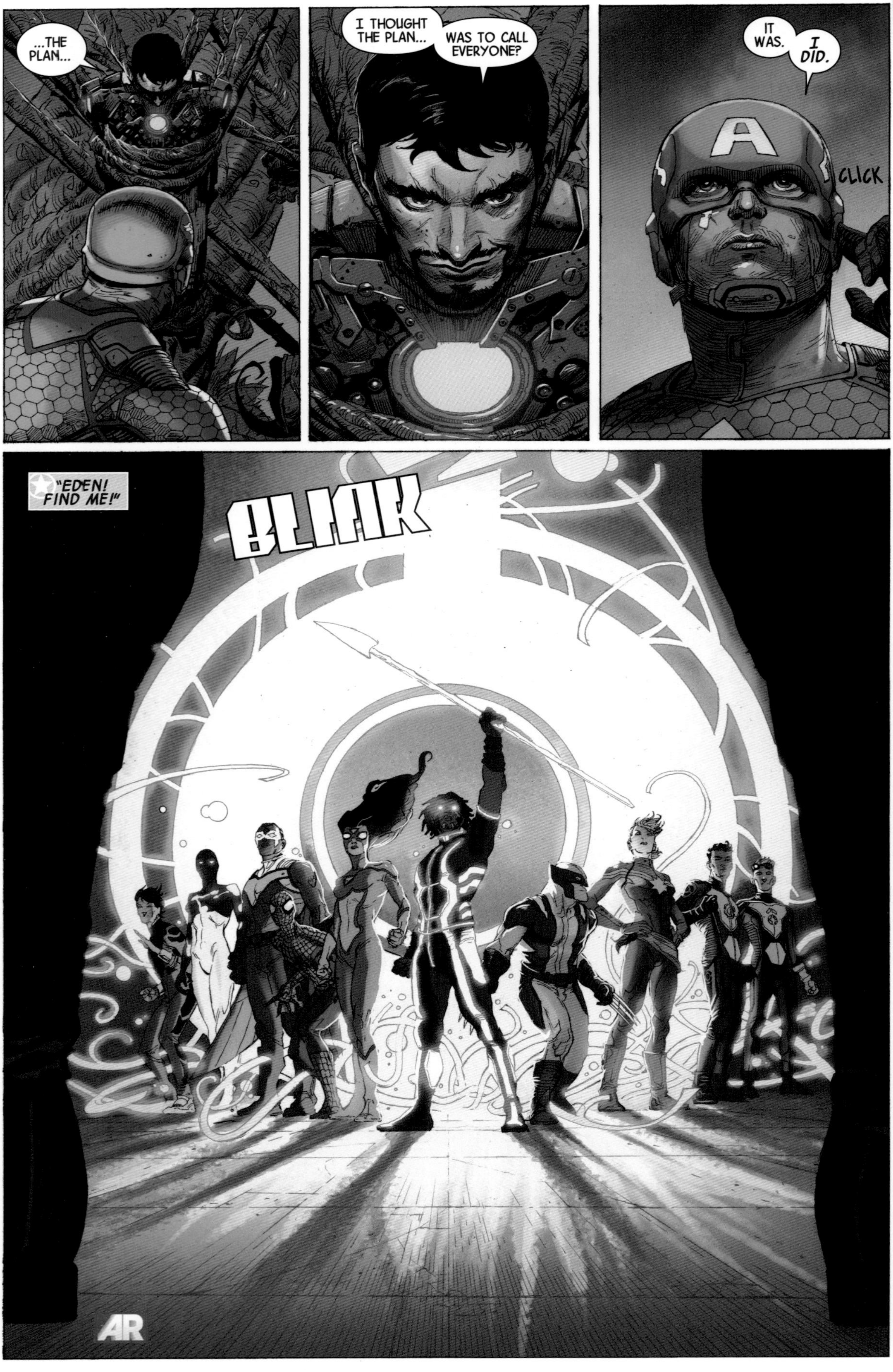
...THE PLAN...
I THOUGHT THE PLAN...
WAS TO CALL EVERYONE?
IT WAS.
I DID.
CLICK
"EDEN! FIND ME!"
BLINK
AR

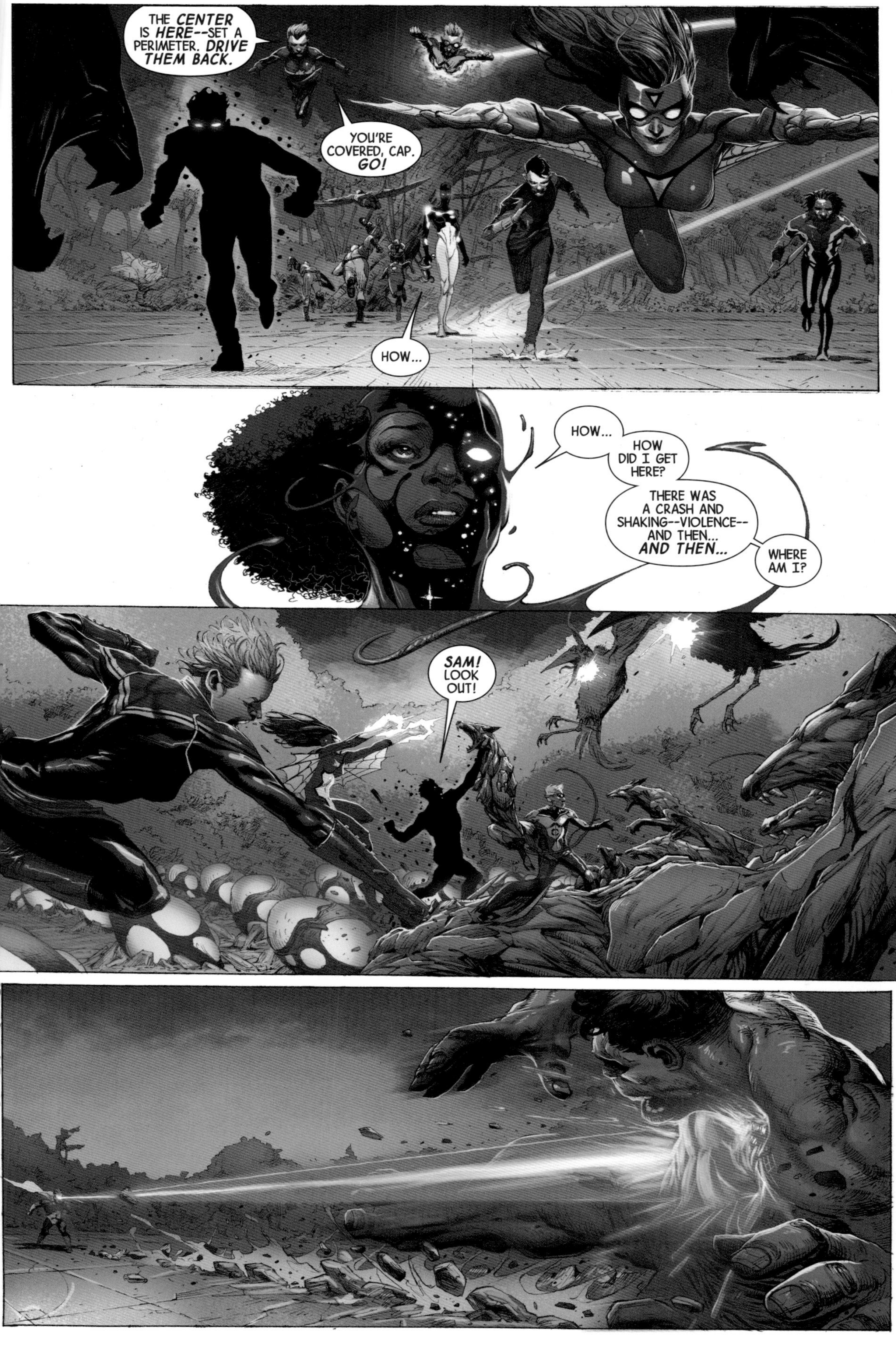
THE CENTER IS HERE--SET A PERIMETER. DRIVE THEM BACK.
YOU'RE COVERED, CAP. GO!
HOW...
HOW...
HOW DID I GET HERE?
THERE WAS A CRASH AND SHAKING--VIOLENCE--AND THEN... AND THEN...
WHERE AM I?
SAM! LOOK OUT!

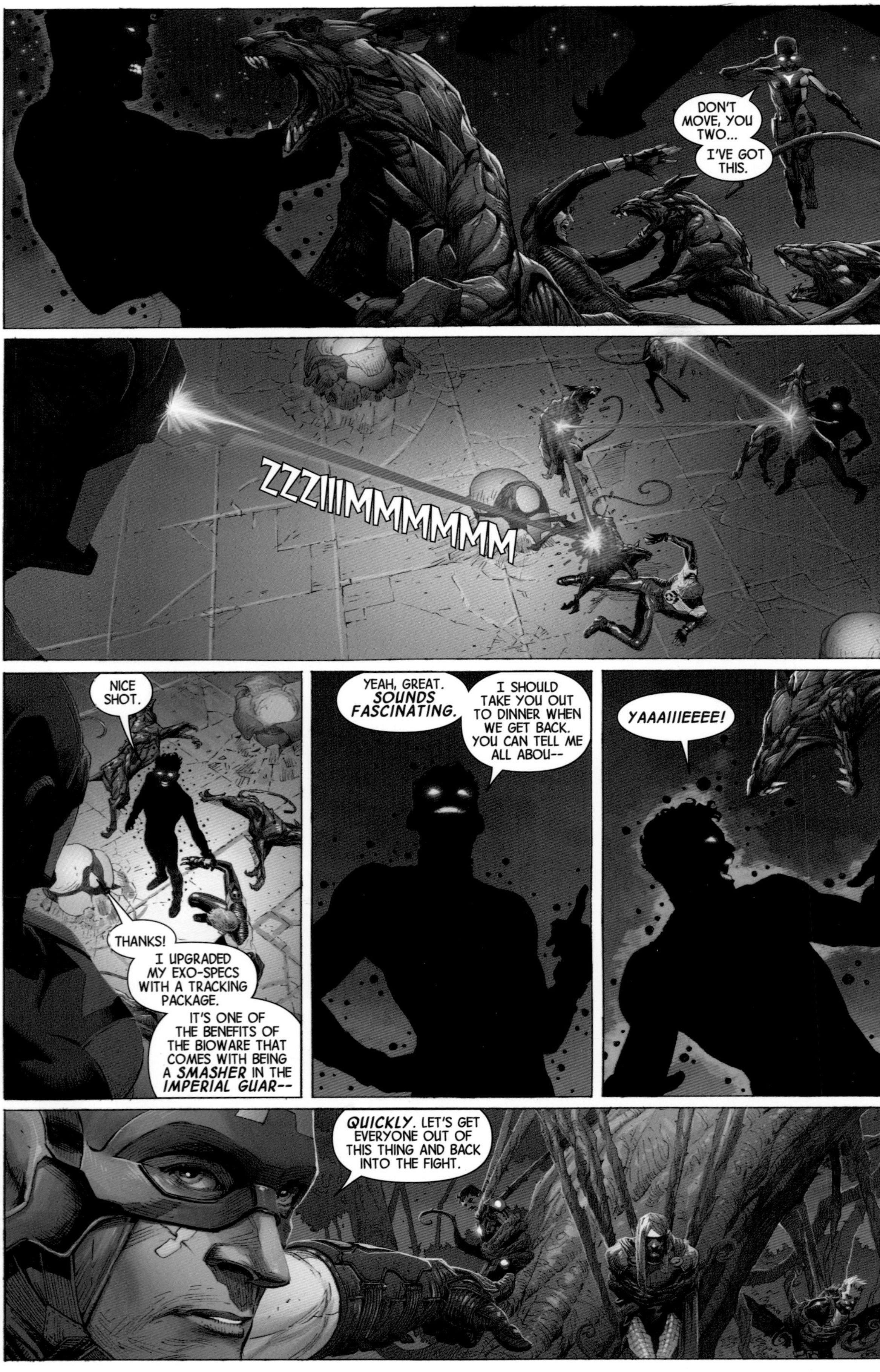
DON'T MOVE, YOU TWO...
I'VE GOT THIS.
ZZZIIIMMMMMMM
NICE SHOT.
THANKS!
I UPGRADED MY EXO-SPECS WITH A TRACKING PACKAGE.
IT'S ONE OF THE BENEFITS OF THE BIOWARE THAT COMES WITH BEING A SMASHER IN THE IMPERIAL GUAR--
YEAH, GREAT. SOUNDS FASCINATING.
I SHOULD TAKE YOU OUT TO DINNER WHEN WE GET BACK. YOU CAN TELL ME ALL ABOU--
YAAAIIIEEEE!
QUICKLY. LET'S GET EVERYONE OUT OF THIS THING AND BACK INTO THE FIGHT.

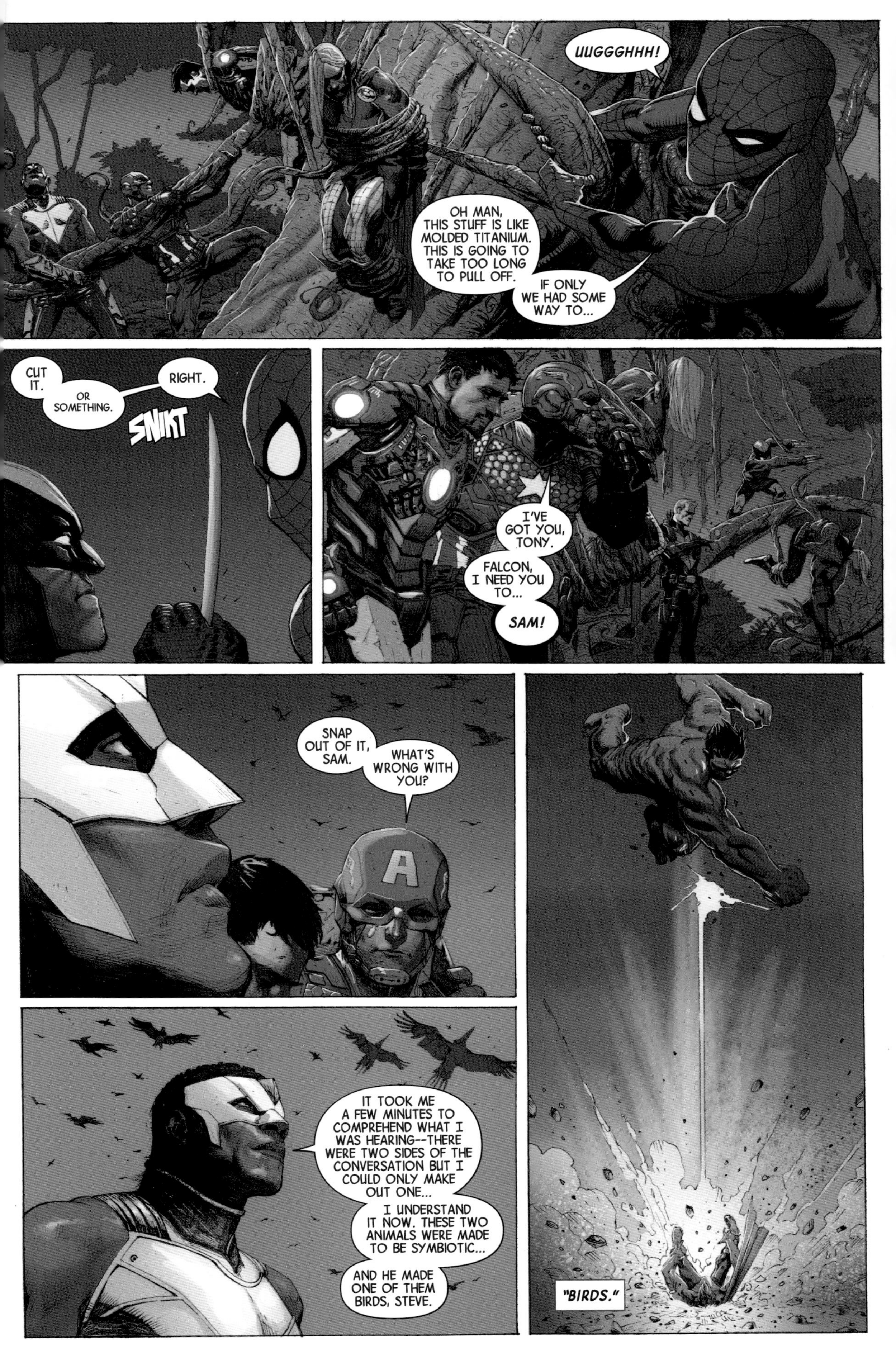
UUGGGHHH!
OH MAN, THIS STUFF IS LIKE MOLDED TITANIUM. THIS IS GOING TO TAKE TOO LONG TO PULL OFF.
IF ONLY WE HAD SOME WAY TO...
CUT IT.
OR SOMETHING.
RIGHT.
SNIKT
I'VE GOT YOU, TONY.
FALCON, I NEED YOU TO...
SAM!
SNAP OUT OF IT, SAM.
WHAT'S WRONG WITH YOU?
IT TOOK ME A FEW MINUTES TO COMPREHEND WHAT I WAS HEARING--THERE WERE TWO SIDES OF THE CONVERSATION BUT I COULD ONLY MAKE OUT ONE...
I UNDERSTAND IT NOW. THESE TWO ANIMALS WERE MADE TO BE SYMBIOTIC...
AND HE MADE ONE OF THEM BIRDS, STEVE.
"BIRDS."

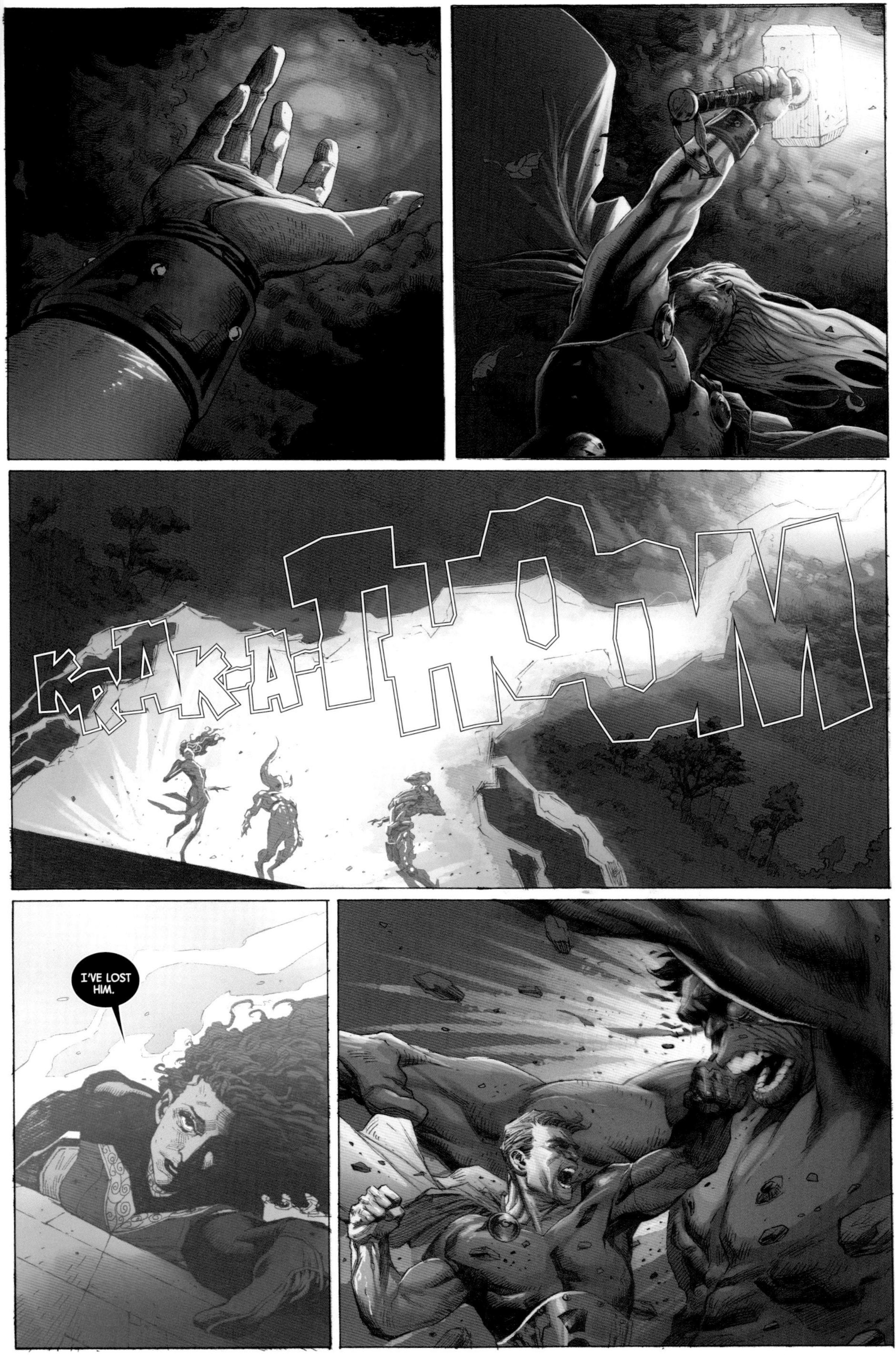
KRAK-A-THOOM
I'VE LOST HIM.

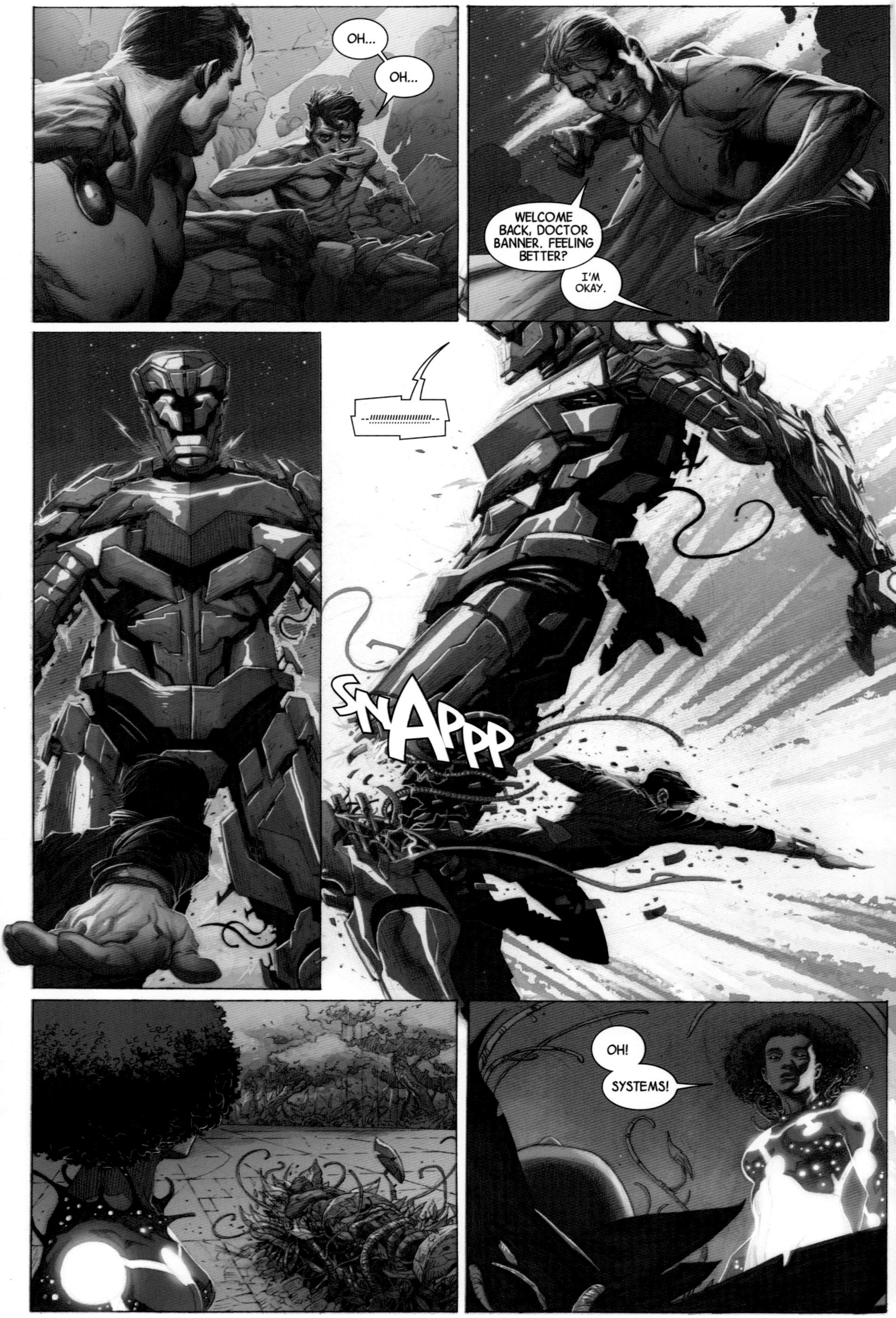
OH...
OH...
WELCOME BACK, DOCTOR BANNER. FEELING BETTER?
I'M OKAY.
--!!!!!!!!!!!!!!!!!!!!!!!!!!!!!--
SNAPPP
OH!
SYSTEMS!

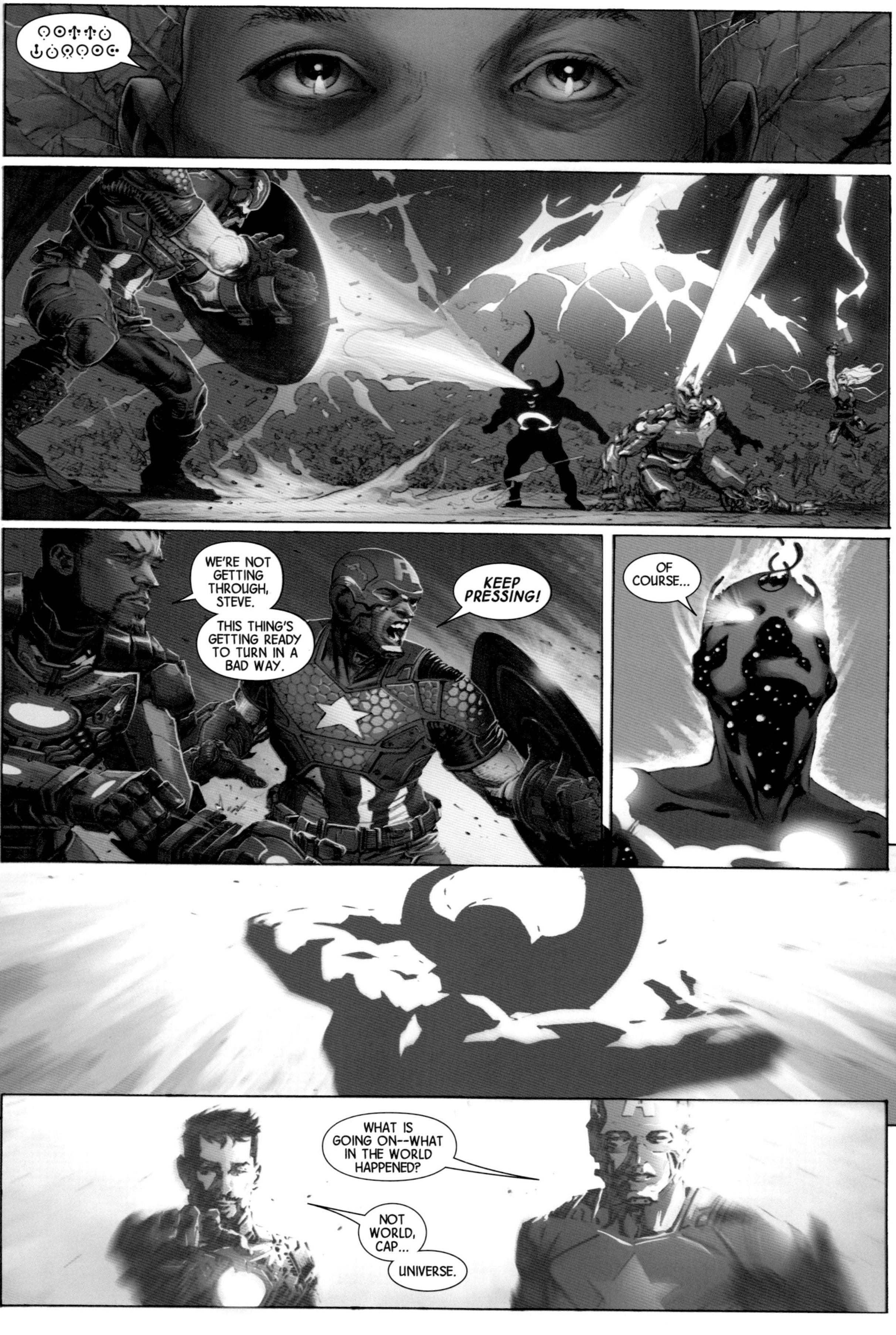

WE'RE NOT GETTING THROUGH, STEVE.
THIS THING'S GETTING READY TO TURN IN A BAD WAY.
KEEP PRESSING!
OF COURSE...
WHAT IS GOING ON--WHAT IN THE WORLD HAPPENED?
NOT WORLD, CAP...
UNIVERSE.

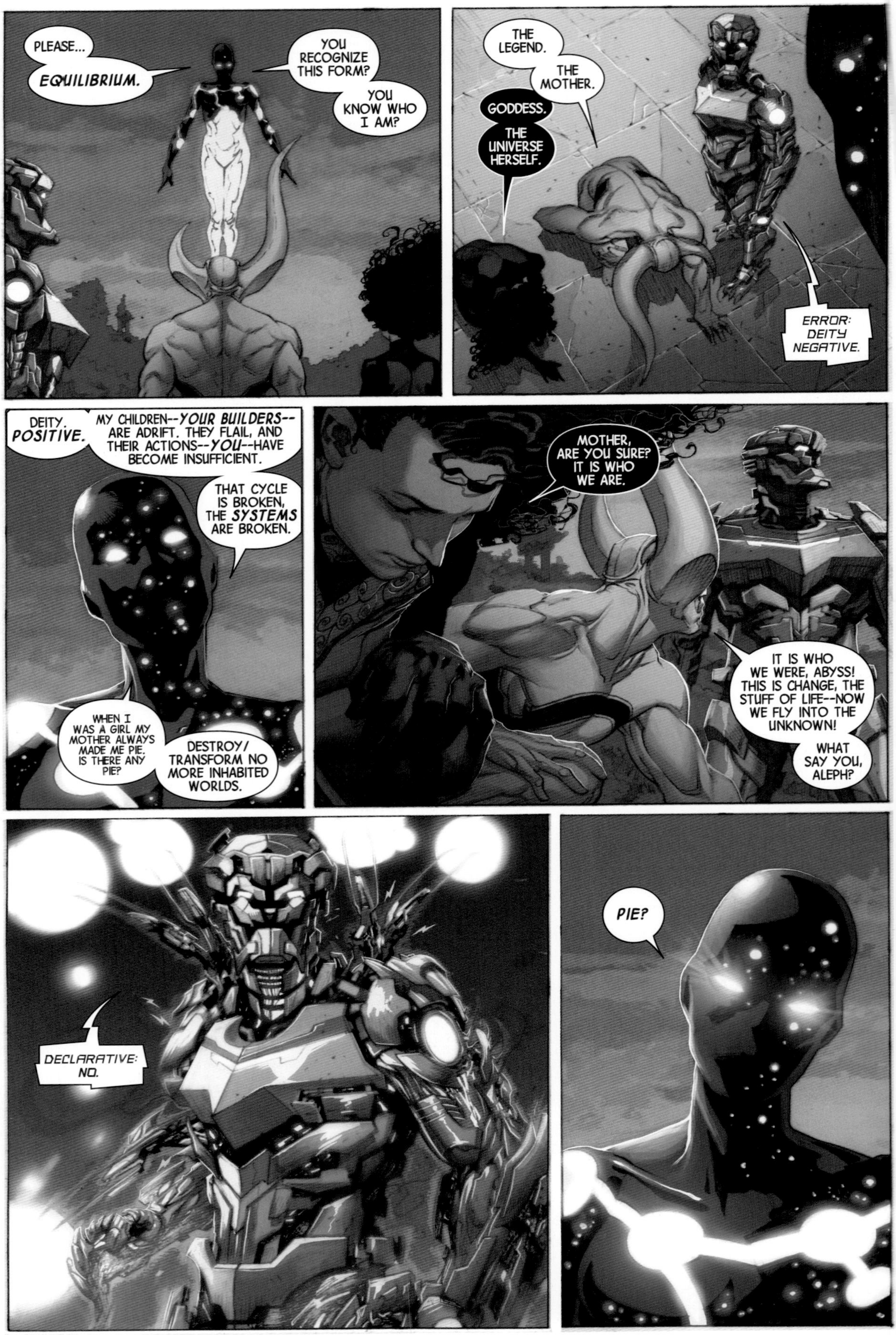
PLEASE...
EQUILIBRIUM.
YOU RECOGNIZE THIS FORM?
YOU KNOW WHO I AM?
THE LEGEND.
THE MOTHER.
GODDESS.
THE UNIVERSE HERSELF.
ERROR: DEITY NEGATIVE.
DEITY. POSITIVE.
MY CHILDREN--YOUR BUILDERS--ARE ADRIFT. THEY FLAIL, AND THEIR ACTIONS--YOU--HAVE BECOME INSUFFICIENT.
THAT CYCLE IS BROKEN, THE SYSTEMS ARE BROKEN.
WHEN I WAS A GIRL MY MOTHER ALWAYS MADE ME PIE. IS THERE ANY PIE?
DESTROY/ TRANSFORM NO MORE INHABITED WORLDS.
MOTHER, ARE YOU SURE? IT IS WHO WE ARE.
IT IS WHO WE WERE, ABYSS! THIS IS CHANGE, THE STUFF OF LIFE--NOW WE FLY INTO THE UNKNOWN!
WHAT SAY YOU, ALEPH?
DECLARATIVE: NO.
PIE?

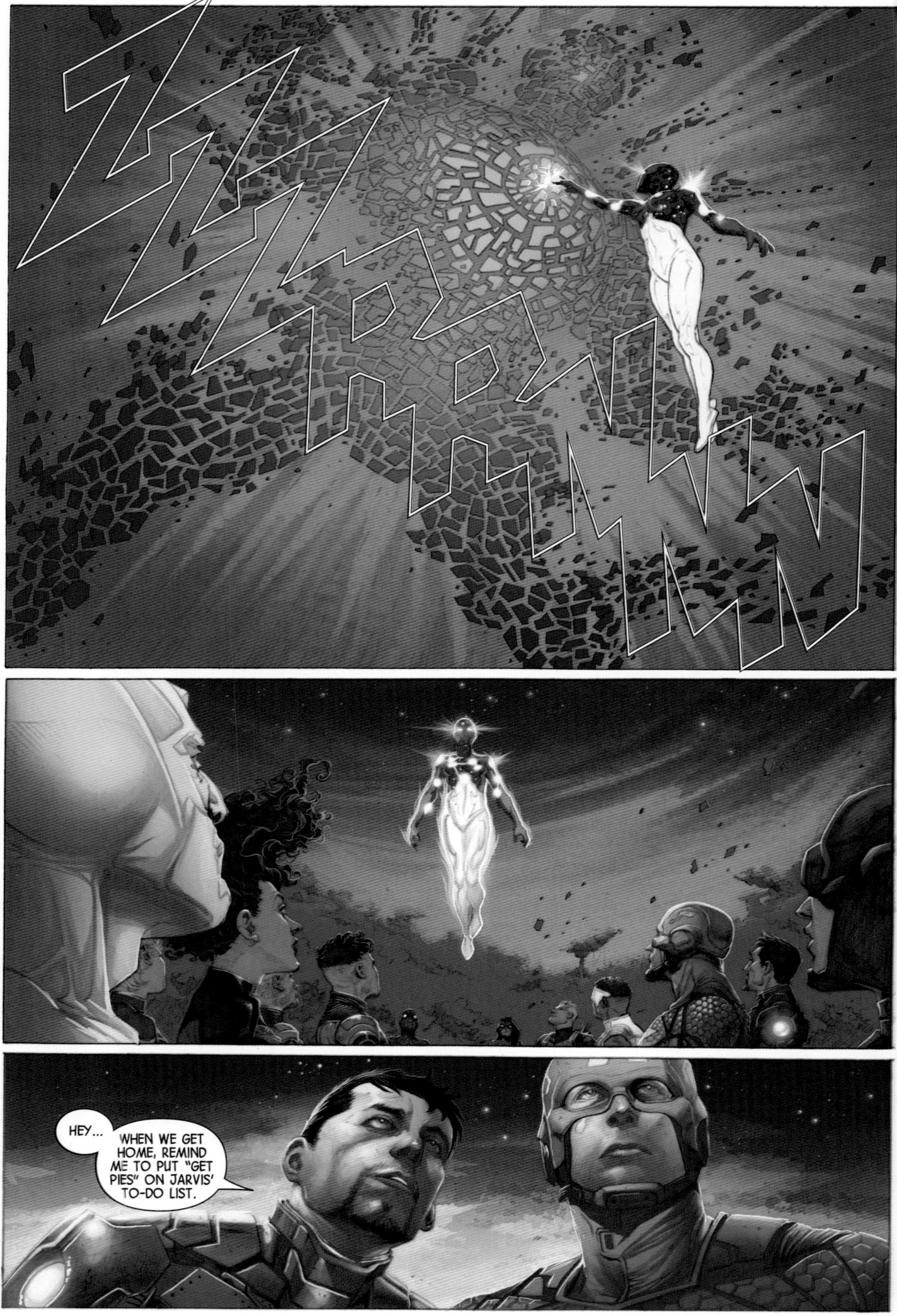
HEY...
WHEN WE GET HOME, REMIND ME TO PUT "GET PIES" ON JARVIS' TO-DO LIST.

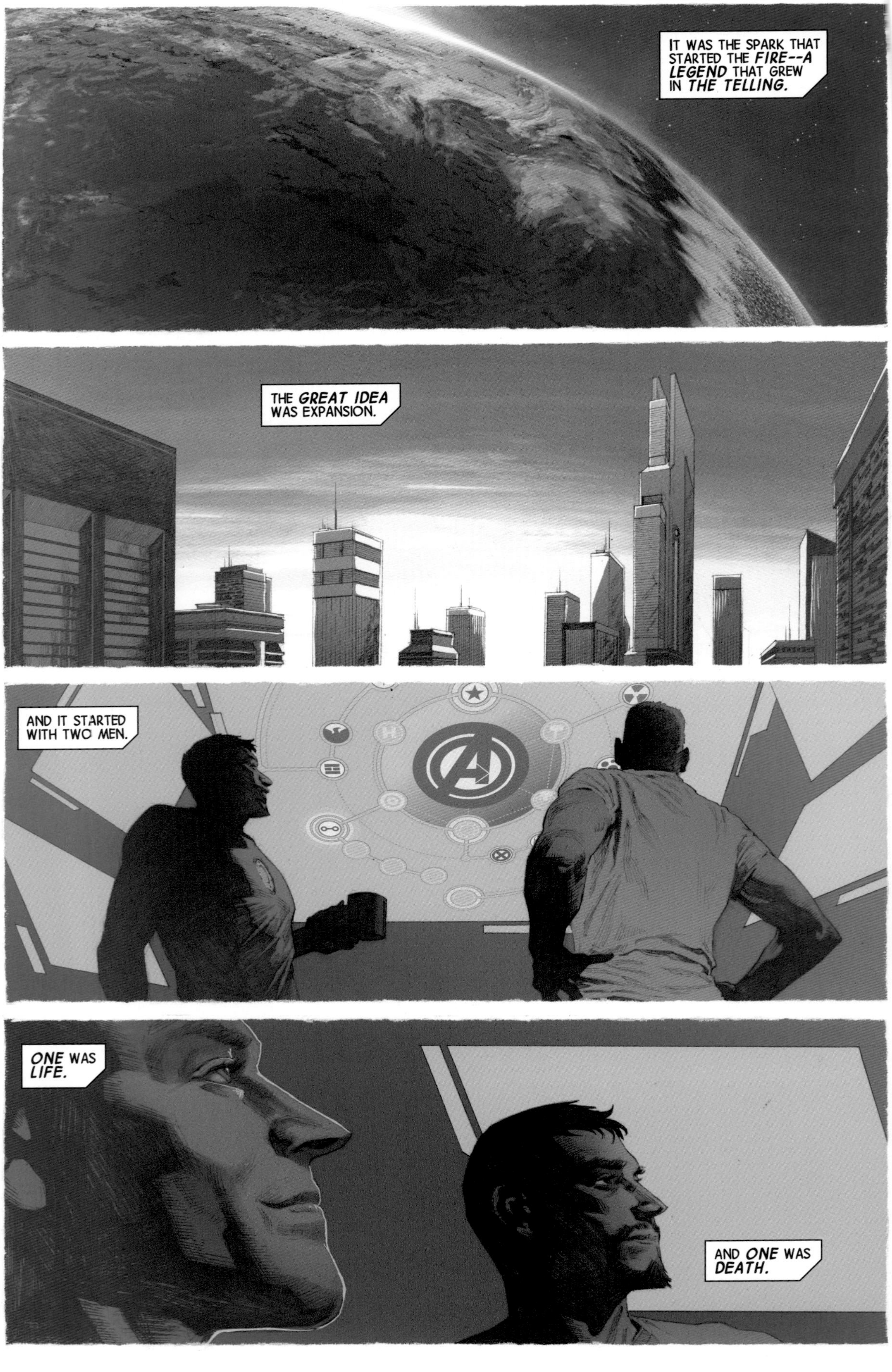
IT WAS THE SPARK THAT STARTED THE FIRE--A LEGEND THAT GREW IN THE TELLING.
THE GREAT IDEA WAS EXPANSION.
AND IT STARTED WITH TWO MEN.
ONE WAS LIFE.
AND ONE WAS DEATH.

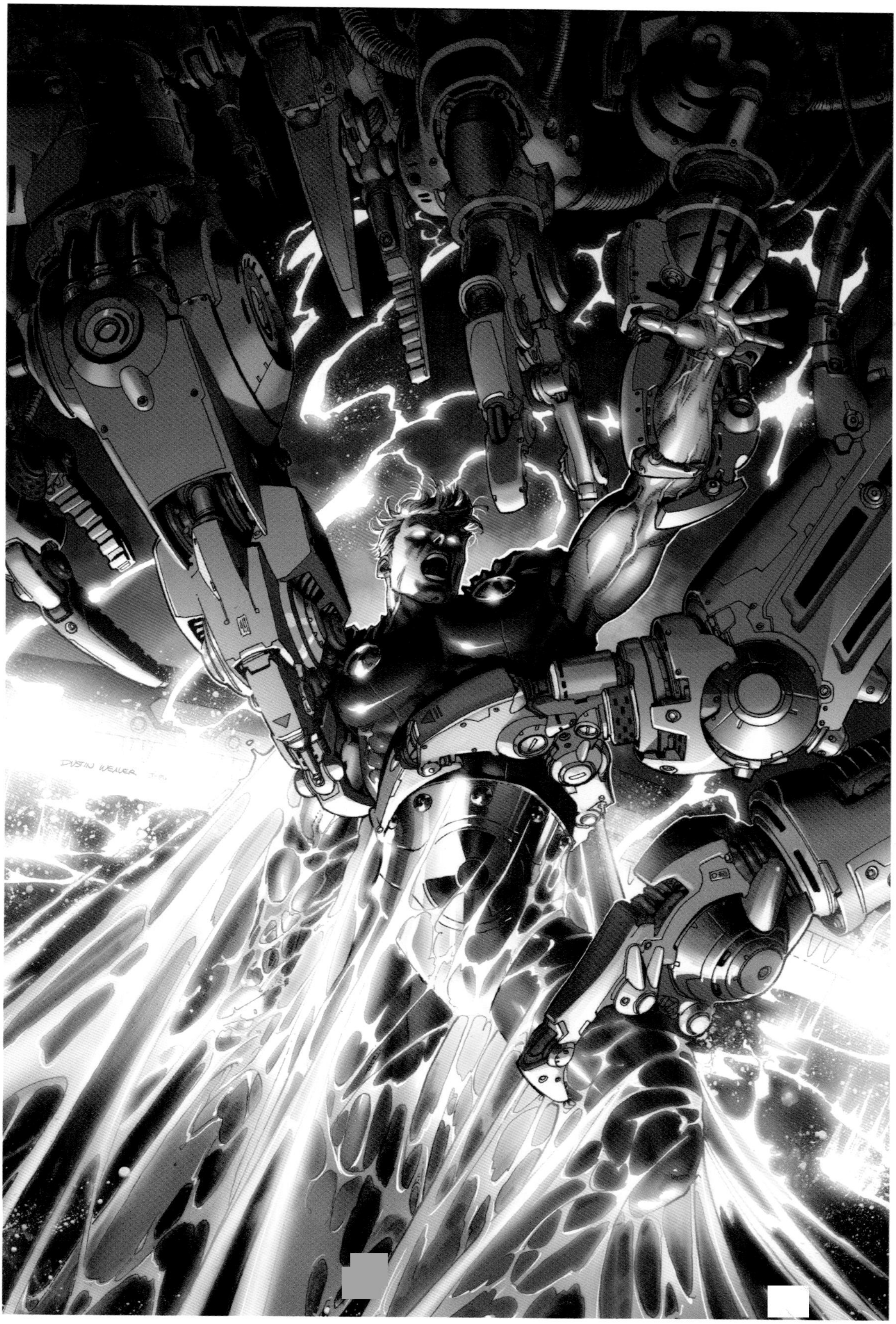
DUSTIN WEAVER

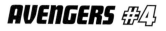

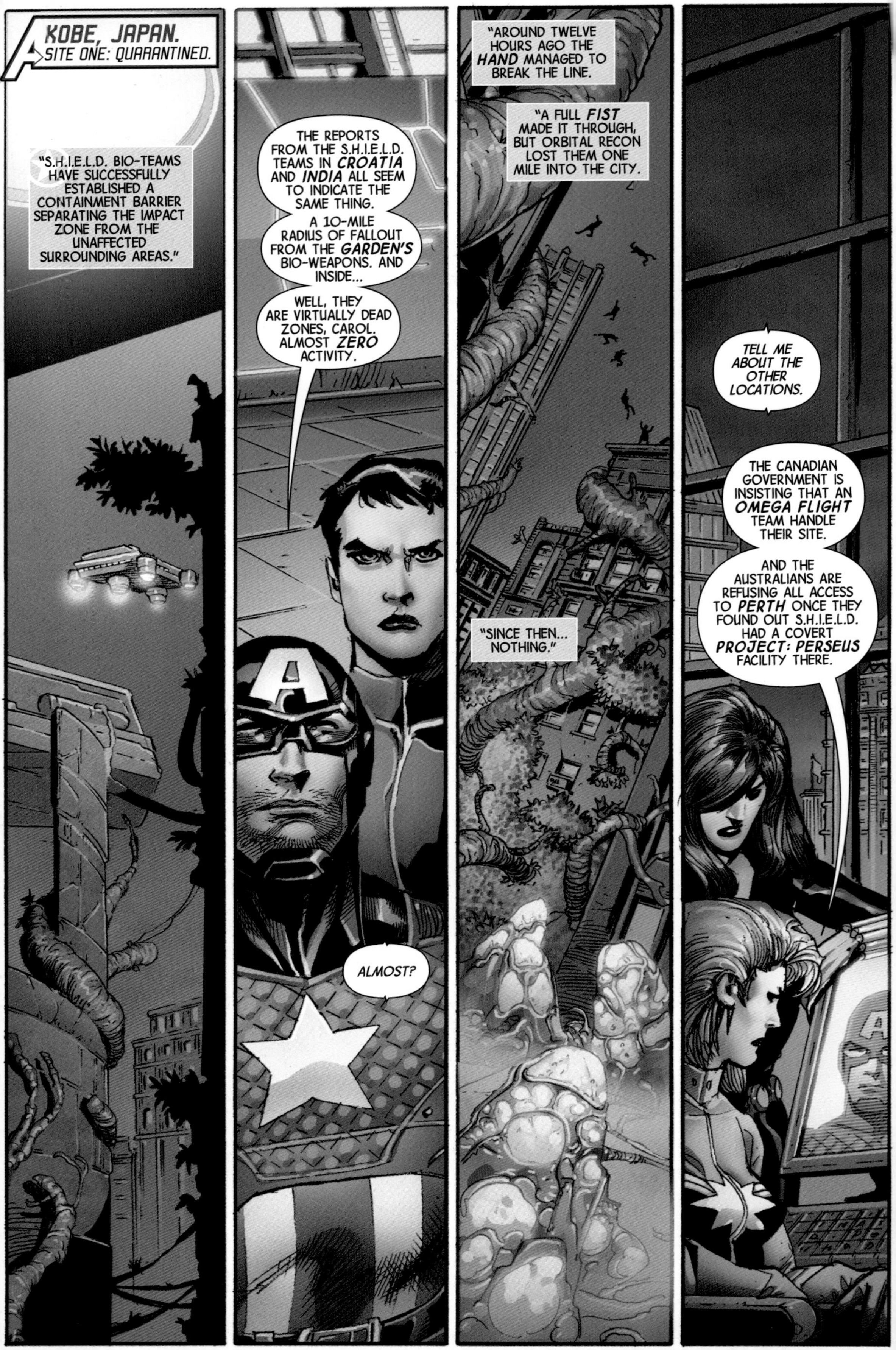
KOBE, JAPAN.
SITE ONE: QUARANTINED.
"S.H.I.E.L.D. BIO-TEAMS HAVE SUCCESSFULLY ESTABLISHED A CONTAINMENT BARRIER SEPARATING THE IMPACT ZONE FROM THE UNAFFECTED SURROUNDING AREAS."
THE REPORTS FROM THE S.H.I.E.L.D. TEAMS IN CROATIA AND INDIA ALL SEEM TO INDICATE THE SAME THING.
A 10-MILE RADIUS OF FALLOUT FROM THE GARDEN'S BIO-WEAPONS. AND INSIDE...
WELL, THEY ARE VIRTUALLY DEAD ZONES, CAROL. ALMOST ZERO ACTIVITY.
ALMOST?
"AROUND TWELVE HOURS AGO THE HAND MANAGED TO BREAK THE LINE.
"A FULL FIST MADE IT THROUGH, BUT ORBITAL RECON LOST THEM ONE MILE INTO THE CITY.
"SINCE THEN... NOTHING."
TELL ME ABOUT THE OTHER LOCATIONS.
THE CANADIAN GOVERNMENT IS INSISTING THAT AN OMEGA FLIGHT TEAM HANDLE THEIR SITE.
AND THE AUSTRALIANS ARE REFUSING ALL ACCESS TO PERTH ONCE THEY FOUND OUT S.H.I.E.L.D. HAD A COVERT PROJECT: PERSEUS FACILITY THERE.

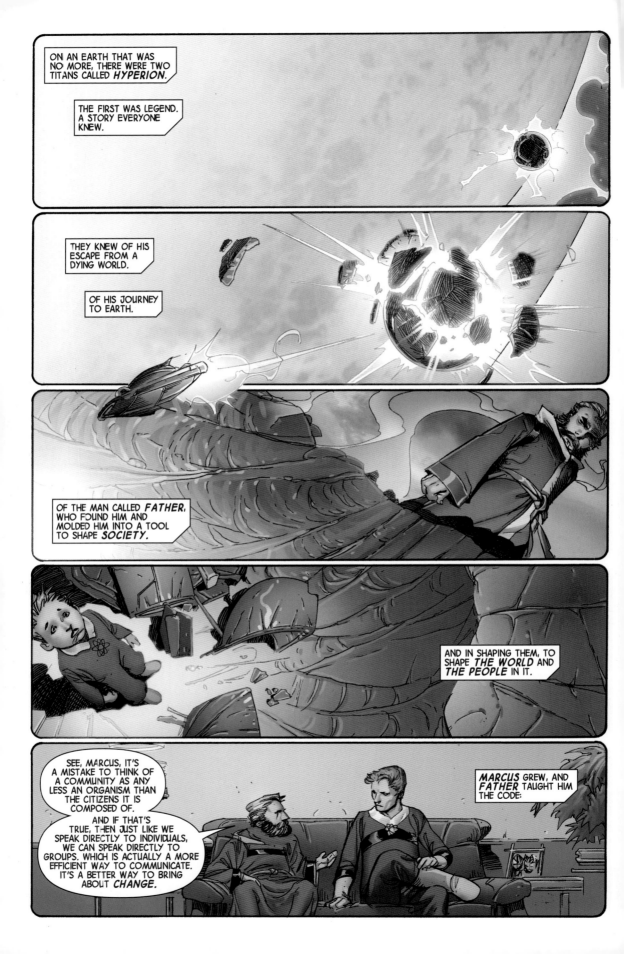

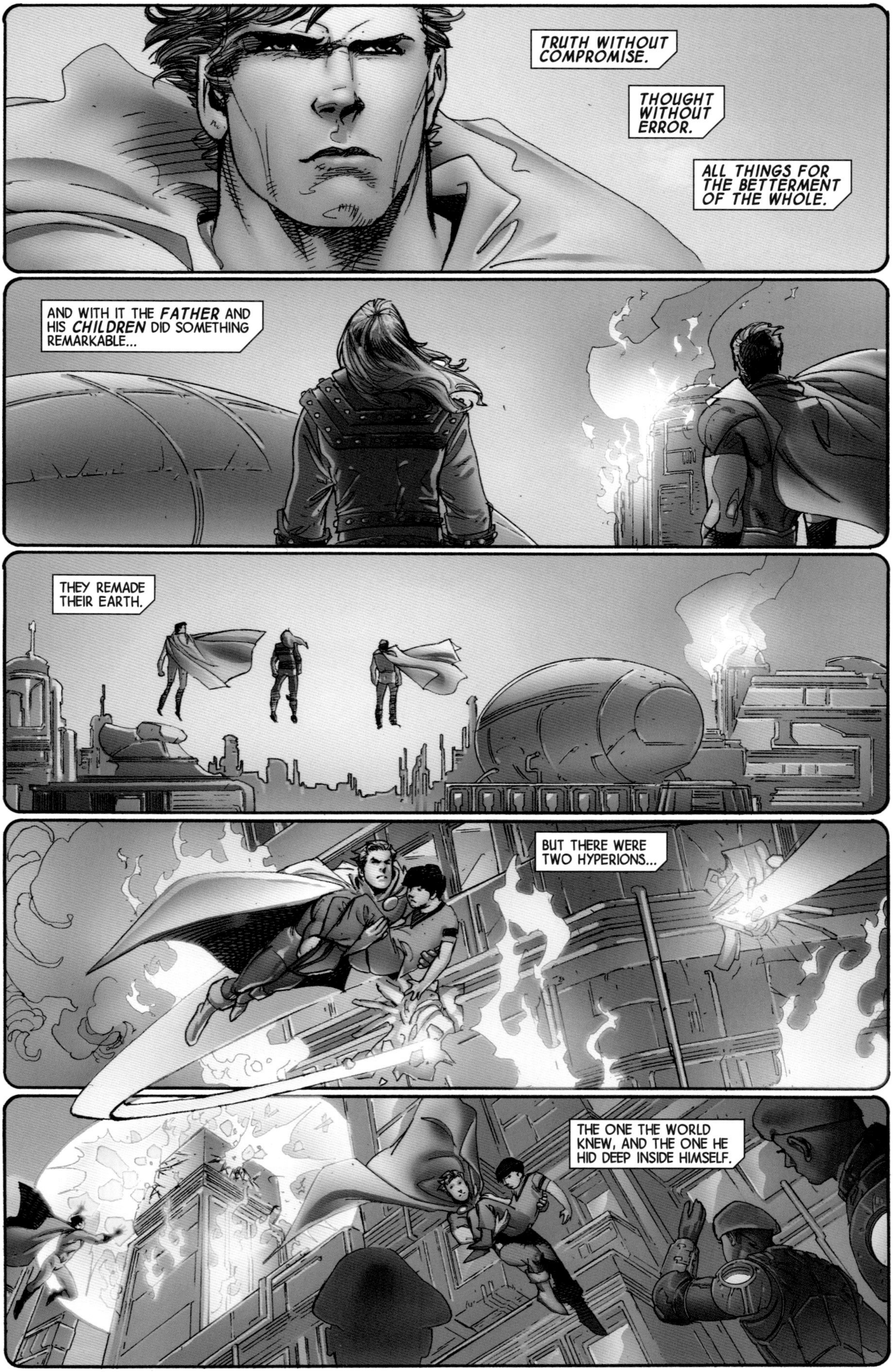
TRUTH WITHOUT COMPROMISE.
THOUGHT WITHOUT ERROR.
ALL THINGS FOR THE BETTERMENT OF THE WHOLE.
AND WITH IT THE FATHER AND HIS CHILDREN DID SOMETHING REMARKABLE...
THEY REMADE THEIR EARTH.
BUT THERE WERE TWO HYPERIONS...
THE ONE THE WORLD KNEW, AND THE ONE HE HID DEEP INSIDE HIMSELF.

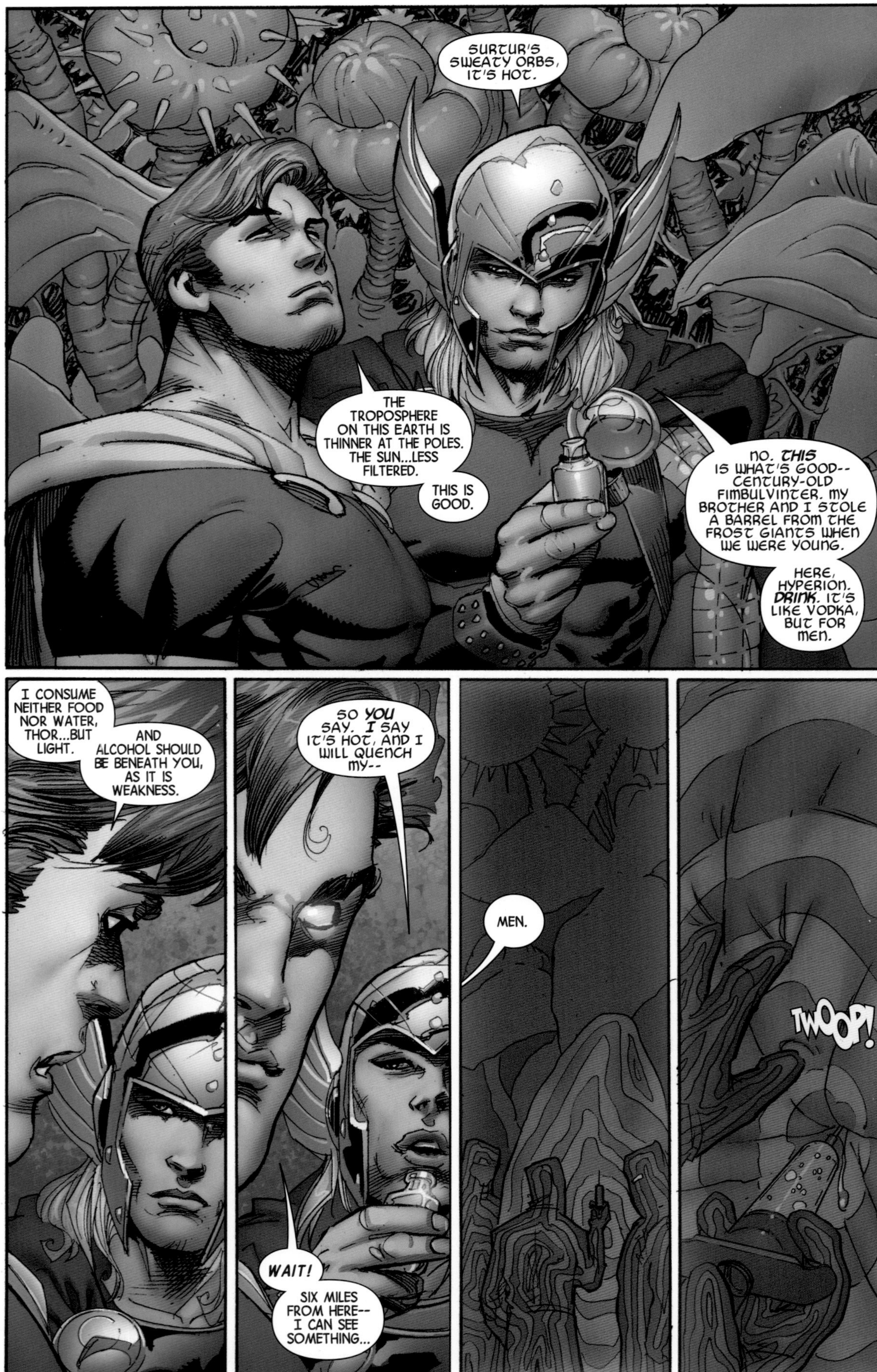
SURTUR'S SWEATY ORBS, IT'S HOT.
THE TROPOSPHERE ON THIS EARTH IS THINNER AT THE POLES. THE SUN...LESS FILTERED.
THIS IS GOOD.
NO. THIS IS WHAT'S GOOD--CENTURY-OLD FIMBULVINTER. MY BROTHER AND I STOLE A BARREL FROM THE FROST GIANTS WHEN WE WERE YOUNG.
HERE, HYPERION. DRINK. IT'S LIKE VODKA, BUT FOR MEN.
I CONSUME NEITHER FOOD NOR WATER, THOR...BUT LIGHT.
AND ALCOHOL SHOULD BE BENEATH YOU, AS IT IS WEAKNESS.
SO YOU SAY. I SAY IT'S HOT, AND I WILL QUENCH MY--
WAIT!
SIX MILES FROM HERE--I CAN SEE SOMETHING...
MEN.
TWOOP!

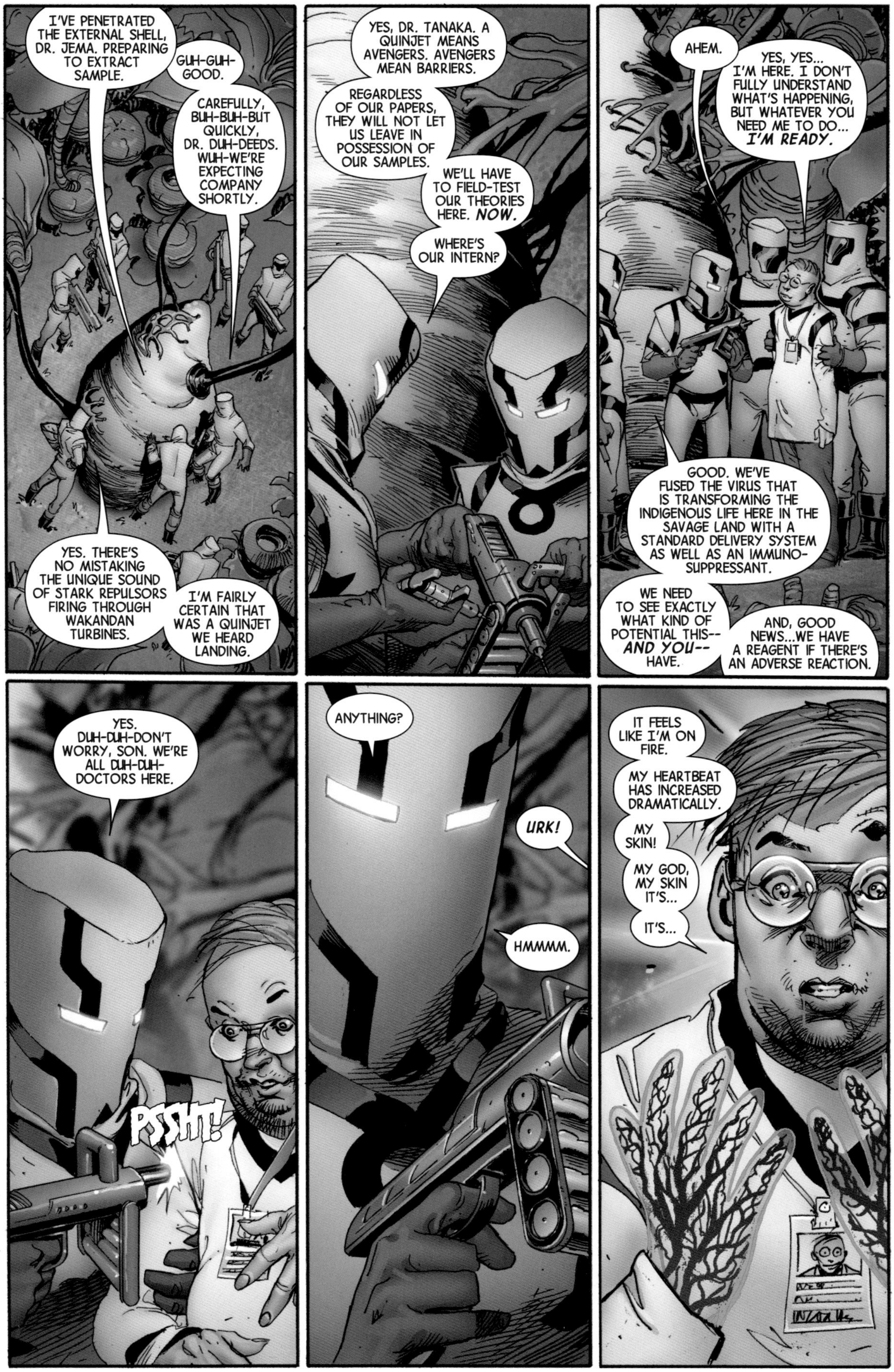
I'VE PENETRATED THE EXTERNAL SHELL, DR. JEMA. PREPARING TO EXTRACT SAMPLE.
GUH-GUH-GOOD.
CAREFULLY, BUH-BUH-BUT QUICKLY, DR. DUH-DEEDS. WUH-WE'RE EXPECTING COMPANY SHORTLY.
YES. THERE'S NO MISTAKING THE UNIQUE SOUND OF STARK REPULSORS FIRING THROUGH WAKANDAN TURBINES.
I'M FAIRLY CERTAIN THAT WAS A QUINJET WE HEARD LANDING.
YES, DR. TANAKA. A QUINJET MEANS AVENGERS. AVENGERS MEAN BARRIERS.
REGARDLESS OF OUR PAPERS, THEY WILL NOT LET US LEAVE IN POSSESSION OF OUR SAMPLES.
WE'LL HAVE TO FIELD-TEST OUR THEORIES HERE. NOW.
WHERE'S OUR INTERN?
AHEM.
YES, YES... I'M HERE. I DON'T FULLY UNDERSTAND WHAT'S HAPPENING, BUT WHATEVER YOU NEED ME TO DO... I'M READY.
GOOD. WE'VE FUSED THE VIRUS THAT IS TRANSFORMING THE INDIGENOUS LIFE HERE IN THE SAVAGE LAND WITH A STANDARD DELIVERY SYSTEM AS WELL AS AN IMMUNO-SUPPRESSANT.
WE NEED TO SEE EXACTLY WHAT KIND OF POTENTIAL THIS-- AND YOU-- HAVE.
AND, GOOD NEWS...WE HAVE A REAGENT IF THERE'S AN ADVERSE REACTION.
YES. DUH-DUH-DON'T WORRY, SON. WE'RE ALL DUH-DUH-DOCTORS HERE.
PSSHT!
ANYTHING?
URK!
HMMMM.
IT FEELS LIKE I'M ON FIRE.
MY HEARTBEAT HAS INCREASED DRAMATICALLY.
MY SKIN!
MY GOD, MY SKIN IT'S...
IT'S...

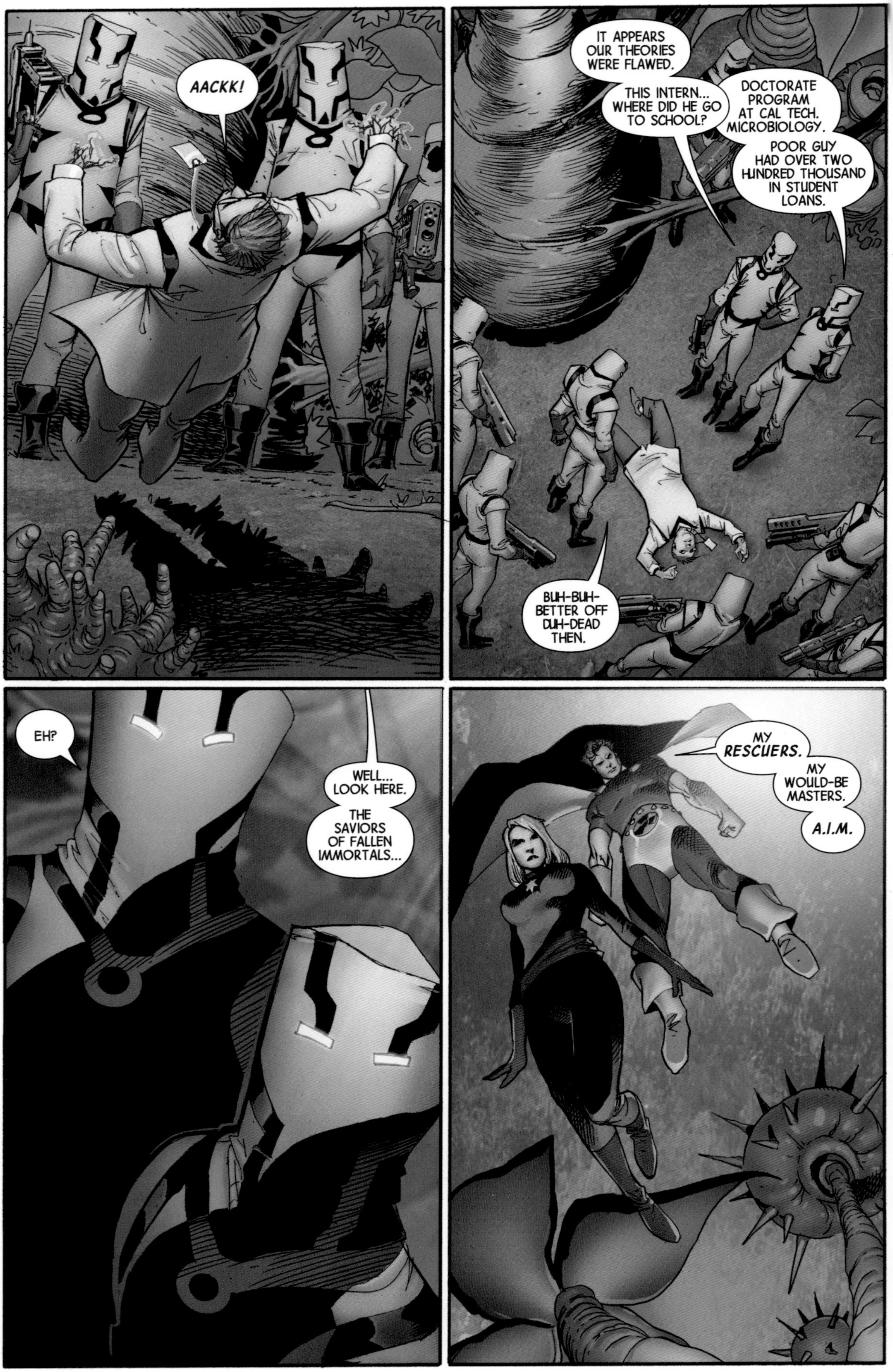
AACKK!
IT APPEARS OUR THEORIES WERE FLAWED.
THIS INTERN... WHERE DID HE GO TO SCHOOL?
DOCTORATE PROGRAM AT CAL TECH. MICROBIOLOGY.
POOR GUY HAD OVER TWO HUNDRED THOUSAND IN STUDENT LOANS.
BUH-BUH-BETTER OFF DUH-DEAD THEN.
EH?
WELL... LOOK HERE.
THE SAVIORS OF FALLEN IMMORTALS...
MY RESCUERS.
MY WOULD-BE MASTERS.
A.I.M.

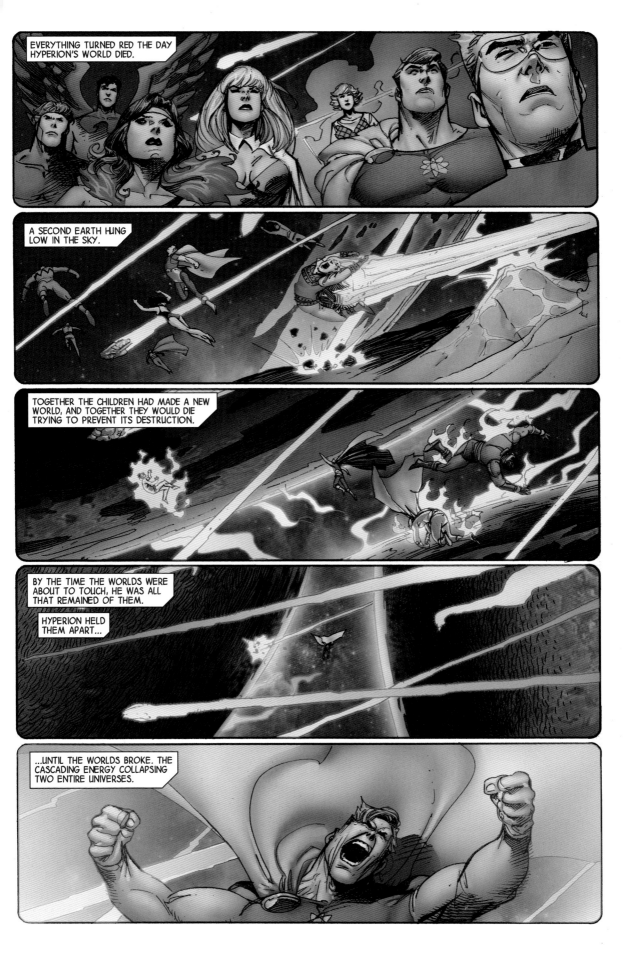

EVERYTHING TURNED RED THE DAY HYPERION'S WORLD DIED.

A SECOND EARTH HUNG LOW IN THE SKY.

TOGETHER THE CHILDREN HAD MADE A NEW WORLD, AND TOGETHER THEY WOULD DIE TRYING TO PREVENT ITS DESTRUCTION.

BY THE TIME THE WORLDS WERE ABOUT TO TOUCH, HE WAS ALL THAT REMAINED OF THEM.

HYPERION HELD THEM APART...

...UNTIL THE WORLDS BROKE. THE CASCADING ENERGY COLLAPSING TWO ENTIRE UNIVERSES.

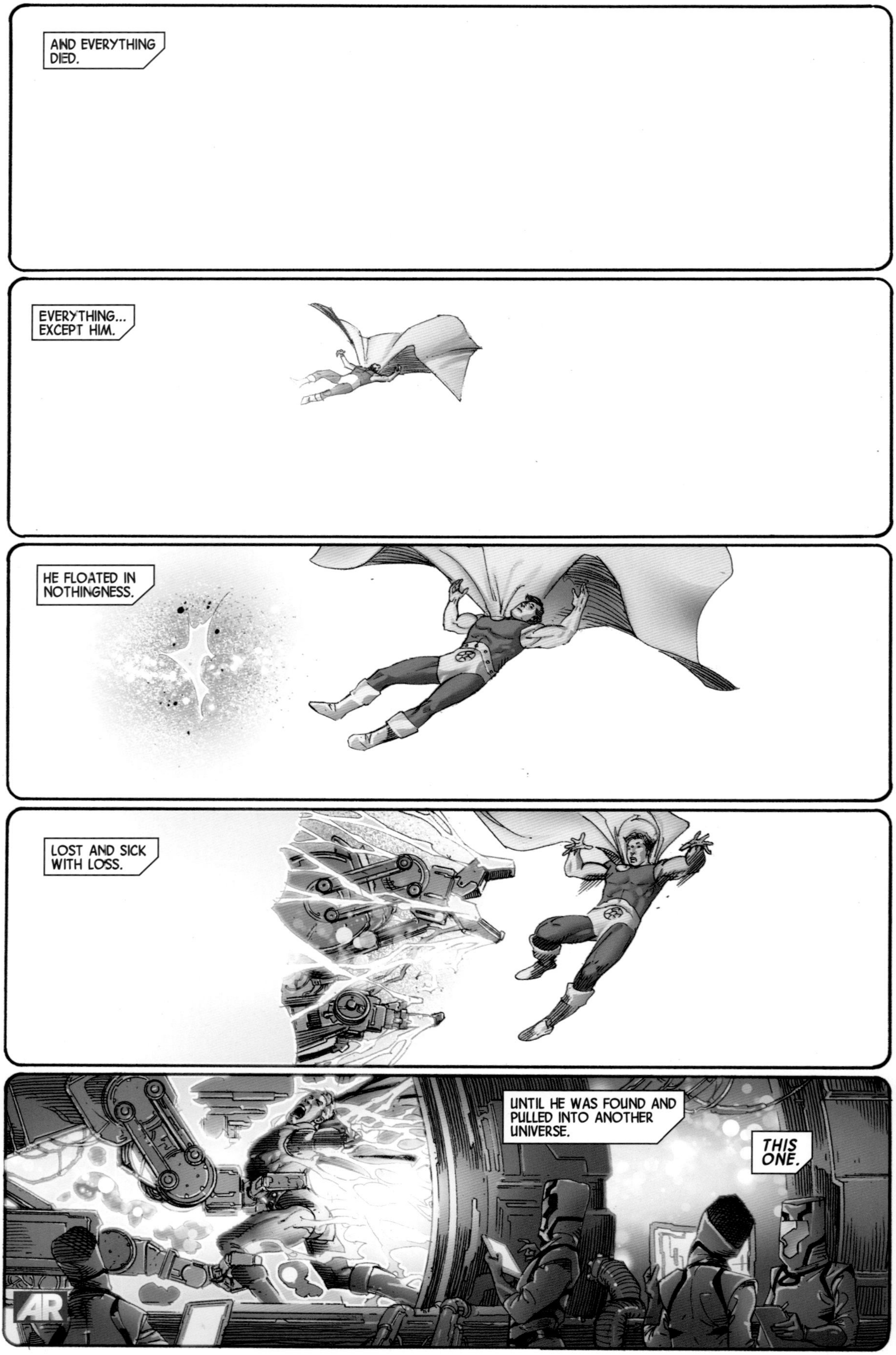
AND EVERYTHING DIED.
EVERYTHING... EXCEPT HIM.
HE FLOATED IN NOTHINGNESS.
LOST AND SICK WITH LOSS.
UNTIL HE WAS FOUND AND PULLED INTO ANOTHER UNIVERSE.
THIS ONE.

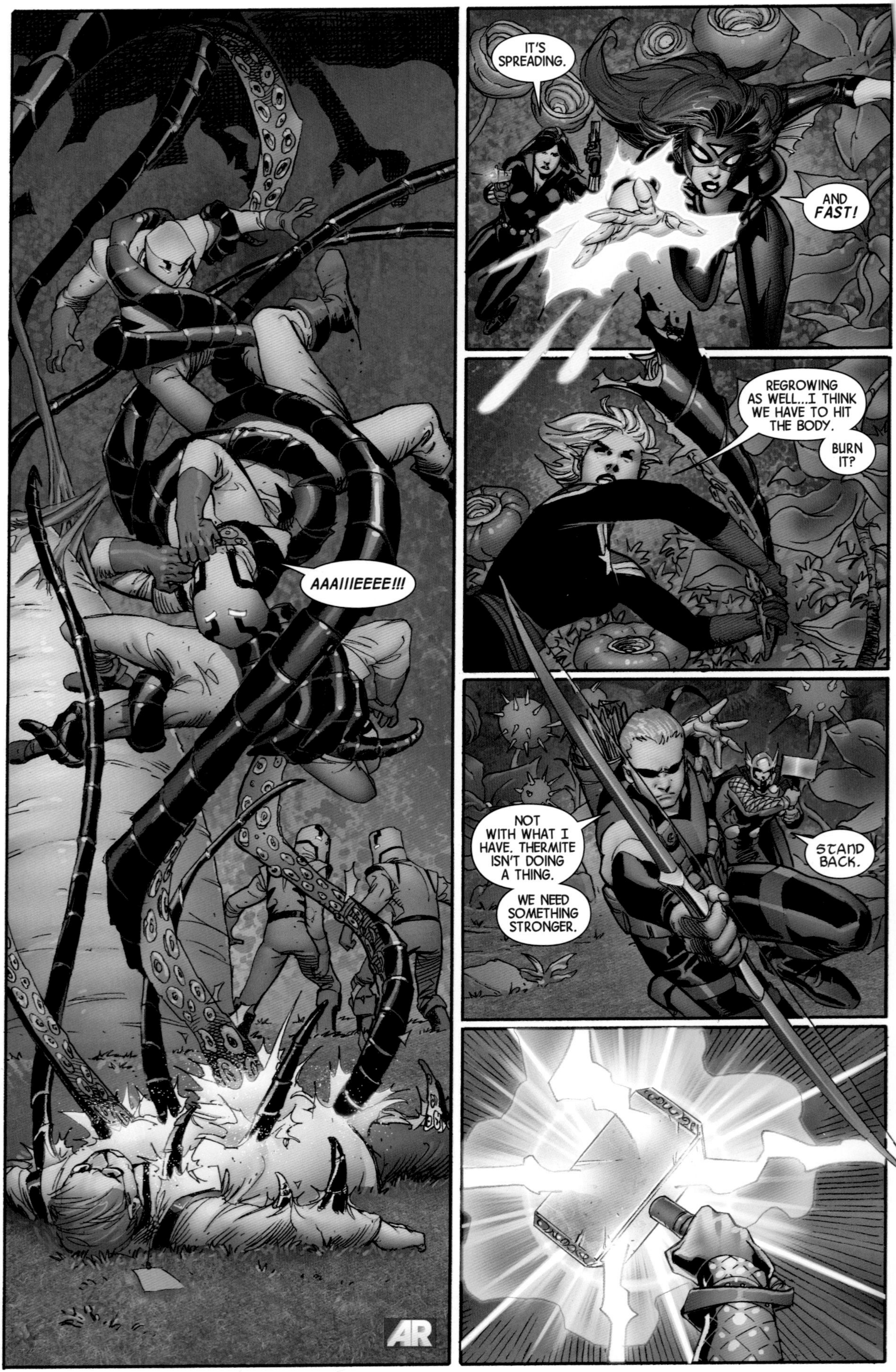

AAAIIIEEEE!!!
IT'S SPREADING.
AND FAST!
REGROWING AS WELL...I THINK WE HAVE TO HIT THE BODY.
BURN IT?
NOT WITH WHAT I HAVE. THERMITE ISN'T DOING A THING.
WE NEED SOMETHING STRONGER.
STAND BACK.

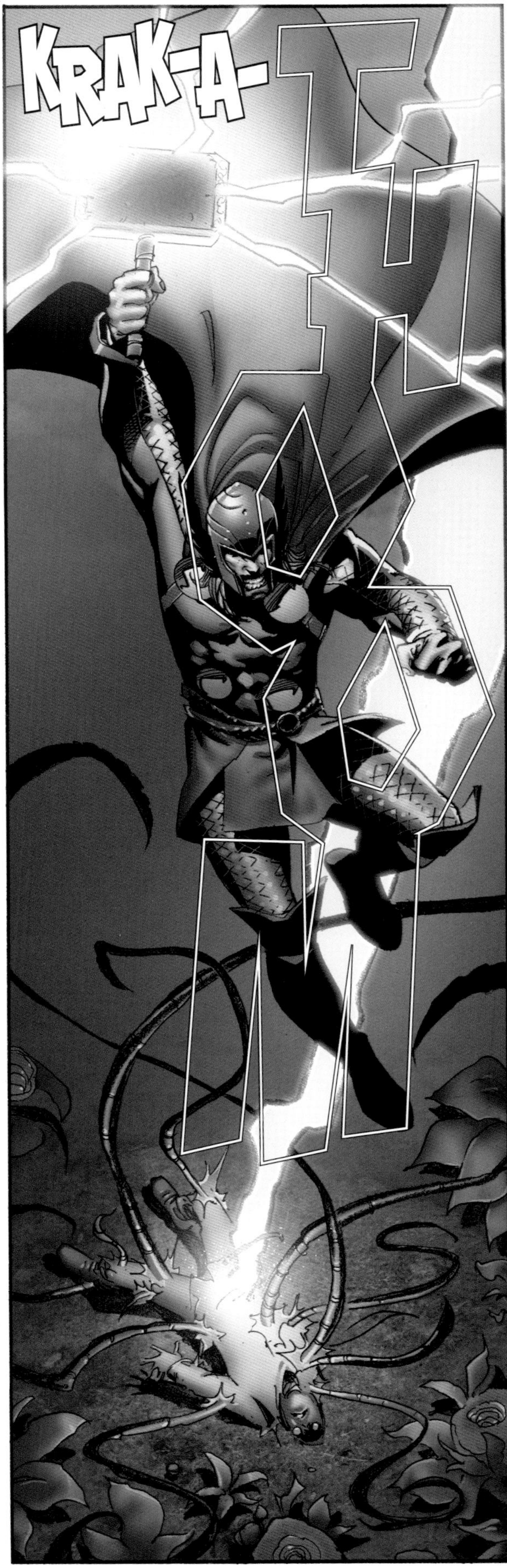
KRAK-A-THOOM

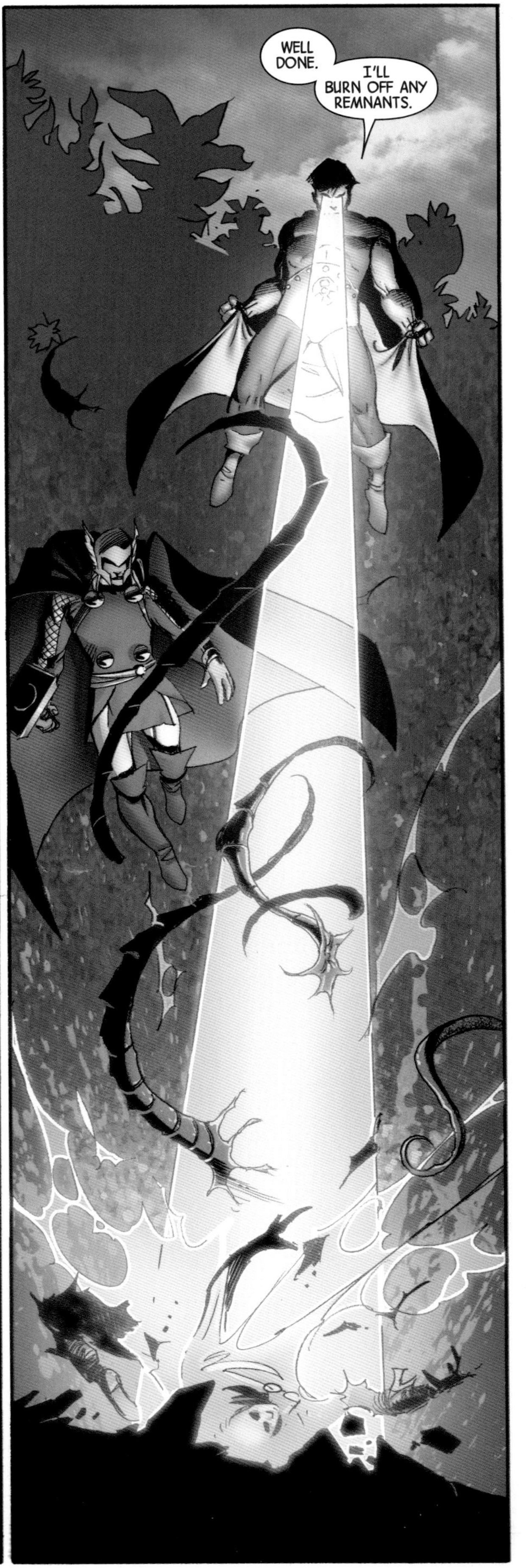
WELL DONE.
I'LL BURN OFF ANY REMNANTS.

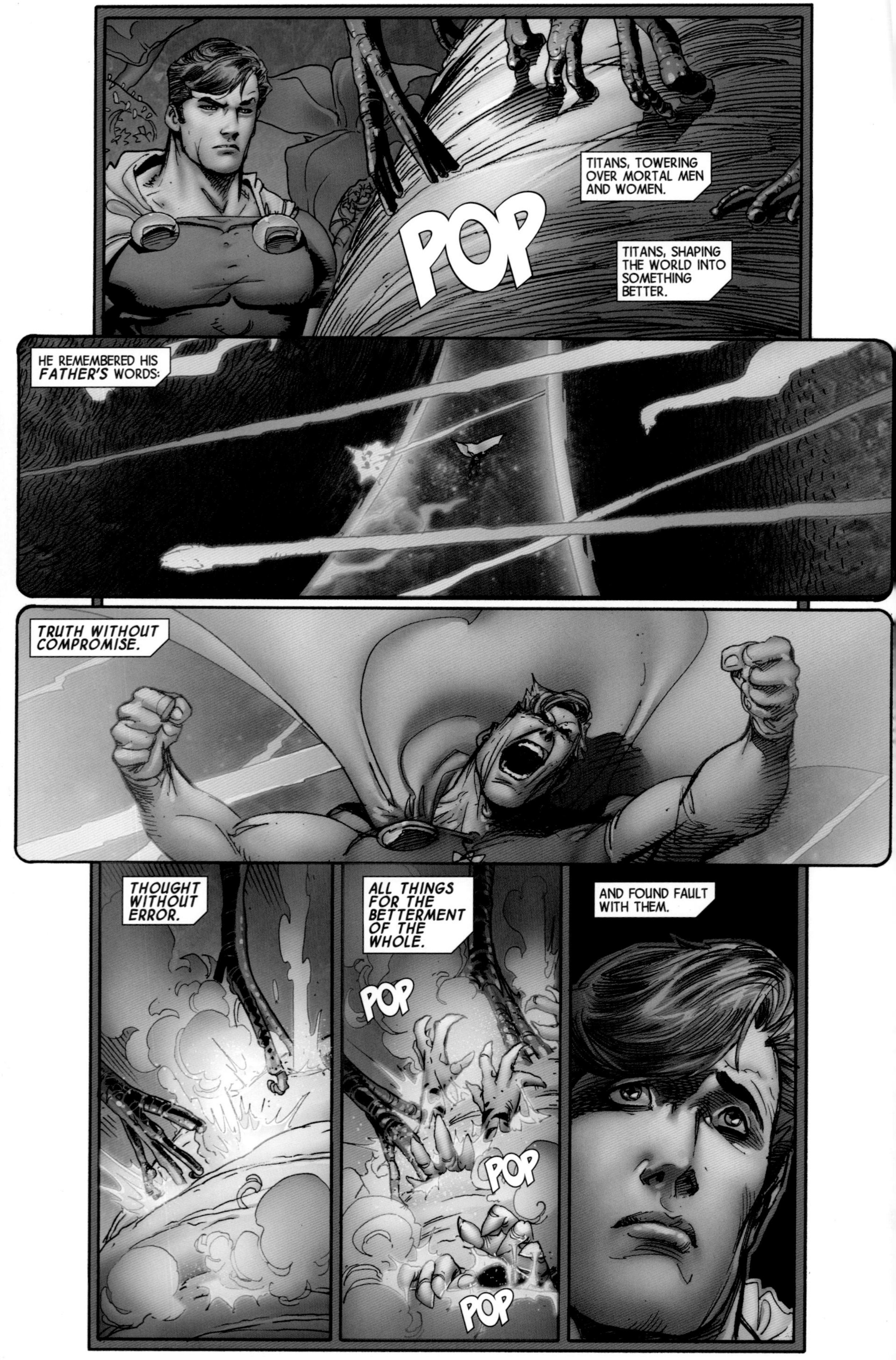
TITANS, TOWERING OVER MORTAL MEN AND WOMEN.
POP
TITANS, SHAPING THE WORLD INTO SOMETHING BETTER.
HE REMEMBERED HIS *FATHER'S* WORDS:
TRUTH WITHOUT COMPROMISE.
THOUGHT WITHOUT ERROR.
ALL THINGS FOR THE BETTERMENT OF THE WHOLE.
POP
POP
POP
AND FOUND FAULT WITH THEM.

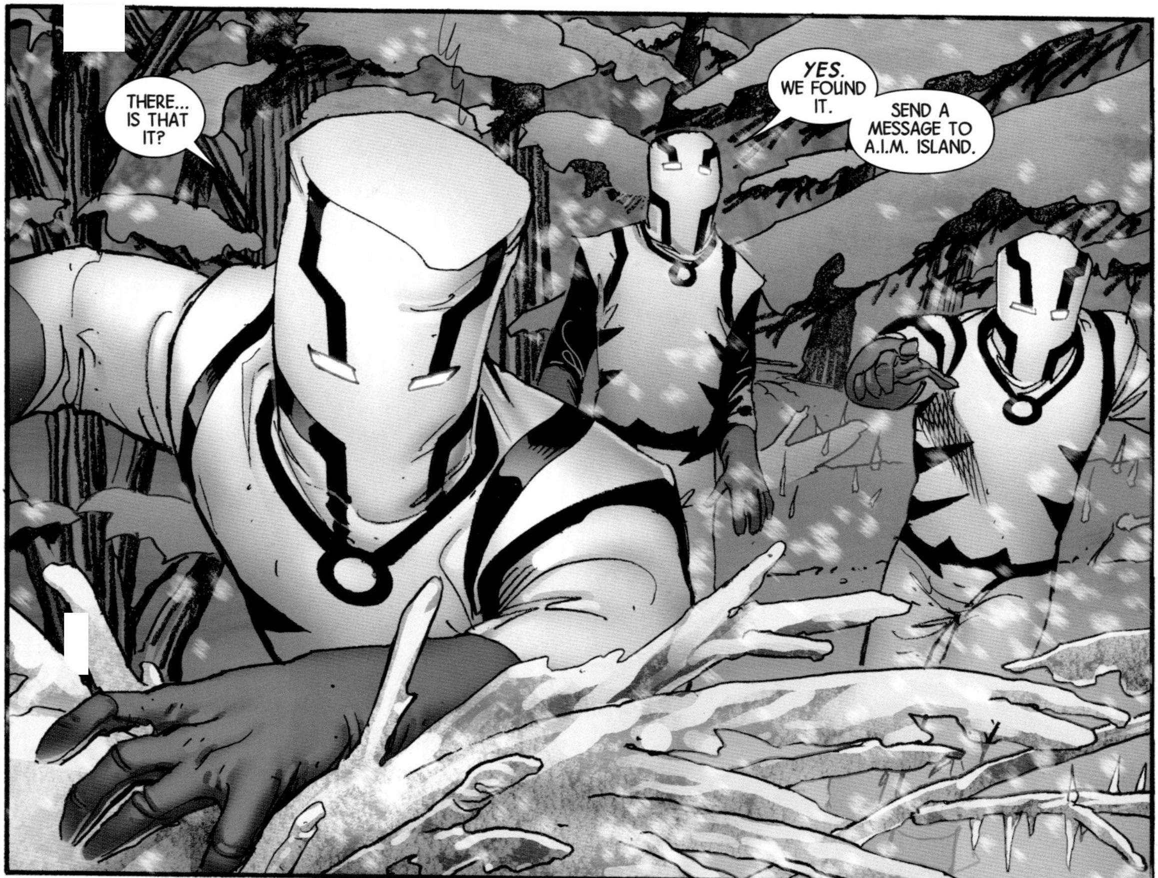
THERE... IS THAT IT?
YES. WE FOUND IT.
SEND A MESSAGE TO A.I.M. ISLAND.
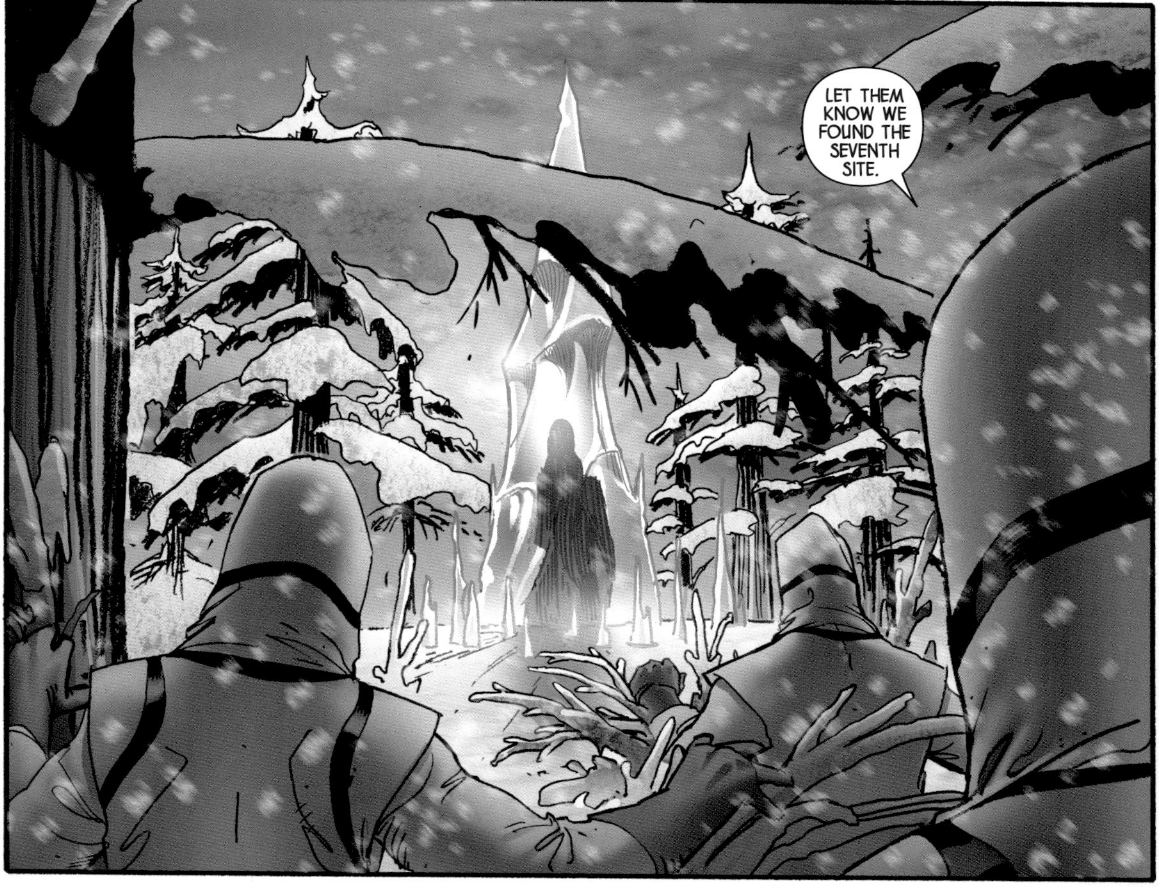
LET THEM KNOW WE FOUND THE SEVENTH SITE.

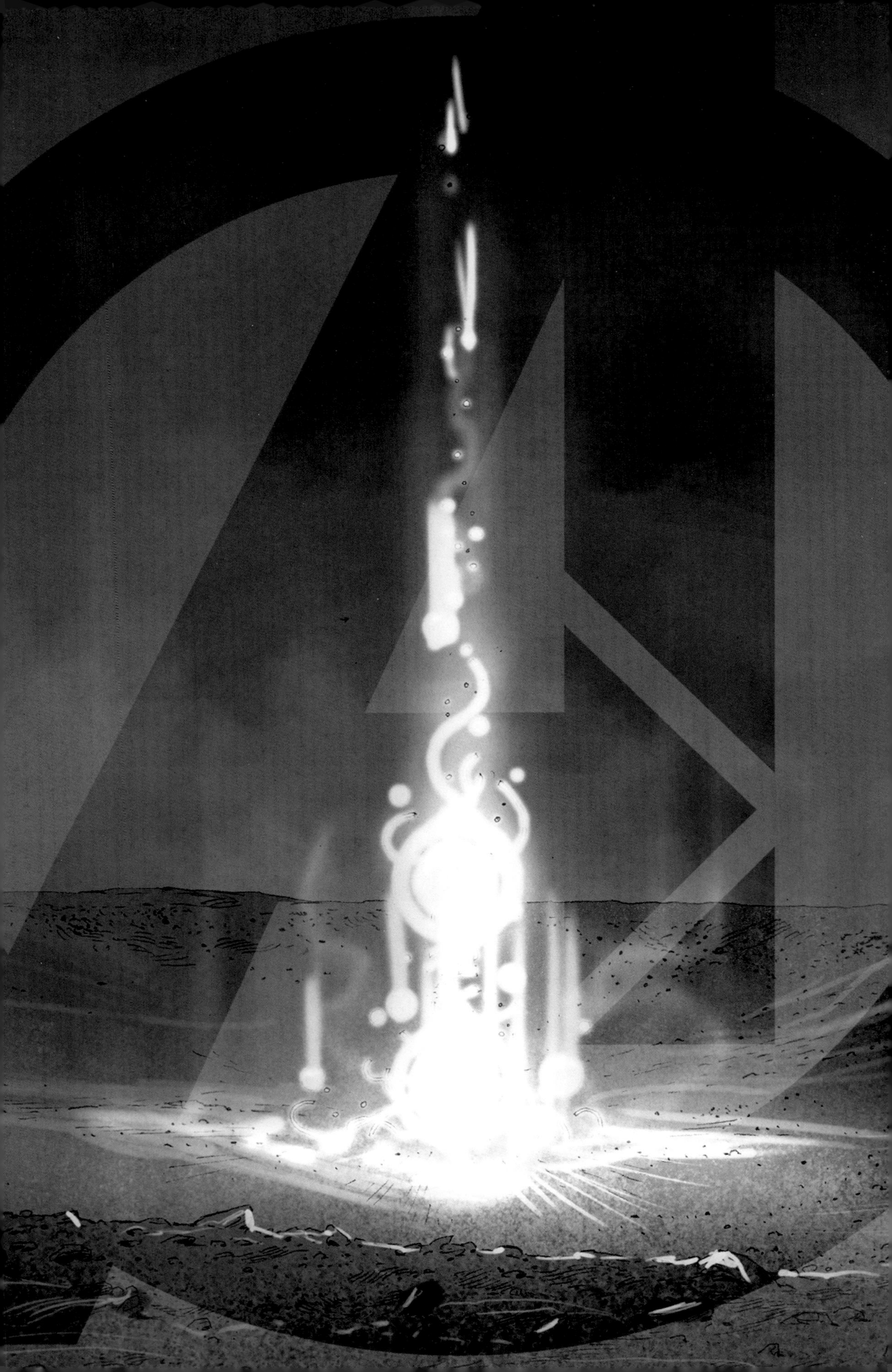

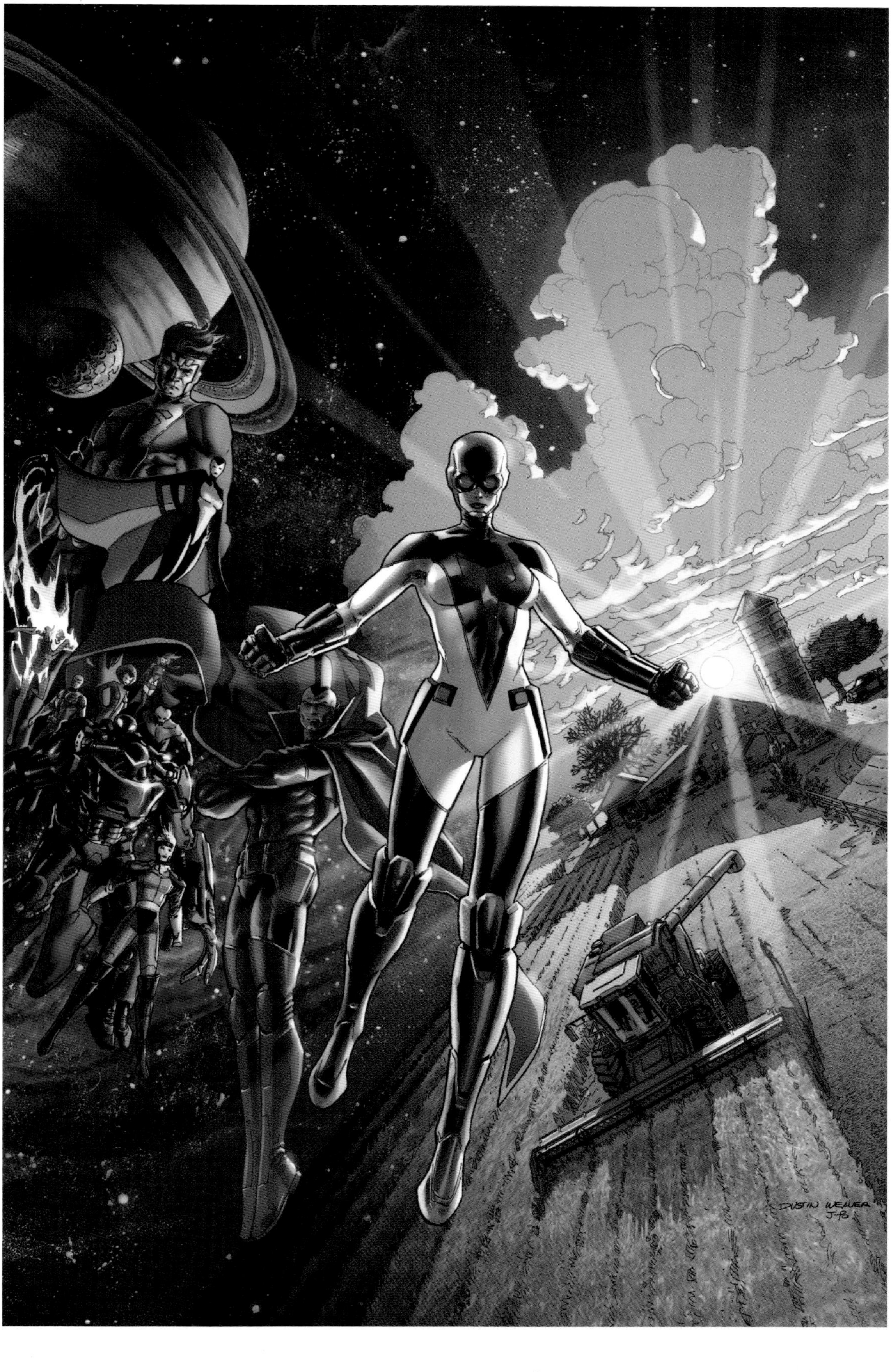
DUSTIN WEAVER
J-P

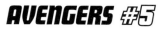

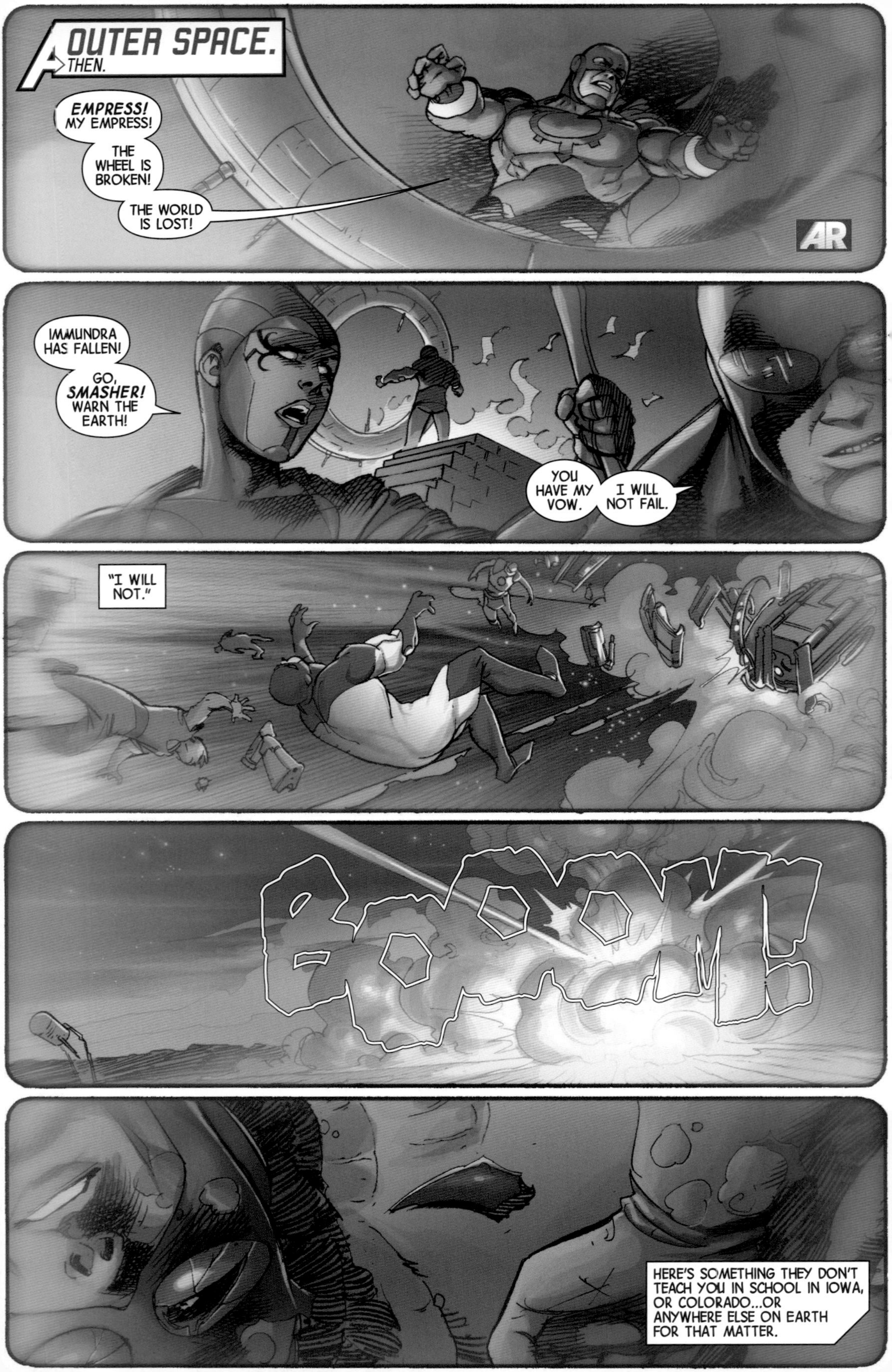
OUTER SPACE.
THEN.
EMPRESS! MY EMPRESS!
THE WHEEL IS BROKEN!
THE WORLD IS LOST!
AR
IMMUNDRA HAS FALLEN!
GO, SMASHER! WARN THE EARTH!
YOU HAVE MY VOW.
I WILL NOT FAIL.
"I WILL NOT."
BOOOOM!
HERE'S SOMETHING THEY DON'T TEACH YOU IN SCHOOL IN IOWA, OR COLORADO...OR ANYWHERE ELSE ON EARTH FOR THAT MATTER.

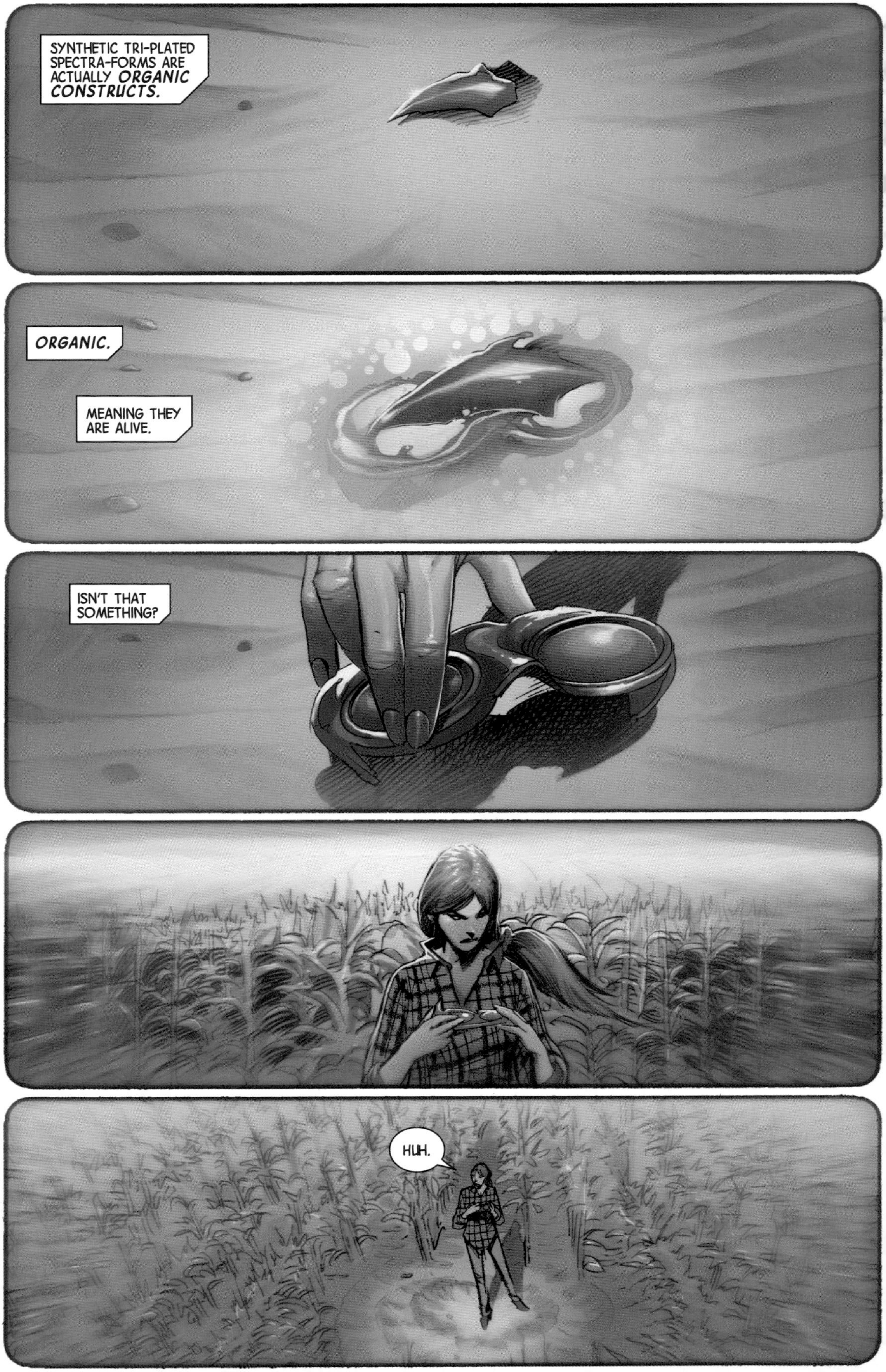
SYNTHETIC TRI-PLATED SPECTRA-FORMS ARE ACTUALLY ORGANIC CONSTRUCTS.
ORGANIC.
MEANING THEY ARE ALIVE.
ISN'T THAT SOMETHING?
HUH.

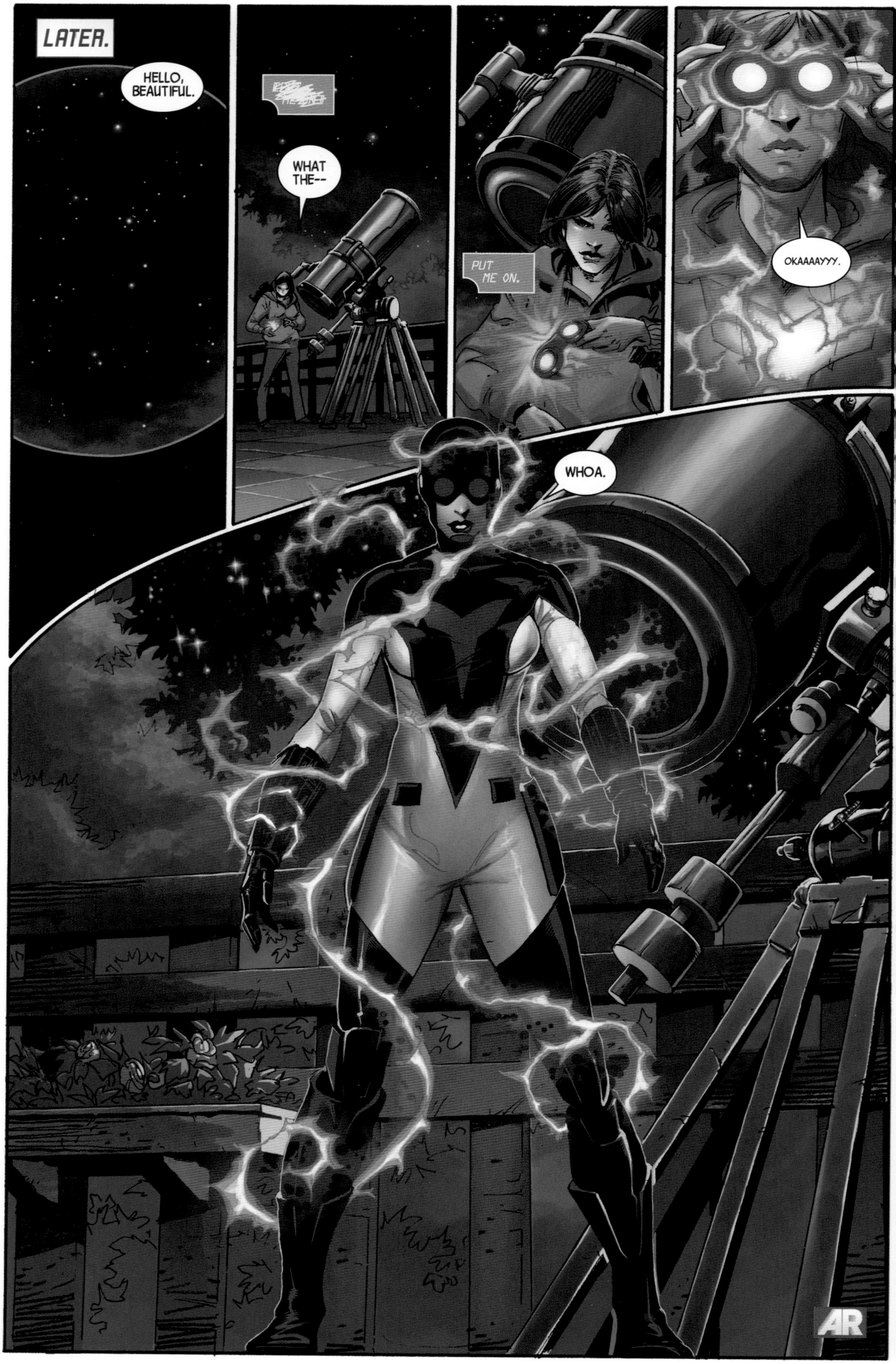
LATER.
HELLO, BEAUTIFUL.
WHAT THE--
PUT ME ON.
OKAAAAYYY.
WHOA.

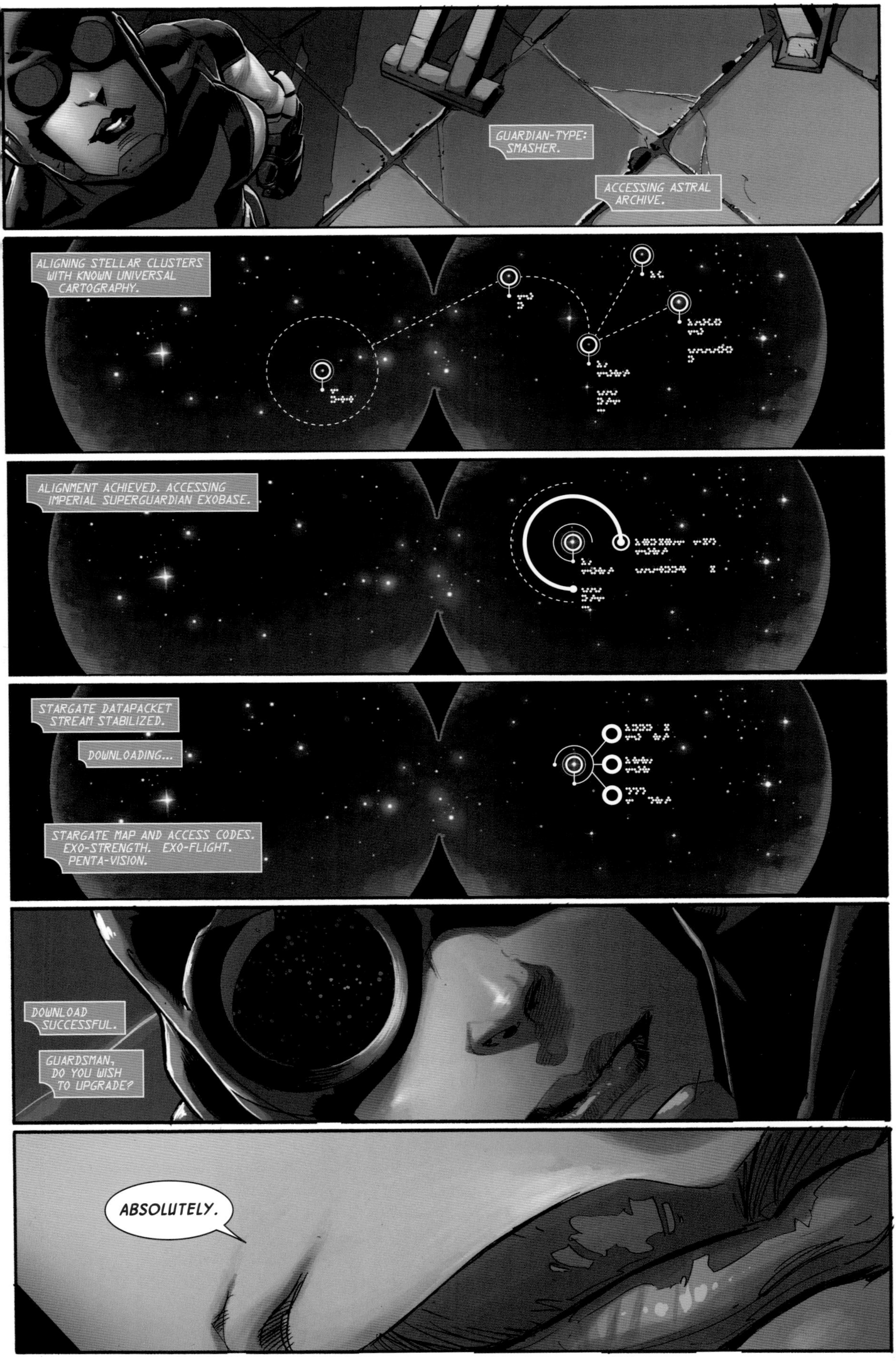
GUARDIAN-TYPE: SMASHER.
ACCESSING ASTRAL ARCHIVE.
ALIGNING STELLAR CLUSTERS WITH KNOWN UNIVERSAL CARTOGRAPHY.
ALIGNMENT ACHIEVED. ACCESSING IMPERIAL SUPERGUARDIAN EXOBASE.
STARGATE DATAPACKET STREAM STABILIZED.
DOWNLOADING...
STARGATE MAP AND ACCESS CODES. EXO-STRENGTH. EXO-FLIGHT. PENTA-VISION.
DOWNLOAD SUCCESSFUL.
GUARDSMAN, DO YOU WISH TO UPGRADE?
ABSOLUTELY.

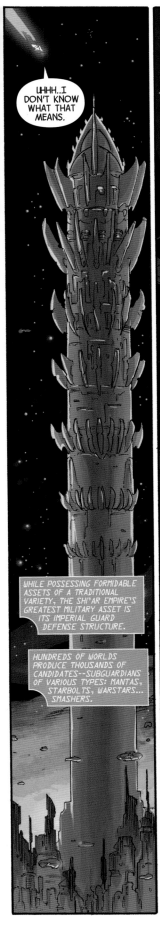

UHHH..I DON'T KNOW WHAT THAT MEANS.

WHILE POSSESSING FORMIDABLE ASSETS OF A TRADITIONAL VARIETY, THE SHI'AR EMPIRE'S GREATEST MILITARY ASSET IS ITS IMPERIAL GUARD DEFENSE STRUCTURE.

HUNDREDS OF WORLDS PRODUCE THOUSANDS OF CANDIDATES--SUBGUARDIANS OF VARIOUS TYPES: MANTAS, STARBOLTS, WARSTARS... SMASHERS.

WAIT, SMASHER-- YOU MEAN LIKE ME?

YES. THERE ARE CURRENTLY 43 SMASHER-CLASS SUBGUARDIANS PREPARING FOR THE CHANCE TO ONE DAY JOIN THE MOST ELITE FIGHTING FORCE IN THE KNOWN UNIVERSE...

THE IMPERIAL GUARD.

OKAY... AND IF I'M A SUBGUARDIAN, WHAT ARE THEY CALLED?

SUPERGUARDIANS.

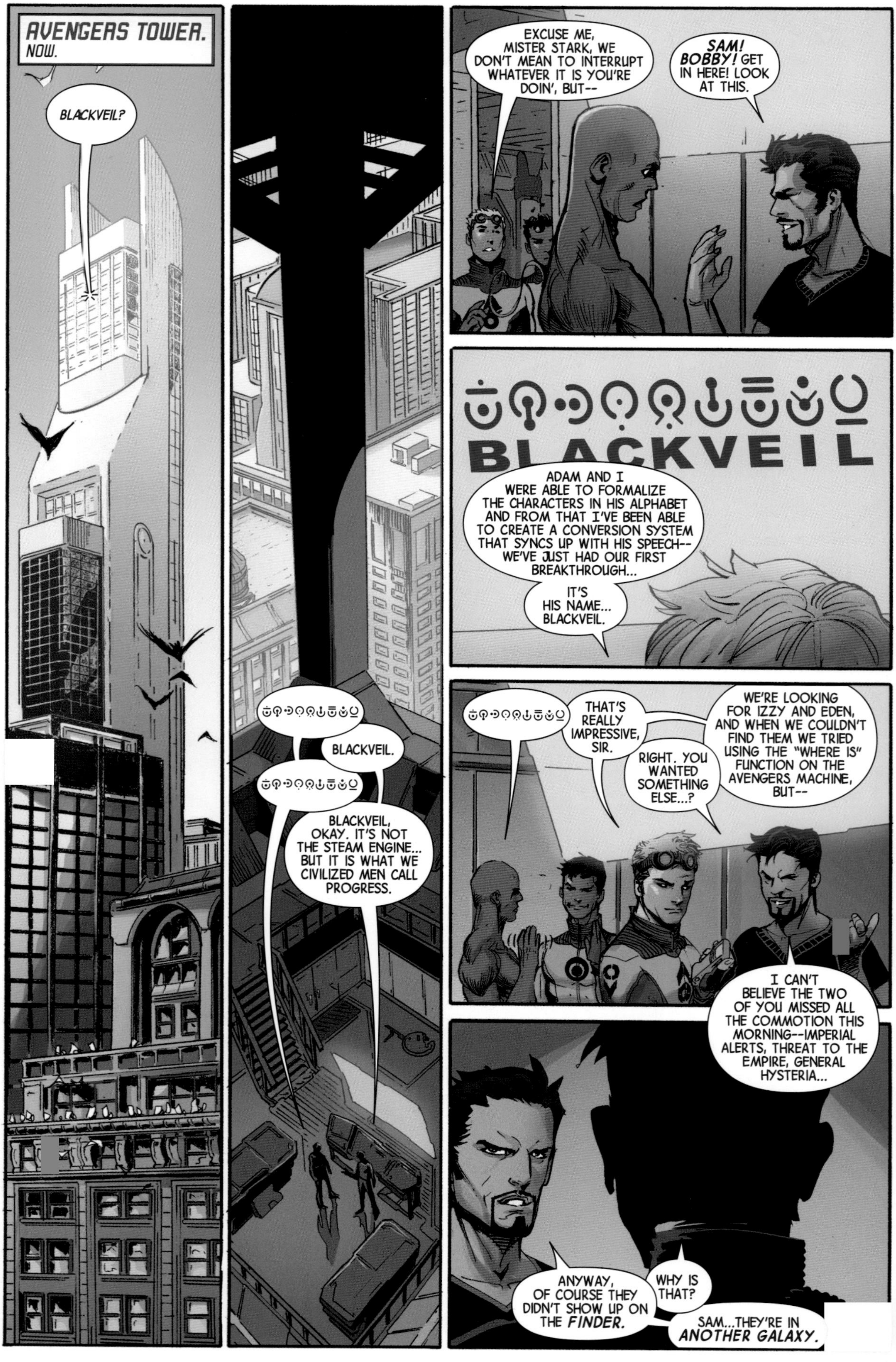
AVENGERS TOWER. NOW.
BLACKVEIL?
BLACKVEIL.
BLACKVEIL, OKAY. IT'S NOT THE STEAM ENGINE... BUT IT IS WHAT WE CIVILIZED MEN CALL PROGRESS.
EXCUSE ME, MISTER STARK, WE DON'T MEAN TO INTERRUPT WHATEVER IT IS YOU'RE DOIN', BUT--
SAM! BOBBY! GET IN HERE! LOOK AT THIS.
BLACKVEIL
ADAM AND I WERE ABLE TO FORMALIZE THE CHARACTERS IN HIS ALPHABET AND FROM THAT I'VE BEEN ABLE TO CREATE A CONVERSION SYSTEM THAT SYNCS UP WITH HIS SPEECH--WE'VE JUST HAD OUR FIRST BREAKTHROUGH...
IT'S HIS NAME... BLACKVEIL.
THAT'S REALLY IMPRESSIVE, SIR.
RIGHT. YOU WANTED SOMETHING ELSE...?
WE'RE LOOKING FOR IZZY AND EDEN, AND WHEN WE COULDN'T FIND THEM WE TRIED USING THE "WHERE IS" FUNCTION ON THE AVENGERS MACHINE, BUT--
I CAN'T BELIEVE THE TWO OF YOU MISSED ALL THE COMMOTION THIS MORNING--IMPERIAL ALERTS, THREAT TO THE EMPIRE, GENERAL HYSTERIA...
ANYWAY, OF COURSE THEY DIDN'T SHOW UP ON THE FINDER.
WHY IS THAT?
SAM...THEY'RE IN ANOTHER GALAXY.

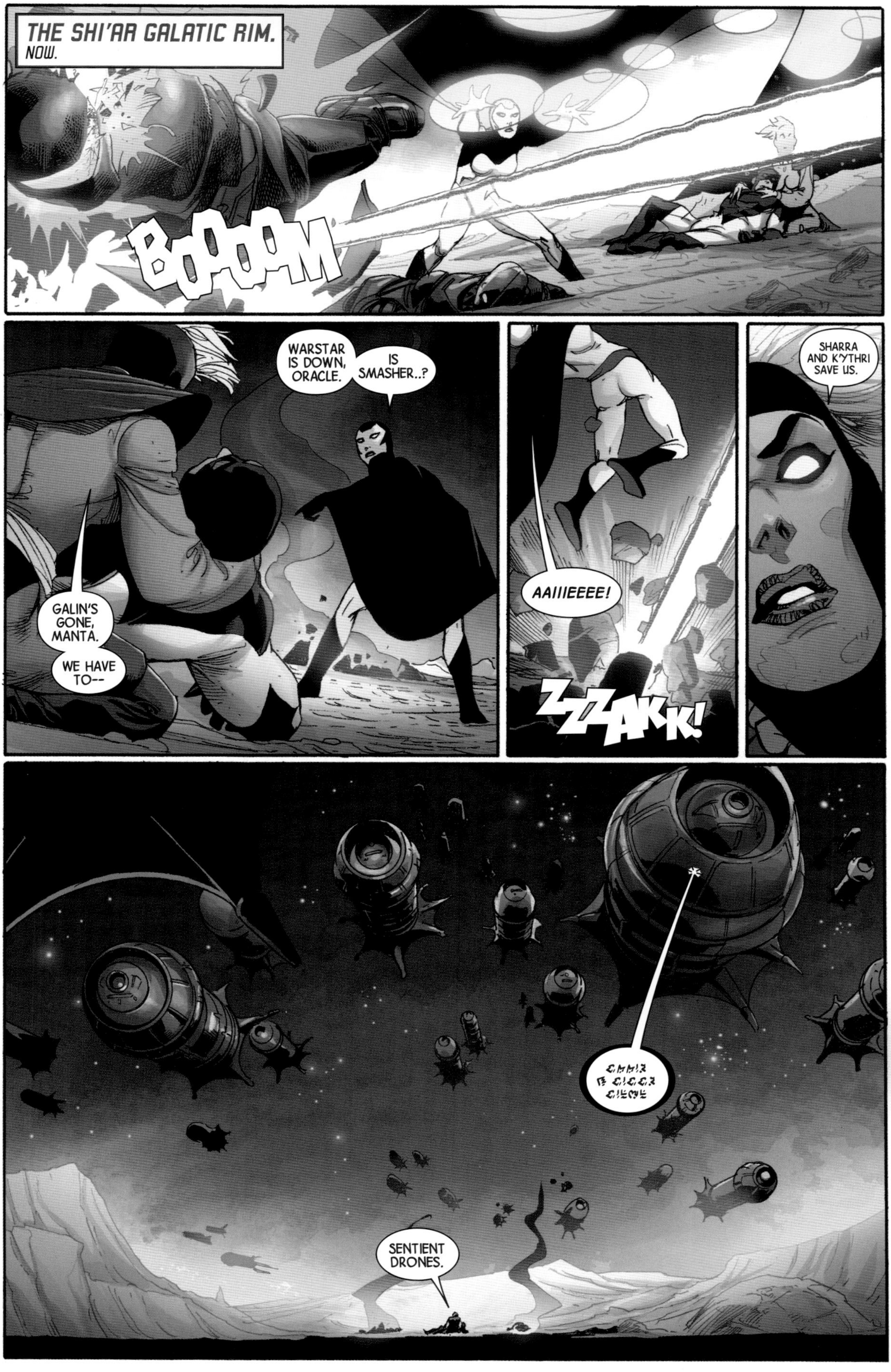
THE SHI'AR GALATIC RIM.
NOW.
BOOOOM
WARSTAR IS DOWN, ORACLE.
IS SMASHER..?
GALIN'S GONE, MANTA.
WE HAVE TO--
AAIIIEEEE!
ZZZAKK!
SHARRA AND K'YTHRI SAVE US.
SENTIENT DRONES.

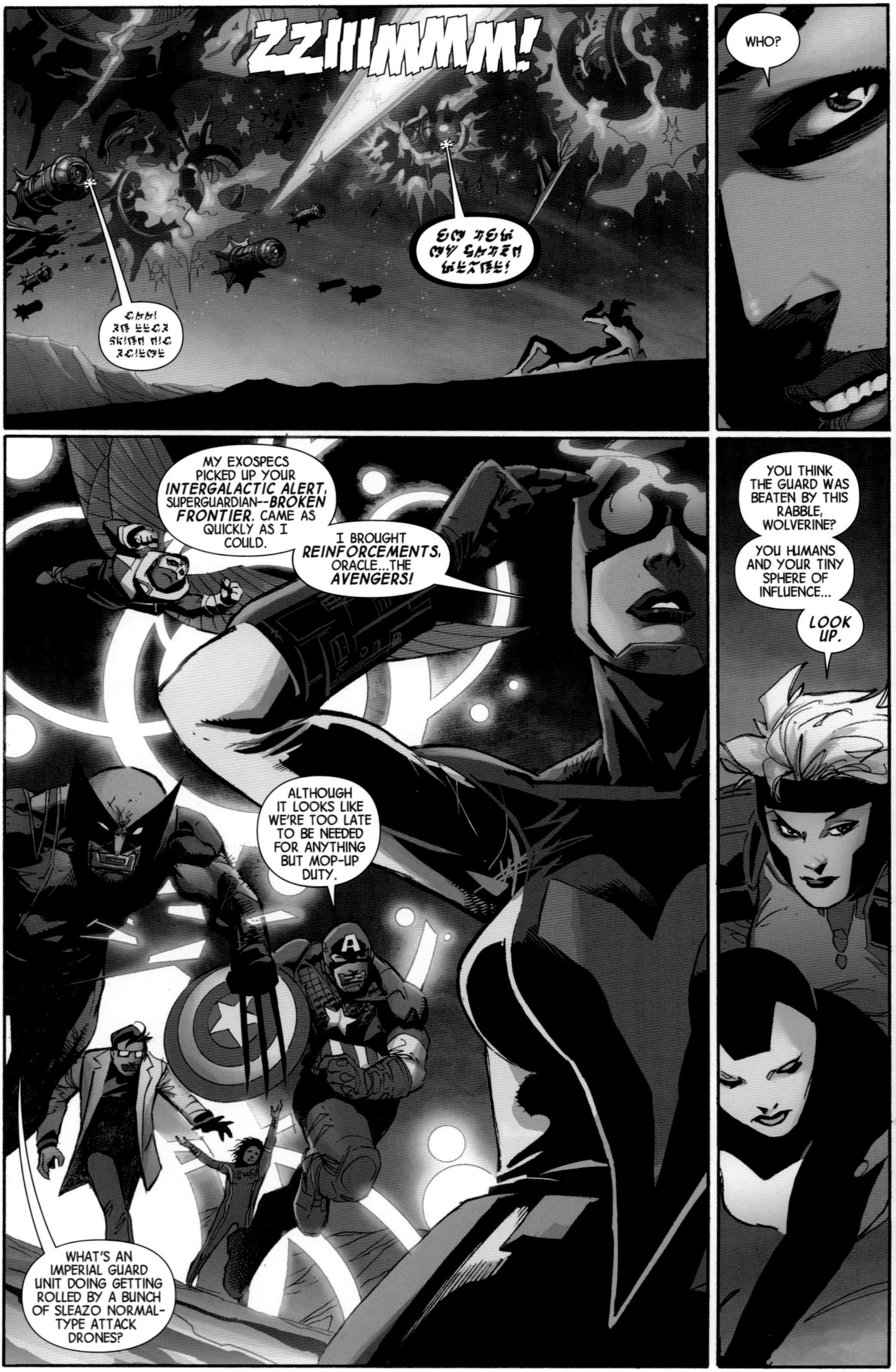
ZZIIIMMM!
WHO?
MY EXOSPECS PICKED UP YOUR INTERGALACTIC ALERT, SUPERGUARDIAN--BROKEN FRONTIER. CAME AS QUICKLY AS I COULD.
I BROUGHT REINFORCEMENTS, ORACLE...THE AVENGERS!
ALTHOUGH IT LOOKS LIKE WE'RE TOO LATE TO BE NEEDED FOR ANYTHING BUT MOP-UP DUTY.
WHAT'S AN IMPERIAL GUARD UNIT DOING GETTING ROLLED BY A BUNCH OF SLEAZO NORMAL-TYPE ATTACK DRONES?
YOU THINK THE GUARD WAS BEATEN BY THIS RABBLE, WOLVERINE?
YOU HUMANS AND YOUR TINY SPHERE OF INFLUENCE...
LOOK UP.

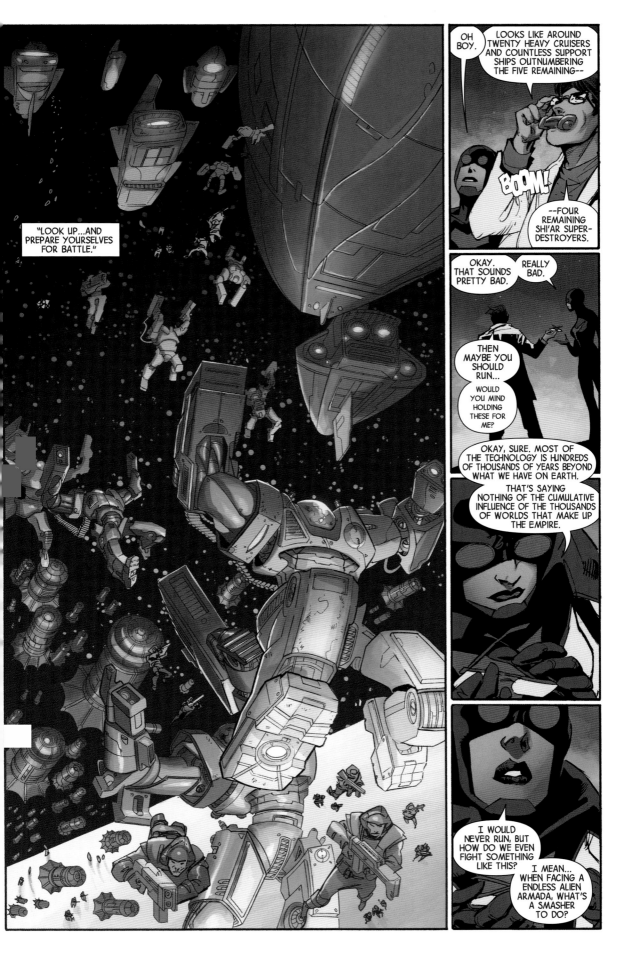

"LOOK UP...AND PREPARE YOURSELVES FOR BATTLE."

OH BOY.

LOOKS LIKE AROUND TWENTY HEAVY CRUISERS AND COUNTLESS SUPPORT SHIPS OUTNUMBERING THE FIVE REMAINING--

BOOM!

--FOUR REMAINING SHI'AR SUPER-DESTROYERS.

OKAY. THAT SOUNDS PRETTY BAD.

REALLY BAD.

THEN MAYBE YOU SHOULD RUN...

WOULD YOU MIND HOLDING THESE FOR ME?

OKAY, SURE. MOST OF THE TECHNOLOGY IS HUNDREDS OF THOUSANDS OF YEARS BEYOND WHAT WE HAVE ON EARTH.

THAT'S SAYING NOTHING OF THE CUMULATIVE INFLUENCE OF THE THOUSANDS OF WORLDS THAT MAKE UP THE EMPIRE.

I WOULD NEVER RUN, BUT HOW DO WE EVEN FIGHT SOMETHING LIKE THIS?

I MEAN... WHEN FACING A ENDLESS ALIEN ARMADA, WHAT'S A SMASHER TO DO?

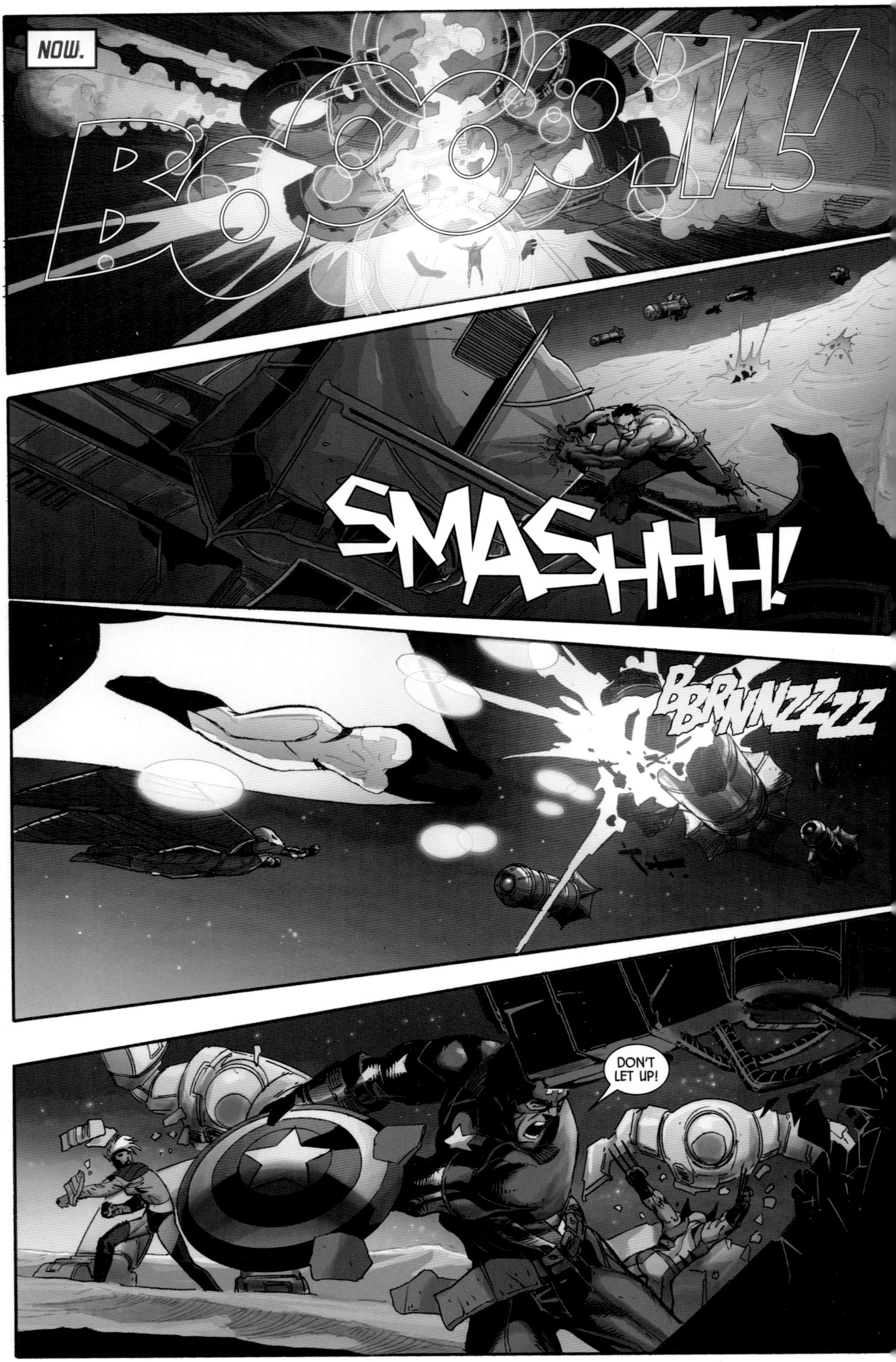
NOW.
BOOOOM!
SMASHHH!
BBRNNZZZzz
DON'T LET UP!

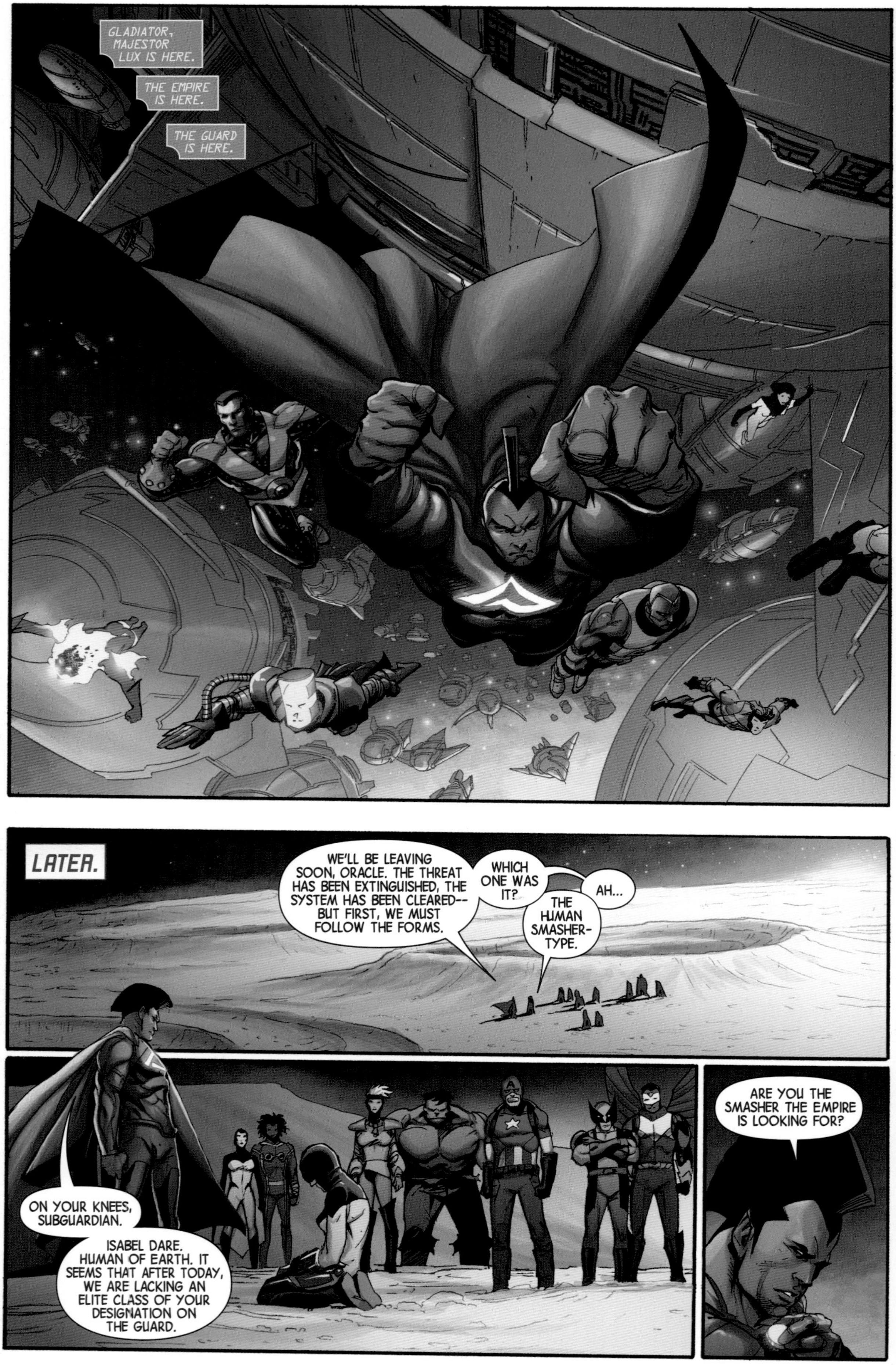
GLADIATOR, MAJESTOR LUX IS HERE.
THE EMPIRE IS HERE.
THE GUARD IS HERE.
LATER.
WE'LL BE LEAVING SOON, ORACLE. THE THREAT HAS BEEN EXTINGUISHED, THE SYSTEM HAS BEEN CLEARED-- BUT FIRST, WE MUST FOLLOW THE FORMS.
WHICH ONE WAS IT?
AH...
THE HUMAN SMASHER-TYPE.
ON YOUR KNEES, SUBGUARDIAN.
ISABEL DARE. HUMAN OF EARTH. IT SEEMS THAT AFTER TODAY, WE ARE LACKING AN ELITE CLASS OF YOUR DESIGNATION ON THE GUARD.
ARE YOU THE SMASHER THE EMPIRE IS LOOKING FOR?

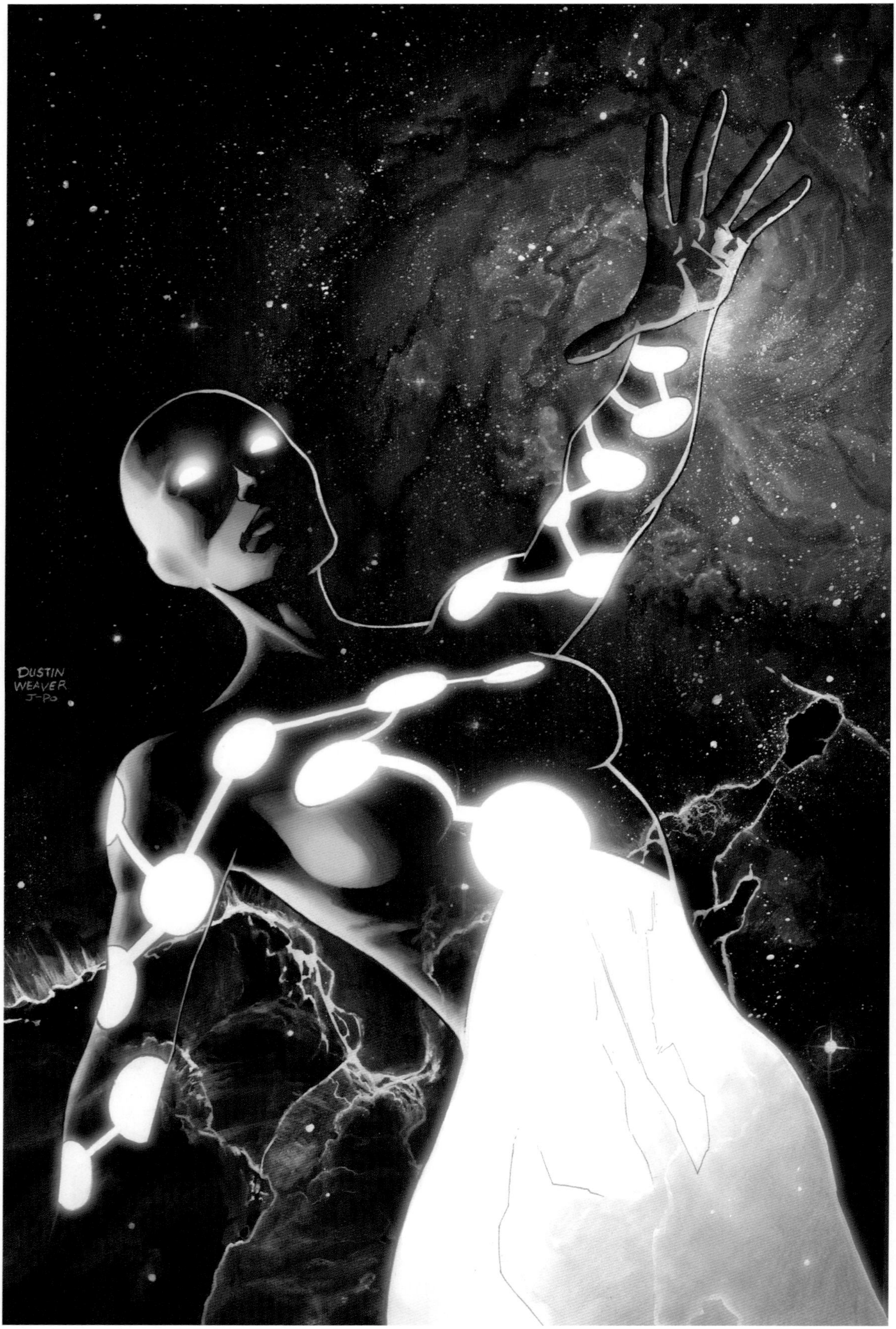
DUSTIN
WEAVER
J-Po

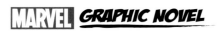

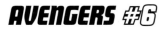

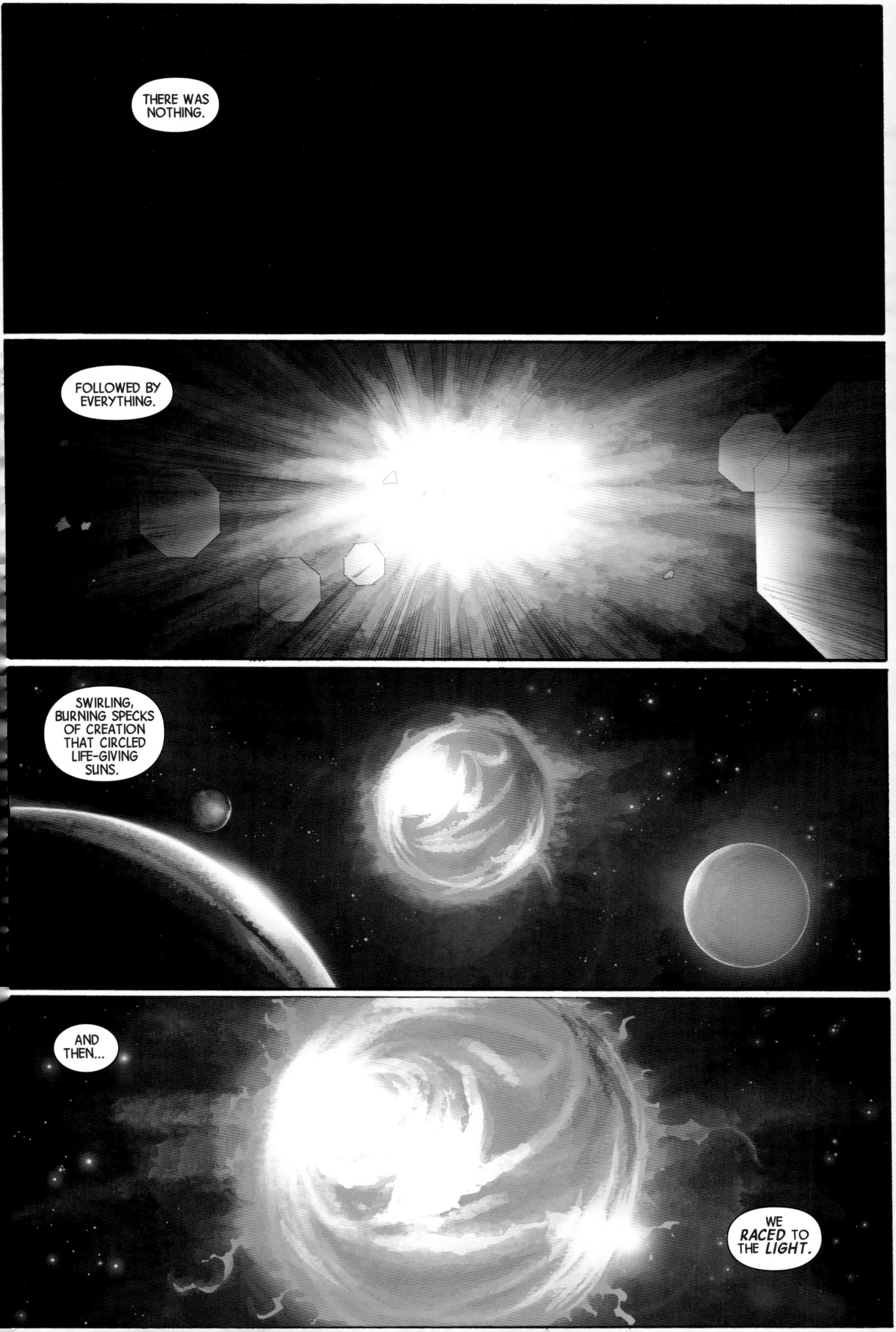

THERE WAS NOTHING.
FOLLOWED BY EVERYTHING.
SWIRLING, BURNING SPECKS OF CREATION THAT CIRCLED LIFE-GIVING SUNS.
AND THEN...
WE *RACED* TO THE *LIGHT*.

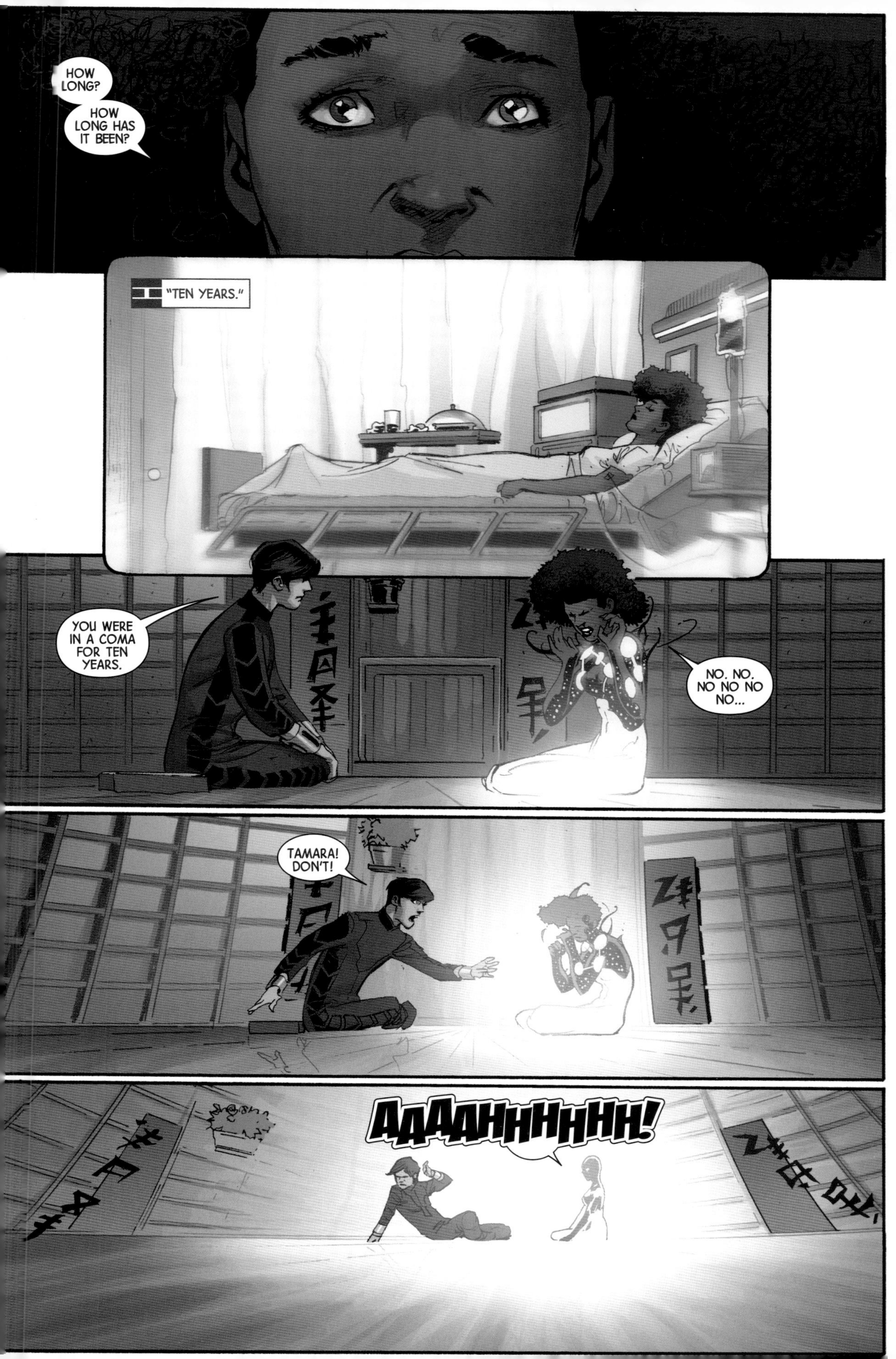
HOW LONG?
HOW LONG HAS IT BEEN?
"TEN YEARS."
YOU WERE IN A COMA FOR TEN YEARS.
NO. NO. NO NO NO NO...
TAMARA! DON'T!
AAAAHHHHHH!

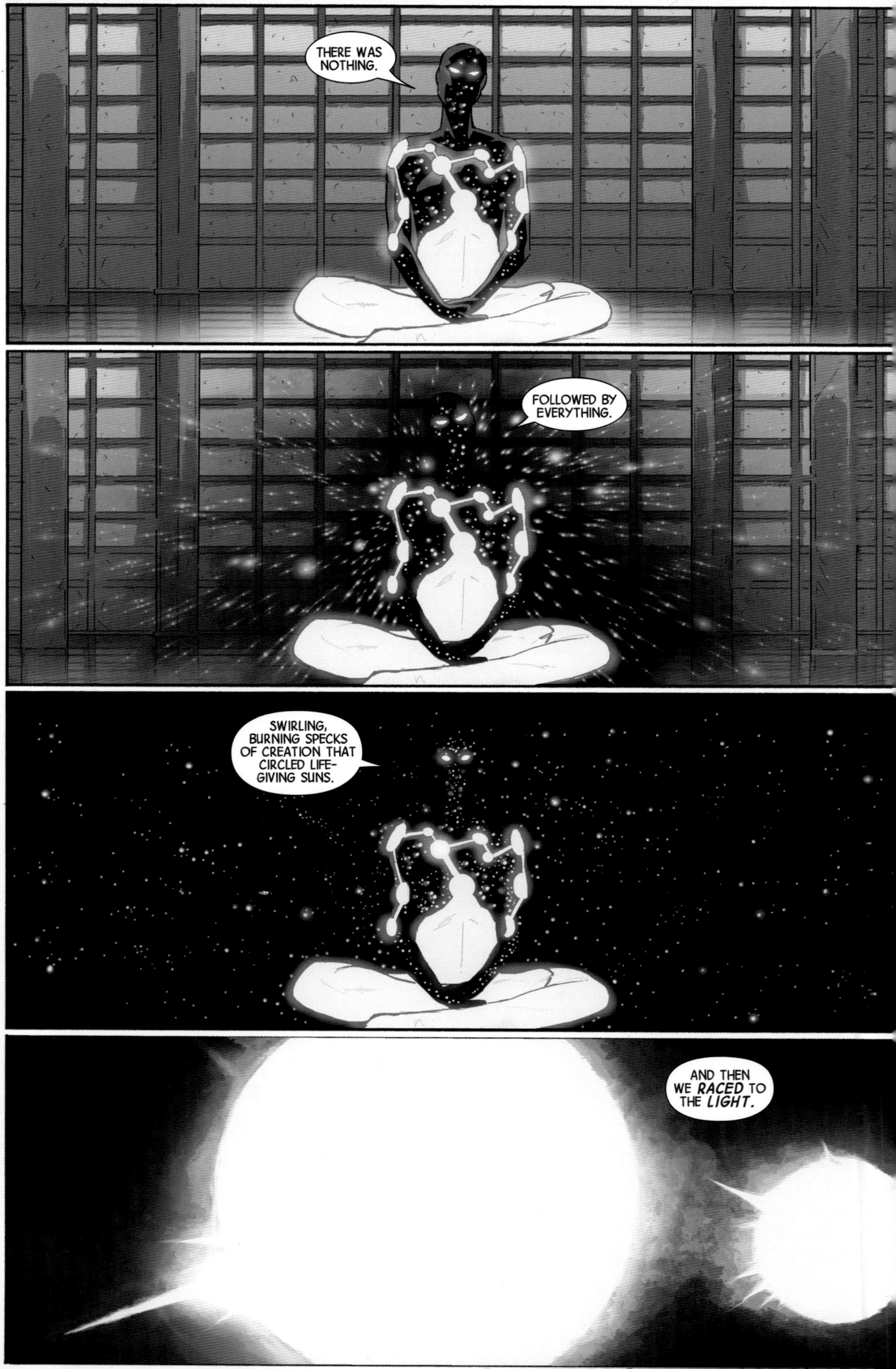
THERE WAS NOTHING.
FOLLOWED BY EVERYTHING.
SWIRLING, BURNING SPECKS OF CREATION THAT CIRCLED LIFE-GIVING SUNS.
AND THEN WE RACED TO THE LIGHT.

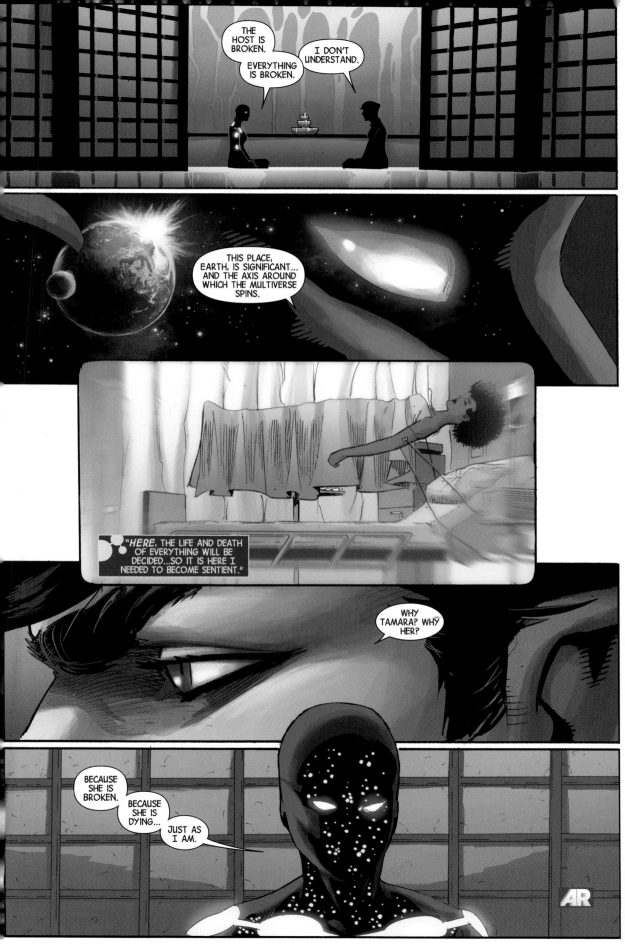

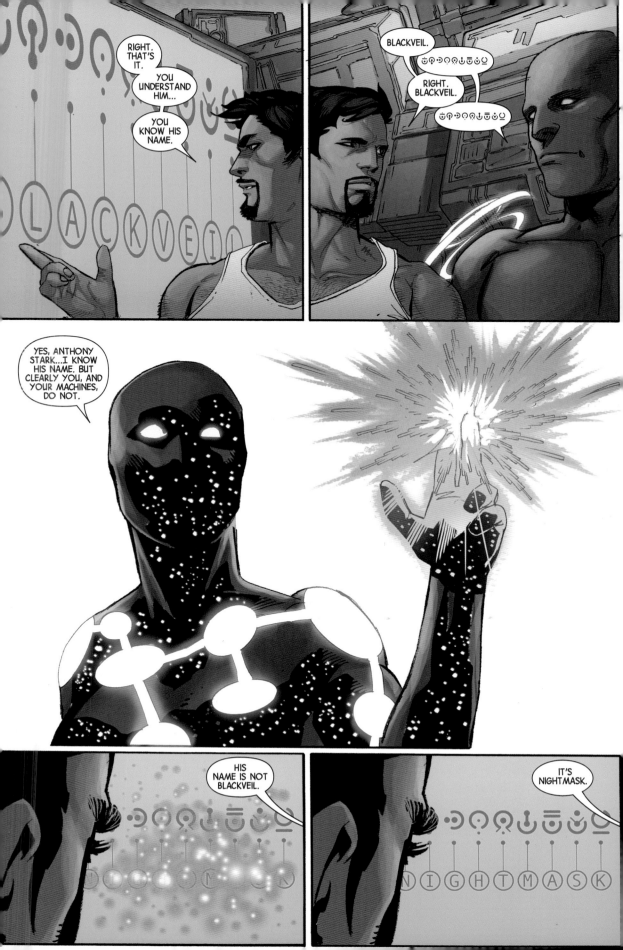

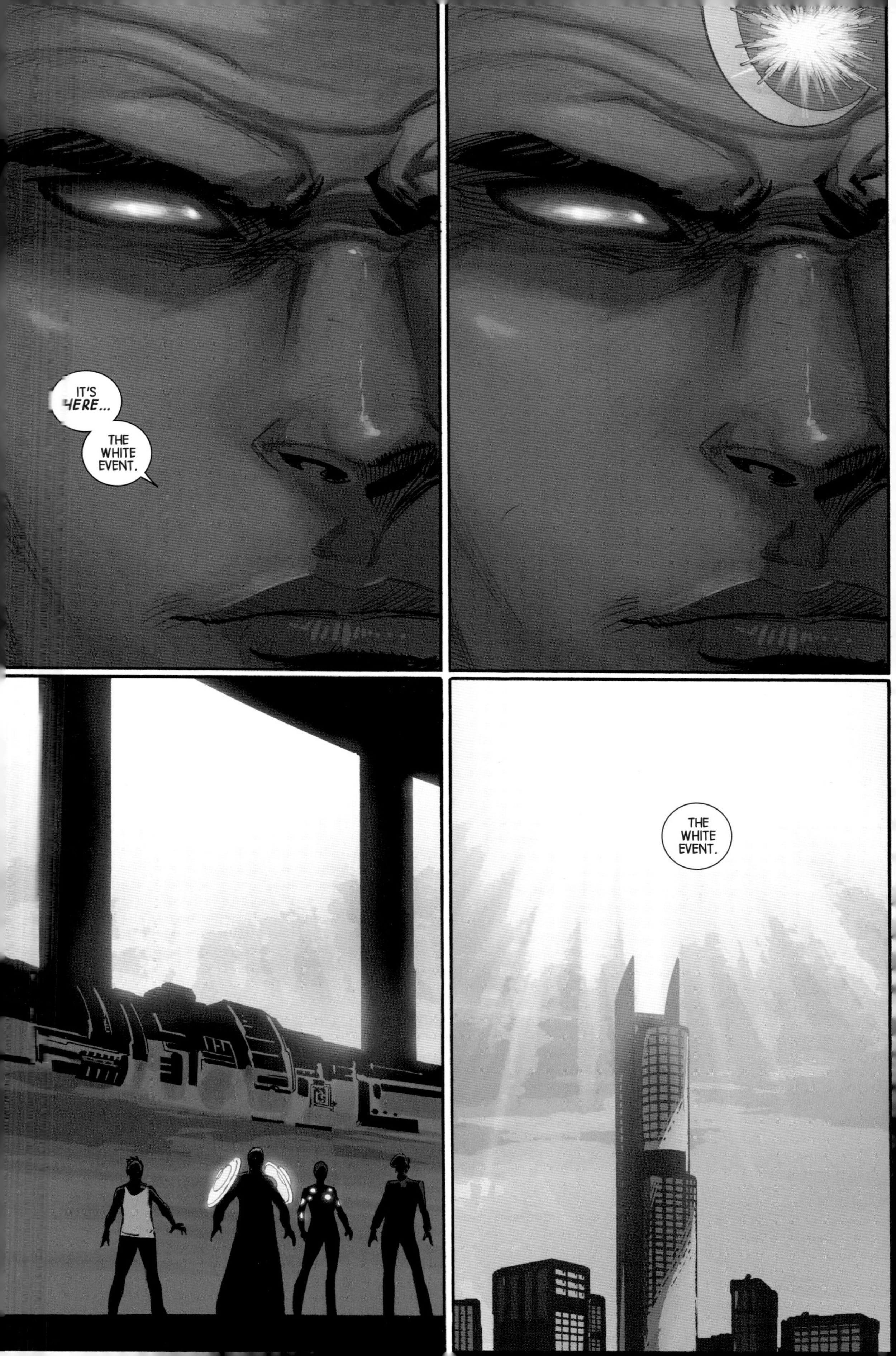
IT'S HERE...
THE WHITE EVENT.
THE WHITE EVENT.

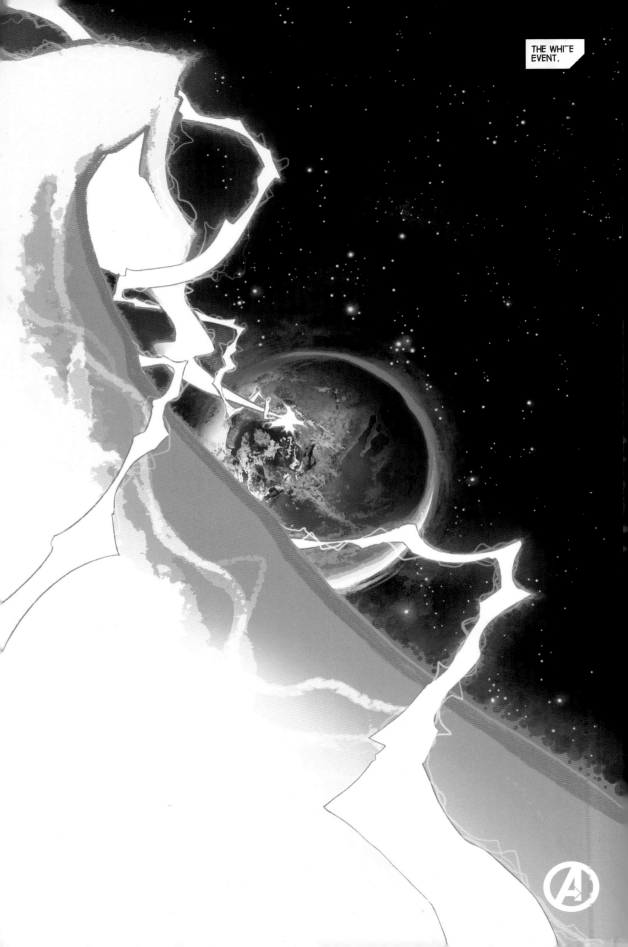

THE WHITE
EVENT.

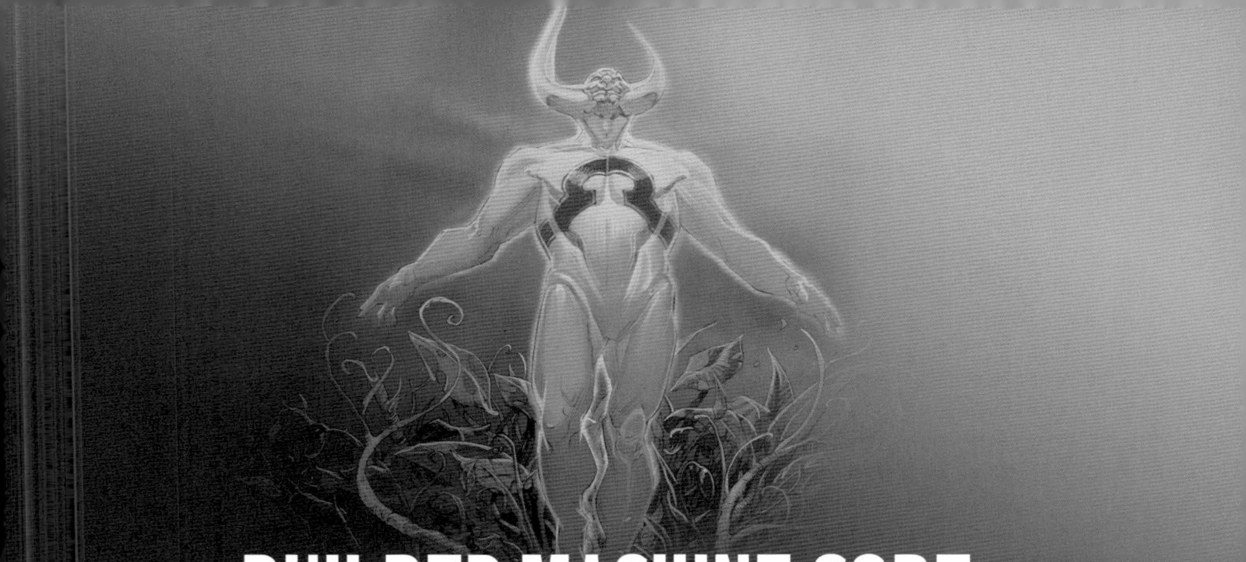

BUILDER MACHINE CODE

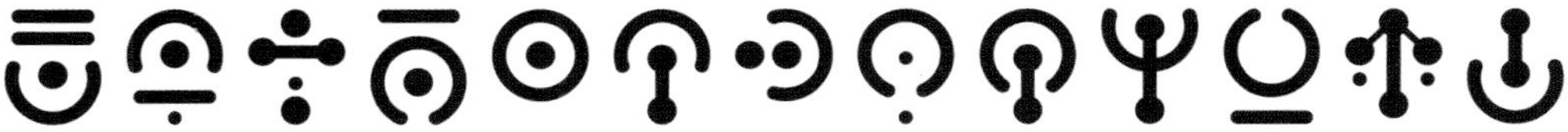

A B C D E F G H I J K L M

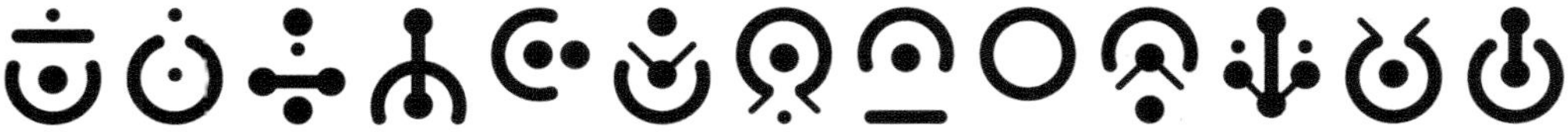

N O P Q R S T U V W X Y Z

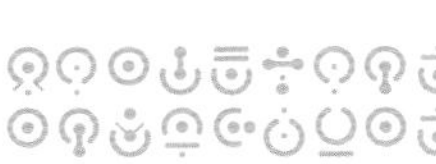

THE AVENGERS:

AVENGERS WORLD

VARIANT COVERS GALLERY

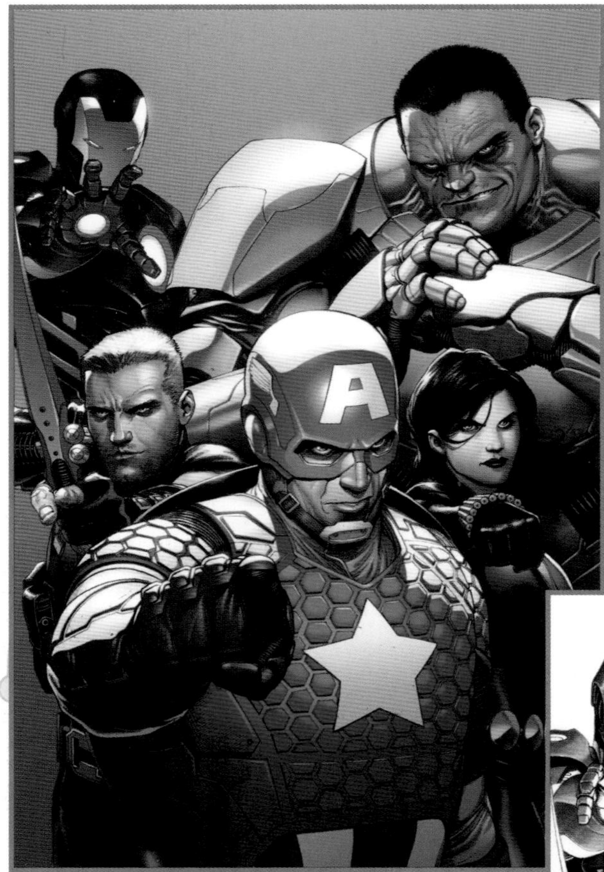

Avengers #1 Variant Cover
By Steve McNiven

Avengers #1 Sketch Variant Cover
By Steve McNiven

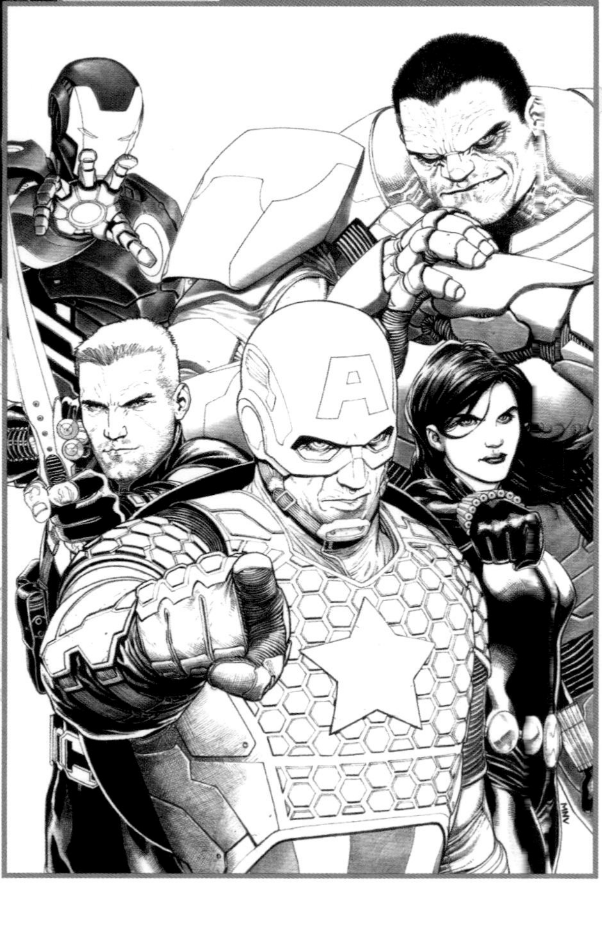

VARIANT COVERS GALLERY

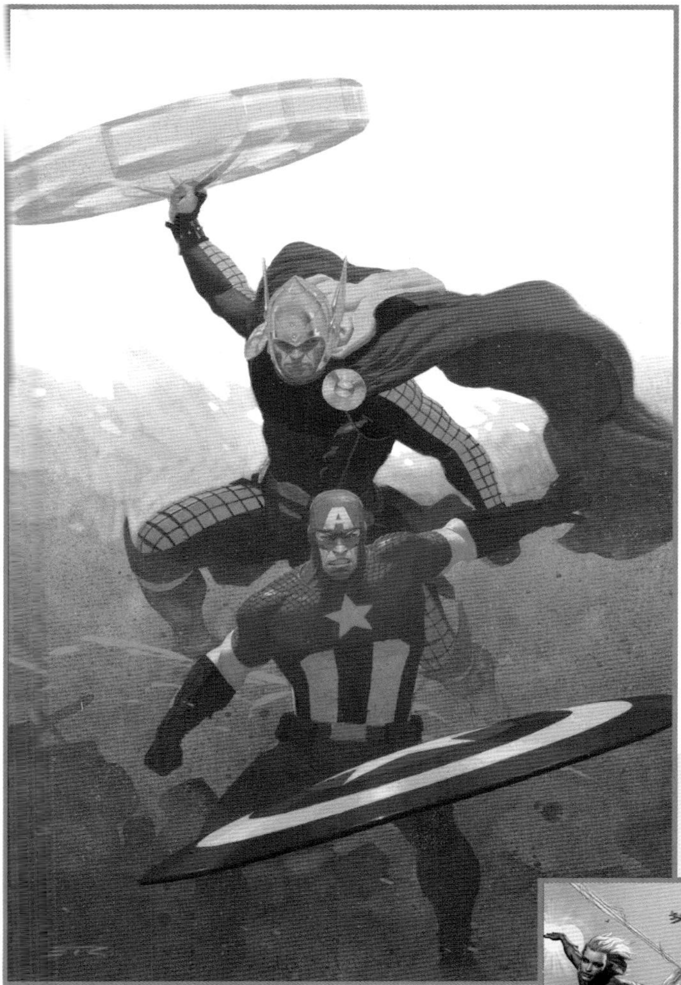

Avengers #1 Variant Cover
By Esad Ribic

Avengers #1 Hastings
Variant Cover

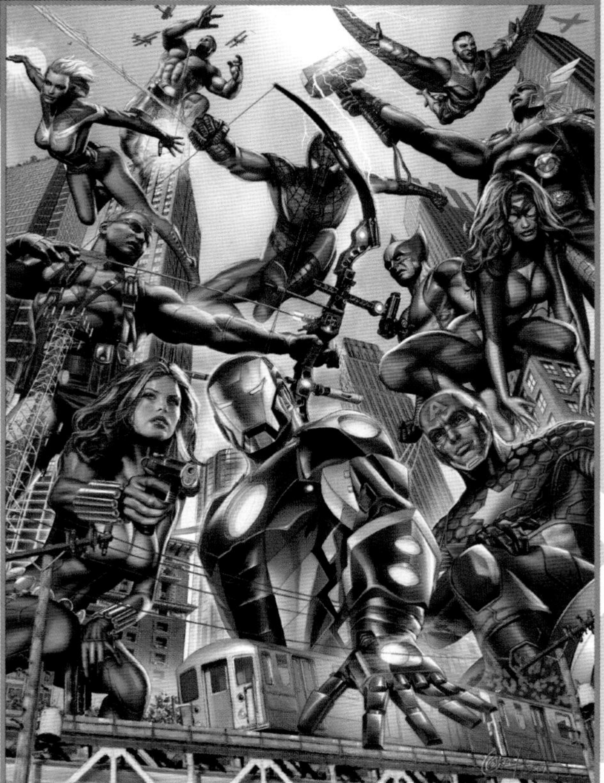

Avengers #1 Midtown Comics
Variant Cover
By Jeff Scott Campbell

VARIANT COVERS GALLERY

Avengers #1 Young Baby
Variant Cover
By Scott Young

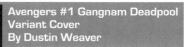

VARIANT COVERS GALLERY

DUSTIN WEAVER

Avengers #1 Gangnam Deadpool
Variant Cover
By Dustin Weaver

DUSTIN WEAVER

Avengers #1 Gangnam Deadpool
Sketch Variant Cover
By Dustin Weaver

VARIANT COVERS GALLERY

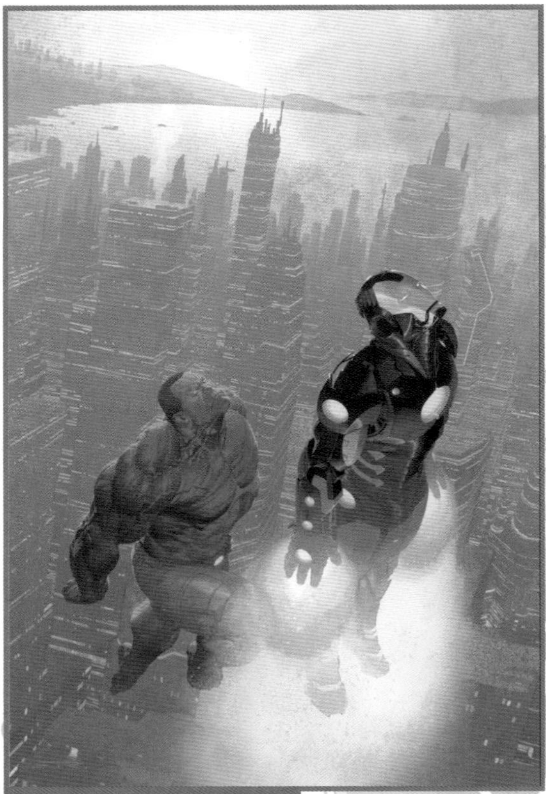

Avengers #2 Variant Cover
By Esad Ribic

Avengers #2 Variant Cover
By John Romita Jr.

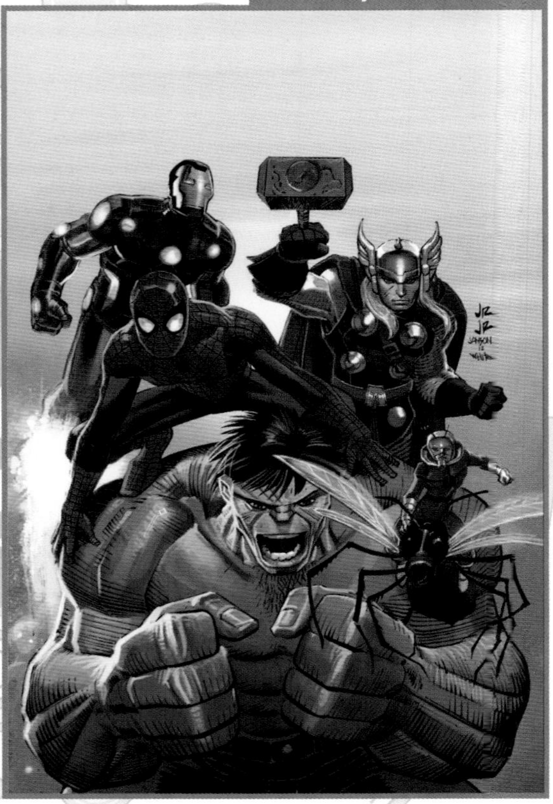

Avengers #1-3 Covers Assembled

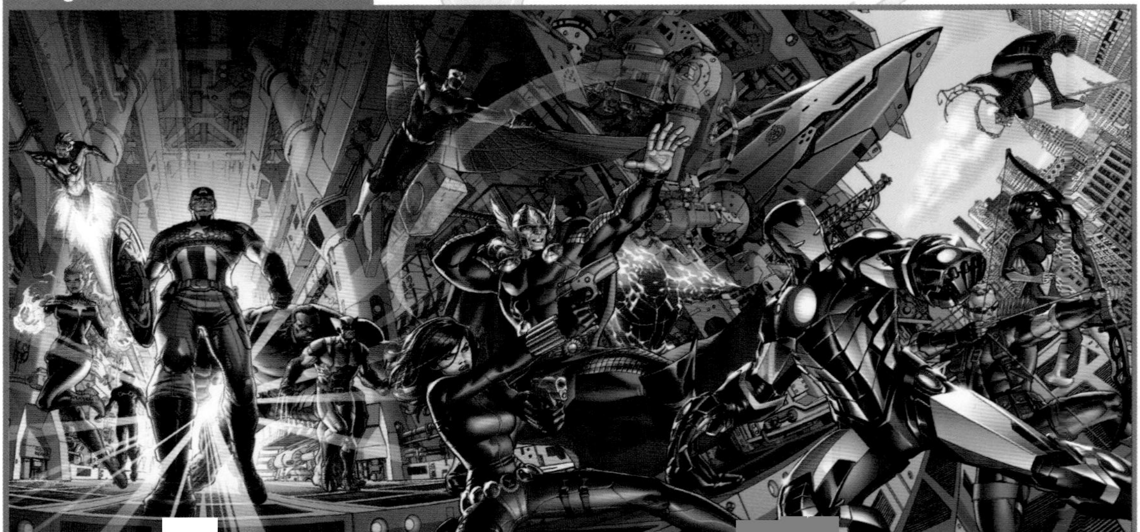

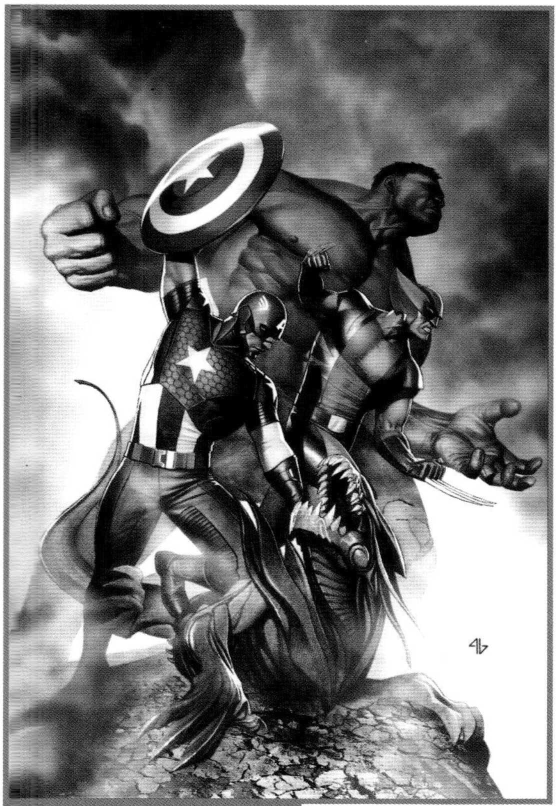

Avengers #3 Variant Cover
By Adi Granov

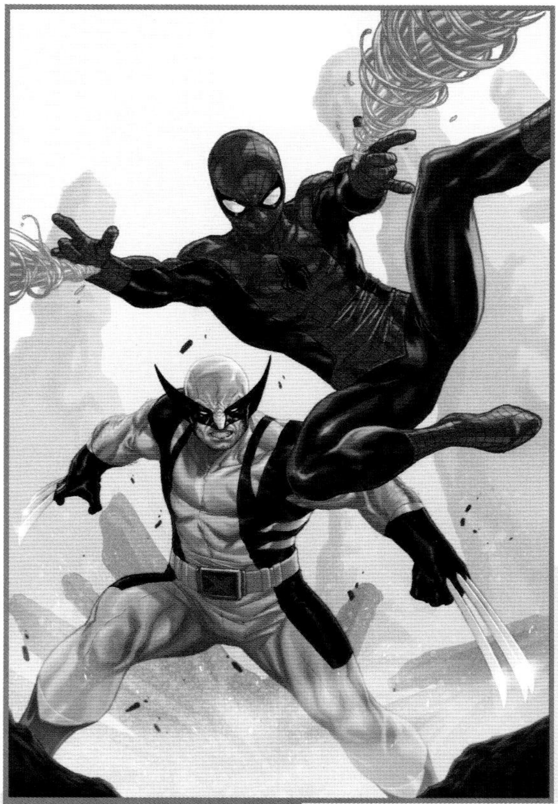

Avengers #3 Variant Cover
By Mark Brooks

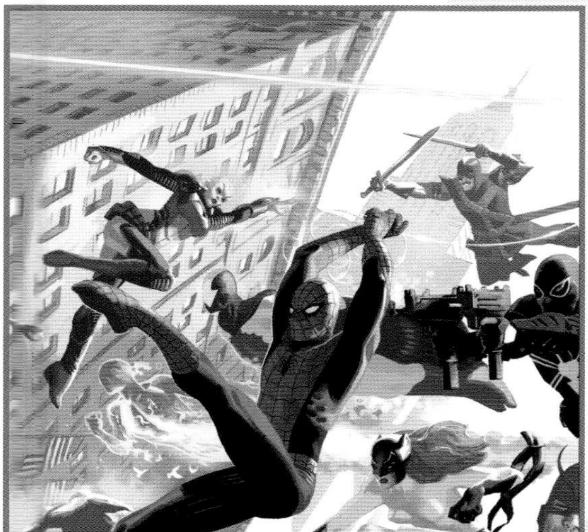

Avengers #3 50th Anniversary
Variant Cover
By Daniel Acuña

VARIANT COVERS GALLERY

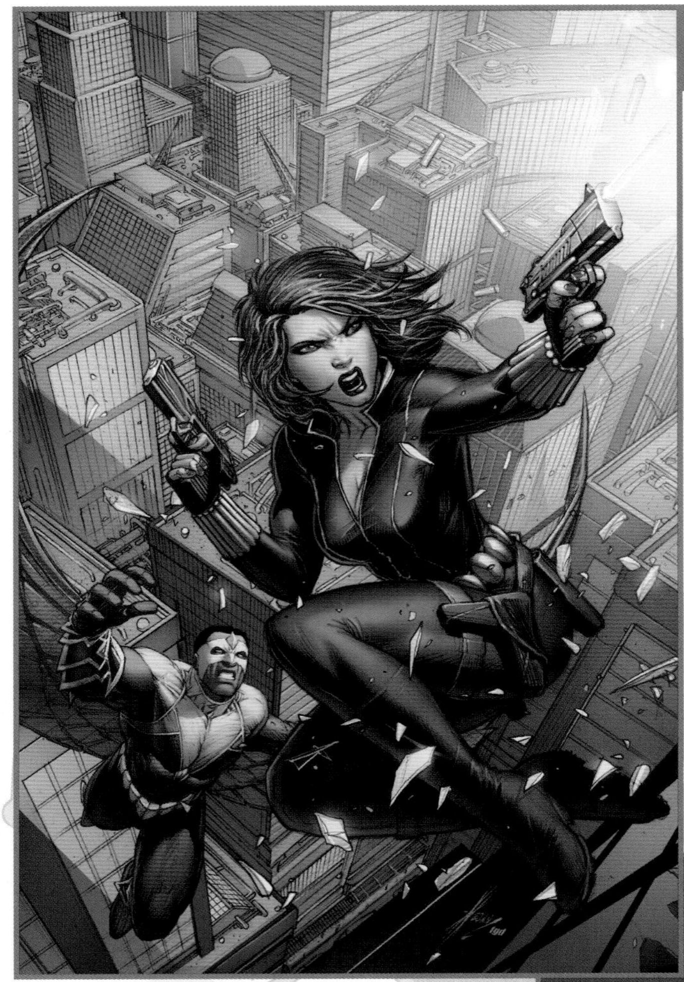

Avengers #4 Variant Cover
By Dale Keown
& Frank G. D'Armata

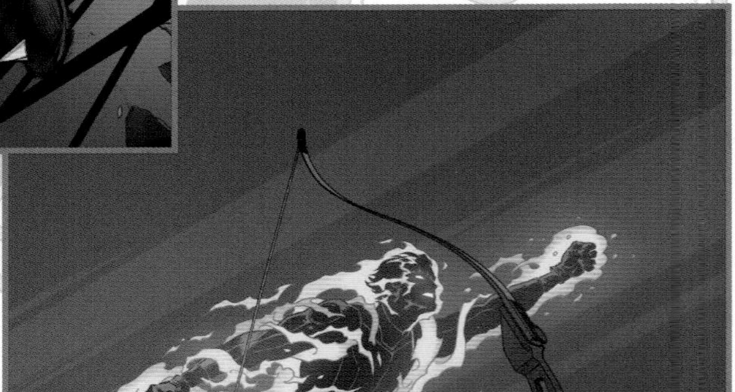

Avengers #5 Variant Cover
By Paolo Manuel Rivera

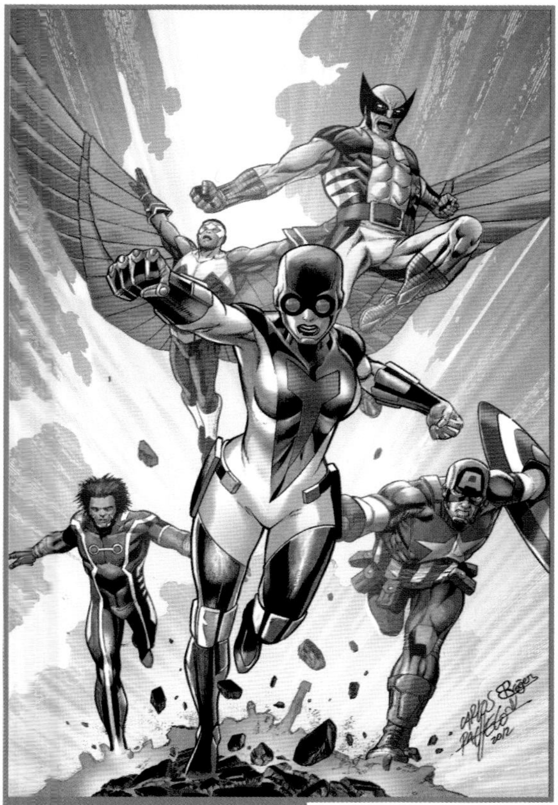

Avengers #5 Variant Cover
By Carlos Pacheco

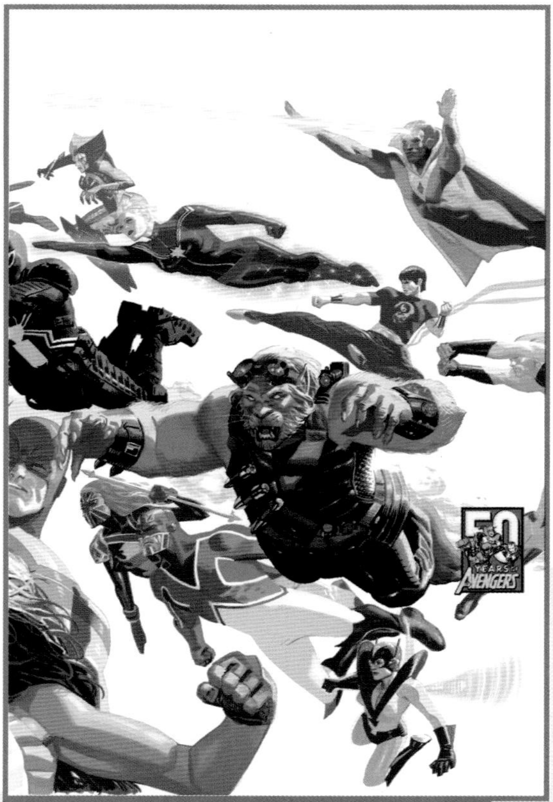
50
YEARS
AVENGERS

Avengers #6 50th Anniversary Variant Cover
By Daniel Acuña

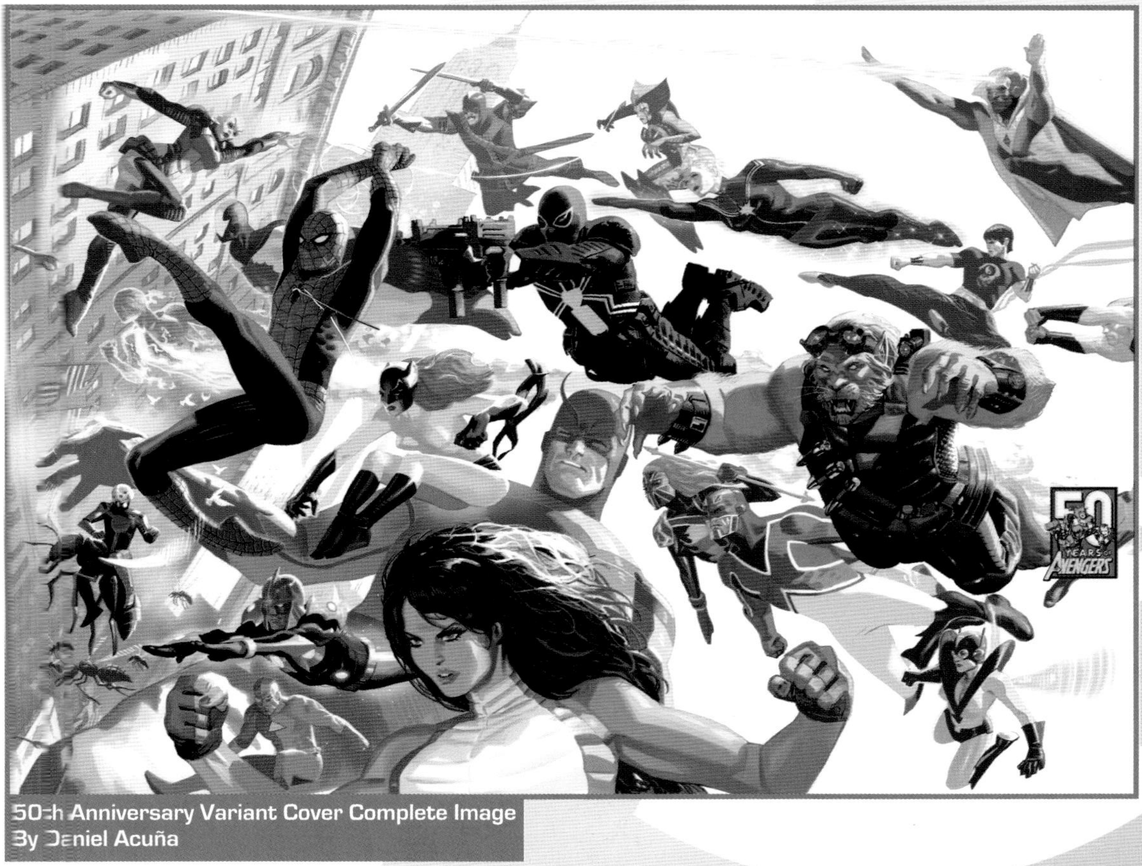
50
YEARS
AVENGERS

50th Anniversary Variant Cover Complete Image
By Daniel Acuña

AVENGERS VS X-MEN

MARVEL

A VS X

MARVEL'S GREATEST HEROES CLASH!

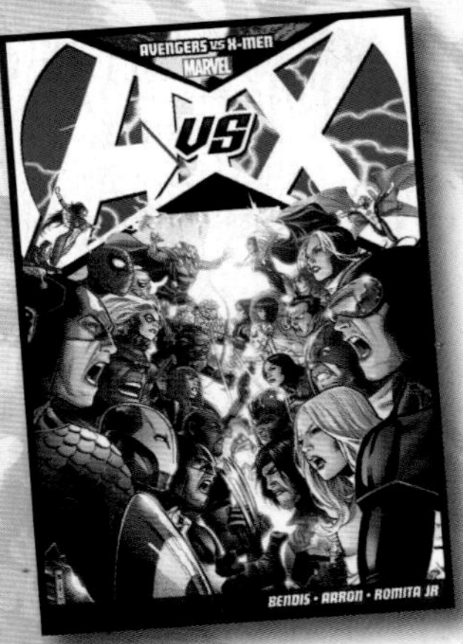
AVENGERS VS X-MEN
MARVEL
A VS X
BENDIS • AARON • ROMITA JR

Avengers Vs. X-Men
ISBN: 978-1-84653-518-5
Pages: 372 **Price: £17.99**

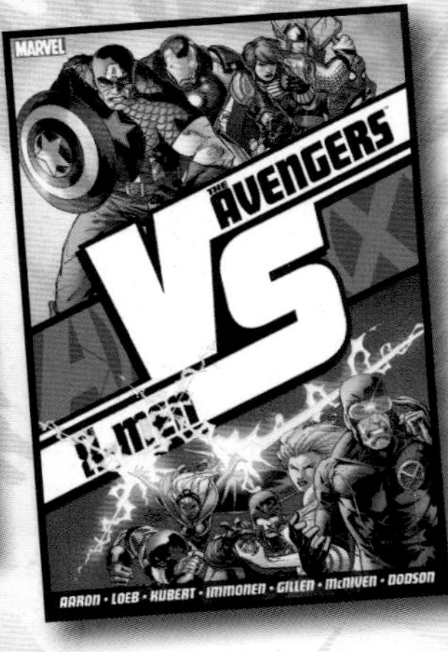
MARVEL
THE AVENGERS
VS
AARON • LOEB • KUBERT • IMMONEN • GILLEN • McNIVEN • DODSON

AVX Versus
ISBN: 978-1-84653-519-2
Pages: 140 **Price: £12.99**

THE FATE OF THE EARTH HANGS IN THE BALANCE, AS WAR BREAKS OUT BETWEEN THE AVENGERS AND THE X-MEN!

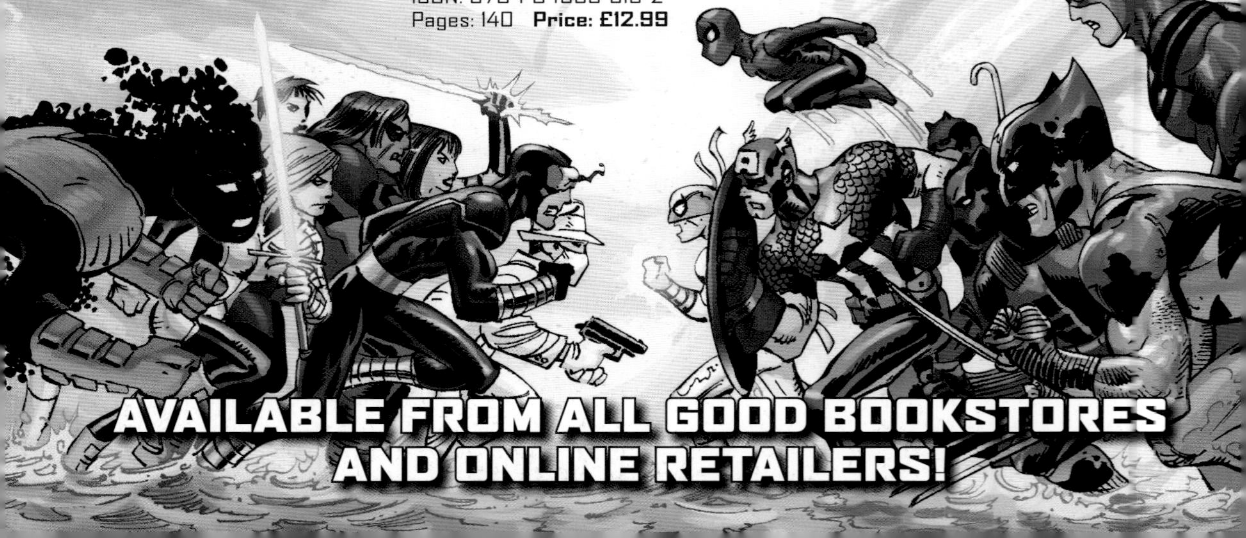

AVAILABLE FROM ALL GOOD BOOKSTORES AND ONLINE RETAILERS!